The Social Self

The Social Self

Hawthorne, Howells,
William James, and
Nineteenth-Century Psychology

Joseph Alkana

THE UNIVERSITY PRESS OF KENTUCKY

Scholarly publisher for the Commonwealth,
serving Bellarmine College, Berea College, Centre
College of Kentucky, Eastern Kentucky University,
The Filson Club, Georgetown College, Kentucky
Historical Society, Kentucky State University,
Morehead State University, Murray State University,
Northern Kentucky University, Transylvania University,
University of Kentucky, University of Louisville,
and Western Kentucky University.

Editorial and Sales Offices: The University Press of Kentucky
663 South Limestone Street, Lexington, Kentucky 40508-4008

96 97 98 99 00   5 4 3 2 1

Library of Congress Cataloging-in-Publication Data

Alkana, Joseph, [date]
The social self : Hawthorne, Howells, William James, and
nineteenth-century psychology / Joseph Alkana.
p. cm.
Includes bibliographical references (p.   ) and index.
ISBN 0-8131-1971-5 (cloth : alk. paper)
1. American fiction—19th century—History and criticism.
2. Social psychology and literature—United States—History—19th
century.   3. Psychological fiction, American—History and criticism.
4. Hawthorne, Nathaniel, 1804-1864—Knowledge—Psychology.
5. Howells, William Dean, 1837-1920—Knowledge—Psychology.
6. American literature—Psychological aspects.   7. James, William,
1842-1910—Influence.   8. Psychology in literature.   9. Self in
literature.   I. Title.
PS374.P7A45   1996
813'.309353—dc20   —dc20
[813'.309353]   96-16404

Contents

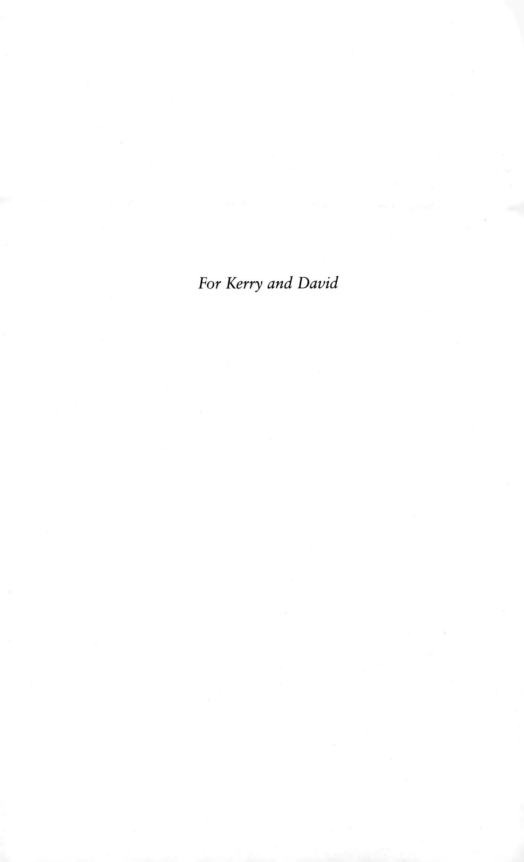

For Kerry and David

Acknowledgments

It seems appropriate that a book on selfhood and sociality should begin by speaking of important interpersonal relationships. William J. Scheick offered indispensable assistance. I am indebted to him for his discerning counsel and his model of professionalism. Evan Carton has been a continuing source of support and valued advice. For his intellectual provocations and insights, I am most grateful to Wayne Lesser.

Other teachers, friends, and colleagues have contributed at various points to the composition of this work. I want to thank Sacvan Bercovitch, C. Glen Colburn, Lester Faigley, Mara Holt, Evan Katz, Jeffrey Meikle, and Thomas Tweed. Janet Gabler-Hover offered a painstaking reading of the manuscript. And the editors at the University Press of Kentucky have been most helpful.

My colleagues at the University of Miami have provided an enlivening intellectual milieu. I especially want to thank Peter J. Bellis for his perceptive advice.

For their early lessons in the importance of language and history, I owe much to Mollie and Jack Alkana. My greatest debts are to my wife, Kerry Alkana, for her loving encouragement, and to our son, David, who reminds me that things other than work also are important.

A portion of chapter 2 appeared in 1990 as "Hawthorne's Drama of the Imagination and the Family" in *Philological Quarterly* and is reprinted here, in revised form, by permission of the publishers.

1

Translating the Self

Between Discord and Individualism
in American Literary History

Selfhood and freedom—in American literature and culture, these two terms have long been linked. The link has seemed so natural that even American sociologist Charles Horton Cooley, whose career was devoted to theorizing the interconnections between the self and society, was moved to declare in 1902, "No matter what a man does, he is not fully sane or human unless there is a spirit of freedom in him."[1] Despite Cooley's theoretical bent and his disciplinary allegiances to the field of sociology, he thus would define the core of human selfhood as that which not only evades predication by social forces but which finds its truest expression in the pursuit of freedom from social strictures. Cooley, not surprisingly, found inspiration for his definition in Thoreau. And why not Thoreau? Although the bond between selfhood and freedom appears strong throughout nineteenth-century literature, a body of writing customarily identified with the emergence of distinctively energetic American selves, it is during the American Renaissance that we encounter Thoreau's solitary, heroic experimenter at Walden, Emerson's Orphic poet, Whitman's omnivorous "I," and Hawthorne's steadfast and passionate Hester Prynne—all characters understood to be committed to strenuous affirmations of the self and the individual consciousness when confronted by the restraints of tradition. With their acts of defiance against social mores, these literary creations have furnished much inspiration to American intellectuals like Cooley.

But the association between selfhood and freedom seems less natural, more strained and tenuous, when questions are posed about their relationship: What kind of freedom is it that can translate us to an ideal state of selfhood? And is the self properly to be understood as the refuge of freedom? Frustration over the self's inability to deliver on an implied promise of liberation would seem to have fueled the poststructuralist drive against the humanist preoccupation with subjectivity. What is especially interesting about the conflict between poststructuralists and humanists is the way each has made its claims about the self in the name of freedom. The humanist view foretold liberation through allegiance to an inviolable subject, and, in an ironically corresponding manner, poststructuralists like Foucault have countered with their own claims of a new liberation, though its fulfillment would come only when the tyranny of the philosophical subject is effectively subverted.

The structure of this theoretical debate over selfhood and subjectivity has been disturbingly reminiscent of Melville's *Typee*, which dramatizes the problems created by an obsession with freedom. *Typee*'s narrator, who calls himself Tommo, jumps ship to escape a tyrannical captain. But, as we know, despite his new, paradisiacal home in the Marquesan Islands, he finds himself continually beset by the urge to escape his extraordinarily gracious Typee hosts, whom he suspects of cannibalistic designs. A century and a half after *Typee*, the rhetoric of freedom has shaped the debate over the philosophical subject, and scholars of literary and cultural studies have been reenacting Tommo's desire for escape. Humanist literary theories have offered ennobling visions of the individual consciousness, visions that have appealed to scholars appalled by the realities of twentieth-century life. But the long-standing dominance of these theories has, perhaps inevitably, seemingly naturalized their association with the academic institutions in which literary scholars have made their careers. Thus, as in *Typee*, in which the captain's history of abusive behaviors vitiated his warning to Tommo and the ship's crew that cannibals would consume deserting sailors, a history within academic institutions of insensitivity to questions of social justice has eroded the moral authority of humanism and its advocates. But when scholars seeking an alternative to a tainted humanism have turned to poststructuralist theory, they, like Tommo, have witnessed how the self stands in danger of being consumed; only this time the threat comes not from suspected cannibals but from linguistic and textual universals. As in *Typee*, theoretical questions about the significance of both selfhood and freedom have been problematically transformed into unworkable dichotomies, choices cast in overly simple contrasts between tyranny and liberation.[2]

This study returns to the topic of American literary selfhood, particularly its nineteenth-century manifestations, and its goal is to challenge understandings of selfhood that are rooted in the logic of dichotomies. I believe that alternative, more complex contemporary descriptions of nineteenth-century selfhood have long been ignored. These descriptions, unlike oppositional and subjectivist visions of selfhood, accommodated the more socially attentive aspects of nineteenth-century selfhood. An awareness of the social orientation of the self, as it was understood by contemporary writers, can effectively reveal a range of nineteenth-century preoccupations. These preoccupations emerge in my examinations of two particular periods—the 1830s through the early 1850s, and the 1890s—and three important figures from those times whose writings display their longstanding interest in and telling anxieties about selfhood: Nathaniel

Hawthorne, William Dean Howells, and William James. In addition, briefer discussions of works by Ralph Waldo Emerson, James Fenimore Cooper, and Harriet Beecher Stowe, among others, will be used to highlight particular issues and raise questions about subjectivity.

The writings of Hawthorne, Howells, and William James reflect a curiosity about questions of subjectivity and the individual consciousness. Yet their fundamental concern was not simply to validate the priority of the individual consciousness. Instead, they, like so many other nineteenth-century writers, were also preoccupied with perceived threats to social cohesion. The dilemma that these writers faced may be formulated in the following question: How can the affirmation of individual consciousness and conscience authorize a commitment to social cohesion, a commitment that simultaneously would assure the possibility of individual experience?

Somewhat surprisingly, perhaps, this commitment to social cohesion was central to that contemporary discourse devoted to questions about the self: psychology. Nineteenth-century psychological discourse dealt with more than just structures of consciousness; it was equally attentive to the interplay between the individual and society. This conceptualization of selfhood from a social perspective characterizes both the Common Sense psychology that predominated during the antebellum years as well as the evolutionist psychology that followed. The fact that such fiction writers as Hawthorne and Howells, each of whom exhibited great awareness of contemporary psychological discourse, shared a social conception of individual psychology is thus no accident. As this study will argue, Hawthorne and Howells used their knowledge to create narratives that would make salient problems in contemporary psychology. William James enters this discussion because in *The Principles of Psychology* he offers more than the innovative ideas and literary charm for which the book is famous. More significantly, he turns to narrative form as a means to resolve the disciplinary problems in psychology that he, along with nonspecialists like Hawthorne and Howells, had posed.

James's turn to narrative in *The Principles of Psychology* also influences the methodology of my study. In the chapter that would have a profound effect on students of literary form, "The Stream of Thought," James describes how the sense of self makes itself known: "The mind is at every stage a theatre of simultaneous possibilities. Consciousness consists in the comparison of these with each other, the selection of some, and the suppression of the rest."[3] James's metaphor of mind as theater is particularly telling—it suggests a series of scenes, a flow of action that presents itself as continuous, a seemingly unbroken "stream of thought, of consciousness, or of subjective life."[4] The self, James's basic unit for study, thereby constitutes itself in narrative form, that is as an ongoing story of itself to itself. The manner by which James perceives narrative to inform selfhood suggests the value of attention to narrative forms in polemics as well as in fictions of selfhood. My approach to particular texts thus is less oriented toward questions of the representation of consciousness or its symbolizations than it is toward the way selfhood arises in narrative and the functions that selfhood assumes, even within texts that do not foreground narrative structures. Obviously, I have *The Principles of Psychology* in mind here as a text that is most revealing when its disciplinary polemics are understood to be working in the service of a guiding dramatic structure. My attention to dramatic structures within nonfictional works leads to the reinterpretation of certain explicit authorial assertions or images.

As an example of this, I would offer Emerson's image of the "transparent eyeball," that most famous—or most notoriously open to ridicule—symbol of the self from *Nature*. As Emerson describes it, in this state, "I am nothing; I see all; the currents of the Universal Being circulate through me; I am part or particle of God."[5] As striking as this statement may be and as forcefully as Emerson poses the visual imagery that informs the piece, its importance within the scheme of *Nature* is limited. Successive chapters develop a repudiation—or, perhaps more properly, a transcendence and recontextualization—of earlier ideas about the lessons of Nature. By the chapter on "Discipline," Emerson has discarded the relative passivity of the transparent eyeball in favor of the "exercise of the Will" and "the lesson of power" (28). And the Orphic poet's conclusion transcends the early lesson of the transparent eyeball and calls instead for the "kingdom of man over nature, which cometh not with observation" (49). The passive observation of the transparent eyeball is here superseded by the dominion of the will. Emerson's recontextualization of the transparent eyeball can be appreciated only when the narrative structure of *Nature*—a structure of continuous revision within this most emphatic, even pressured, discussion of an ideal selfhood—is foregrounded.

Why, however, return yet again to questions about the self within canonical nineteenth-century American writing? Now that critics of American literature and culture have been furnishing newer disciplinary questions, discussing alternative literary genres, and restoring neglected literary figures for scholarly consideration, such a return might seem to signal a renewed willingness to undergo enchantment by images of selfhood. Yet the idea that the self within canonical writing must necessarily be understood in terms established by an academic tradition of American literary history that antedates Matthiessen's *American Renaissance*—that is to say, a tradition in which the self is apprehended as the primary indicator of a transcendental impulse that effectively diverts attention away from questions about social arrangements—overly simplifies and as a result obscures the complex ways in which canonical writers have treated selfhood. The relationship between canonical and noncanonical visions of selfhood and subjectivity is one that, I would suggest, we may not yet be adequately prepared to judge. For example, feminist scholars have articulated Harriet Beecher Stowe's radical vision in *Uncle Tom's Cabin*, a vision which presents an ideal social realm that is not based on the self's opposition to society. But questions remain as to precisely which aspects of her vision, a conception of family and community guided by female insight and moral suasion, should be considered radical. After all, Stowe was not the only writer to suggest that the self achieves its ideal state within a family structure.[6] The notoriously conventional Hawthorne *also* attempted to resolve narrative crises through recourse to images of family and, most famously in *The Scarlet Letter*, by asserting the moral centrality of an antipatriarchal woman. Both Hawthorne and Stowe were deeply committed to what politicians now call family values; and they were both concerned with issues of morality and politics.

In order to disentangle the roots and comparative significance of their differing commitments, we must develop a greater historical sensibility as we speak to the question of how canonical writers represented selfhood. Accordingly, in place of narratives of either transcendent selfhood or determinant language structures, this study stresses a return to particular intellectual and cultural situations. Works by Hawthorne, Howells, and James will be discussed with respect to specific contemporary psychological discourses. In addition, I think it is important to acknowledge the fact that selfhood, even if no longer understood to be a vehicle of transcendence and freedom, has endured as a forceful symbol in American culture. The endurance of this symbol may be best understood, I suspect, as a reaction against a recurrent sense of social crisis and as an expression of anxiety over the possibility of social disintegration.

• • •

What is man when no longer connected with society, or when he finds himself surrounded by a convulsed and a half-dissolved one? He cannot live in solitude; he must belong to some community bound by some ties, however imperfect.
—J. Hector St. John de Crèvecoeur[7]

The fear that American society may be decomposing is repeatedly voiced by journalists and politicians who decry the disappearance of a purportedly unified, peaceable, and homelike past. But fears of social disintegration are hardly new. When we listen, for example, to Crèvecoeur's complaints from two centuries ago, we may detect a surprising resemblance to modern (or postmodern) despair over the destruction of social cohesion. Crèvecoeur's narrator, in the final chapter of *Letters from an American Farmer,* claims to have had his sensibilities utterly shaken by recent events. Prior to what he calls "these calamitous times," he had "labored and prospered, without having ever studied on what the security of my life and the foundation of my prosperity were established: I perceived them just as they left me."[8] And what was the lamentable event that fractured the narrator's security, his sense of a coherent community, leaving him so devastated? It was precisely the founding episode of the United States, the American Revolution. The very creation of a national identity thus is linked by Crèvecoeur with the dissolution of community.

Crèvecoeur's crisis of social dissolution has profound psychological ramifications, as he indicates when asking his almost despairing question, "What is man when no longer connected with society?" He has discovered that his formerly stable sense of selfhood was tightly bound to social order, and, now that this order appears to be unraveling, Crèvecoeur panics. Such concern during the late eighteenth-century over the possibility of social disintegration is not unique to Crèvecoeur. What makes his complaint distinctive is the way he associates potential social dissolution with what we now would more likely describe as a crisis of personal identity. He responds to this crisis by seeking the consolation of a community, "however imperfect," because he cannot "live in solitude." The community he finds, as he soon tells us, is that of Native Americans, and he retreats to the very wilderness he had earlier in his *Letters* disparaged as a place of "lawless profligacy."[9] In short, his struggle to create and maintain a stable self in the midst of accelerating social disintegration takes precedence over all else, and he is willing to dissociate himself from that idealized American society whose emergence he earlier had celebrated.

Crèvecoeur's images of selfhood and society in crisis are the polar opposite of those offered in what customarily stands as the representative text of the early republic, Franklin's *Autobiography.* Franklin, too, exhibits anxieties about social cohesion when in *The Autobiography* he repeatedly regrets the way theology leads to disputation; along similar lines, James Madison speculates in *The Federalist Papers* that perhaps the most important thing a government can do is "to break and control the violence of faction."[10] But Madison articulates a faith that government is up to the task, and Franklin's account of self-improvement ultimately provides a reassuring link between the personal and the national. Franklin's personal transformation from a hungry neophyte, who awkwardly carries his three huge loaves of bread up Market Street, into the stately, most prominent citizen of Philadelphia reinforces—and is reinforced by—his descriptions of national formation. But while Franklin's intertwined stories of personal and national progress historically have exercised a hold over the national imagination, it is Crèvecoeur's anxiety that may indeed reflect a more enduring, typically American literary preoccupation.

What I am suggesting here is that American literary concepts of selfhood have deeply social roots. By this I mean that selfhood is typically presented as arising within particular social networks and in response to conventions, and that, like Crèvecoeur's narrator, literary selves routinely find themselves in crisis states when social cohesion is threatened. In this important respect, nineteenth-century literary selfhood has much in common with its eighteenth-century precursors.

The idea that the nineteenth century witnessed the development of the "Imperial Self," to use Quentin Anderson's well-known term, has long been a critical commonplace. And in recent years, this commonplace has served as a foil against which revisionist critics have juxtaposed the literatures of women and ethnic minorities. Thus, for example, in her introduction to a recent paperback edition of *The House of Mirth*, Martha Banta begins by mentioning "the two most famous narrative traditions that secure other American classics": Franklin's rise and Emerson's faith in his ability "to attain self-sufficiency."[11] Banta's introduction addresses a popular, presumably collegiate, audience rather than scholars. What makes it noteworthy is the fact that one as immersed in American cultural history as is Banta is comfortable casually presenting the Emersonian, transcendent self to her audience. She does not need to speak of Emerson in any detail; he simply serves as a stable launching point for a discussion of Wharton's more complex and highly socialized narrative of self-possession.

But perhaps Emerson is not quite so consistently Emersonian. A classic work of Emersonian idealism, "The Transcendentalist," features Emerson in a mood more equivocal than that of *Nature*, a mood that may be understood to express a typically nineteenth-century anxiety about selfhood. "The Transcendentalist" opens by gesturing toward a dichotomy between "Materialists and Idealists; the first class founding on experience, the second on consciousness" (193). Emerson, of course, will find idealism logically prior and morally preferable to materialism, but such findings may finally be less significant than the manner by which he presents mental processes as an ongoing struggle. Accordingly, he finds that "two states of thought diverge every moment, and stand in wild contrast" (205). And this struggle is itself constitutive of the mind and of the self: "The worst feature of this double consciousness is, that the two lives, of the understanding and of the soul, which we lead, really show very little relation to each other, never meet and measure each other: one prevails now, all buzz and din; and the other prevails then, all infinitude and paradise; and, with the progress of life, the two discover no greater disposition to reconcile

themselves" (205-6). Since Emerson offers here no possibility for reconciliation between "the two lives," it is the transcendentalist's hope to
make the condition in which the ideal prevails permanent. But, as he pes-
simistically observes, "moments of illumination" are, at best, passing, and
the mind remains fractured (205).

It is this divided state, rather than faith in mental unity and self-
sufficiency, that truly characterizes nineteenth-century American depictions of the self. Can it be an accident that two turn-of-the-century writers
with backgrounds as dissimilar as those of W.E.B. Du Bois and Henry
Adams would both home in on the same Emersonian image of internal division? Du Bois opens *The Souls of Black Folk* with his famous description
of "double-consciousness, this sense of always looking at one's self through
the eyes of others."[12] This state of double consciousness reflects an Emersonian attitude toward internal division, and it also conveys the sense that
the racial essence on which Du Bois would comment, the "black folk," is
itself multiple, comprised of "souls."[13] Du Bois was writing in response to
the crises faced by African Americans in the decades after Reconstruction,
crises that presumably were distant from the more generalized anxiety of
Henry Adams, who remarks, "The child born in 1900 would, then, be
born into a new world which would not be a unity but a multiple."[14] To
Adams the great shift in Western civilization, a "movement from unity to
multiplicity," manifests itself not only on the largest social scale but within
the individual as well.[15] Hence, the historian Adams would feel it appropriate to look within. It follows that *The Education of Henry Adams*
begins with an image surprisingly similar to that of Du Bois: "The boy inherited his double nature," and, as a result, "for him, life was double."[16]
This "double nature" of the self and the corresponding "multiplicity" of
society stand against Adams's more famous symbol of cultural unity in
The Education, that of the medieval Virgin. Juxtaposed against the historical backdrop of unity, the same image of unity that he pursues through
Mont-Saint-Michel and Chartres, double nature is to Adams the representative state of nineteenth-century American selfhood just as to Du Bois it is
the state of African American consciousness.

These accounts of selfhood internally divided and in crisis are not
being offered here as simple displacements of the more well-known images
of transcendent nineteenth-century selfhood. Rather, I am arguing for a
recognition that when read with a sensitivity to the ways it situates itself
socially even the transcendentalist rhetoric of an arch-individualist such as
Emerson can be understood as continuous with his more clearly socially
oriented writings. Emersonian transcendence may well constitute a
compensatory rhetorical strategy, one that corresponds to Du Bois's and
Adams's more straightforward acknowledgments of internal division. All

three look inward, and where they had anticipated some sort of integral unity of selfhood they find double nature instead.

The internal tension that Emerson describes in "The Transcendentalist" is further complicated in such later works as *Representative Men* and *Society and Solitude* by more explicit discussions of social allegiances and obligations. A succinct example of the way the later Emerson uses the individual consciousness as the site for a debate between competing allegiances may be found in "Solitude and Society." The rhetorically balanced title of the essay contains a tension amplified by a statement which presents Emerson's response to his dilemma: "Solitude is impracticable, and society fatal. We must keep our head in the one, and our hands in the other. The conditions are met, if we keep our independence, yet do not lose our sympathy."[17] Emerson here uncritically relies on three crucial, commonplace assumptions of antebellum psychology: the idea that the self possesses certain essential qualities (or faculties) that furnish the basis for conceiving "our independence"; the certainty that society possesses coherent, authoritative, adjudicative functions in response to claims made on behalf of individual knowledge; and a belief in the importance of social cohesion. Emerson's contemporaries agreed on these three points; his argument with them had to do with precisely where and how one is to demarcate the boundaries between self and society. Accordingly, the Emerson who reminds us that we must "keep our independence" also warns that we must "not lose our sympathy." *Sympathy* is the key word here because to an antebellum audience it connoted an affective (and even physical) force of social cohesion.

The importance of sympathy correlates with the interpersonal focus of antebellum psychology, a focus that has been largely lost in discussions of American literary history. When discussed by twentieth-century literary scholars, this psychology, rooted in Scottish Common Sense philosophy, generally has been taken to represent the conservative force of social repression, an obstacle to the artistic imagination. For Common Sense thinkers the essence of the individual was a relatively conventional Christian idea of the soul; nevertheless, in practice, their psychology was concerned not only with the state of the individual soul but with that of society, as illustrated by their interest in terms such as *sympathy*. Social cohesion and sympathy were important to Common Sense thinkers who also suggested that psychological truths were subject to communal affirmation (i.e., any thought process observed by the individual should be present in other people). The contradictory nature of this disciplinary structure is suggested by the yoking of two ostensibly contrasting terms in the phrase *common sense*. *Sense* implies individual perception and consciousness, while *common* refers to the idea that the perceptions and components of the individual consciousness are shared. That these things are presumed to be shared indicates the normative function of this psychology. But while others must be relied upon to affirm the validity of one's perceptions, the individual is directed to introspect in order to discover psychological truths. The tension between the introspective methodology and the need for social validation of individual experience would create uncertainty over their relative importance within the system of Common Sense psychology. It was that space between *common* and *sense* which Hawthorne would explore in his narratives of interiority and sociality.[18]

By the late 1800s, evolutionist thought and the advent of physiological psychology had substantially transformed the field of inquiry into the discipline that more closely resembles modern psychology. The individual will, a basic Common Sense category, seemed almost vestigial in the face of evolutionary determinism. Popularizers of evolution theory proposed that sciences which concentrated on thought processes or social structures were secondary to those scientific studies of the physical environment that purportedly determined individual and social development. From the environmentalist perspective, thought appeared epiphenomenal and introspective discourse embarrassingly primitive. Moreover, the new emphasis on physiology rendered introspection an outmoded philosophical, hence unscientific, methodology. This rapid disciplinary transition from the earlier philosophical orientation had profound effects on both the theory of psychology and the interpretation of earlier disciplinary history. The idea that Common Sense psychology was unredeemably moralistic results from polemics by physiological psychologists against the old school of academic holdouts. Despite the accusation of moralism, Common Sense thought provided a framework for American writers, not usually considered moralistic pedants, who wished to explore selfhood. A fairly explicit example of the Common Sense tension between allegiances to introspective knowledge and social validation of this knowledge may be found in Emerson's *Representative Men.*

The inherent tension within *Representative Men* immediately emerges in the competition over the word *representative.* Does *representation* denote a metonymic reduction of some higher transcendent principle into the material realm? Or does *representation* operate as the synecdochic distillation of the ordinary, a raising up of banality into a principle? The essay on Swedenborg serves to model the former, the understanding of *representative* as metonymic reduction. In this essay, Emerson repeatedly lauds Swedenborg's platonic vision. Before long, however, he complains of how Swedenborg's abstractions oppress: "Swedenborg's system of the world wants central spontaneity; it is dynamic, not vital, and lacks power to generate life. There is no individual in it" (682). Emerson finds solipsism in

Swedenborg's attempt to inhabit exclusively the transcendental realm, but also, paradoxically, the weight of transcendental universals extinguishes the personal. The corrective to this transcendental oppression is a return to worldly and material circumstances. When Emerson descends from the spiritual Swedenborgian plane to the mundane realm, he switches to a competing rhetorical figure to define *representative*, that of synecdoche. The representative man now acts in a political capacity: "the constituency determines the vote of the representative" (619). This political, synecdochic logic predominates in "Napoleon; or, the Man of the World." Napoleon's significant characteristics, his strengths and weaknesses, all derive from his status as representative of the mass of people: "He had the virtues of the masses of his constituents: he had also their vices" (742). In the too-worldly Napoleon, Emerson finds the most radical embodiment of synecdochic representation. But without the presence of transcendent principles, materialized in the figure of Swedenborg, synecdochic representation fails to transform society properly. Neither form of representation by itself effectively changes the world, and Emerson vacillates between the two rhetorical figures of synecdoche and metonymy, and the respective social significance of each, in *Representative Men*.

Emerson reveals this ambivalence early in his introduction, "Uses of Great Men." The divided relationship between the great man and society leads him to declare: "Men are also representative; first, of things, and, secondly, of ideas" (618). This counterpoint between material and ideal corresponds to that between Napoleon and Swedenborg, political representation and idealist leadership, synecdoche and metonymy. The oscillation between opposite poles creates a situation in which Emerson will value the great man for his social effects. For example, early in the "Uses of Great Men," Emerson declares: "We have social strengths. Our affection towards others creates a sort of vantage or purchase which nothing will supply. I can do that by another which I cannot do alone" (616). The great man assumes a social role, and he draws out the individuality of those who surround him. Despite such an inquiry into sociality, Emerson may never be regarded as primarily a socially oriented thinker. But in *Representative Men*, he substantially criticizes the goal of individualistic transcendence, and he presents a vision of individualism that is consistent with sociality.[19] What may be most significant about the interplay between claims on behalf of the individual consciousness as opposed to the social validation of truth claims is that the entire debate takes place within the framework of an overarching desire for social cohesion and a corresponding fear of social disintegration.

The fear that society was disintegrating informed nineteenth-century thought about the relationship of the individual to the community.[20] The radical changes of post–Civil War society included such well-known developments as Reconstruction and its aftermath, the growth of cities, the increase of immigration, shifting patterns of immigration from northern Europe to eastern and southern Europe, and the rise of labor unionism. Literary realists and naturalists more clearly responded to these changes than did their precursors—no antebellum novel could claim, for example, to dramatize the development of Lowell, Massachusetts, as a factory town in a manner parallel to that of Frank Norris's chronicle of California railroads and agribusiness in *The Octopus*—yet the relative omission of such direct commentaries on the mechanics of social change should not obscure its importance. Antebellum fears were inspired by such forces as the expansion of the market economy, the social disruptions that accompanied industrialization, and the regional and ideological conflicts that led to the Civil War. The fear of potential social chaos found expression, for example, in Lincoln's 1838 Lyceum address, in which he decried "the wild and furious" individual "passions" that collectively grew into "the worse than savage mobs."[21] The idea that social order was under siege recurred throughout the nineteenth century, and it corresponds, I believe, with the figuration of selfhood by Emerson, Du Bois, and Adams as fractured and multiple. This fear of chaos generated nineteenth-century attempts to redefine both the bases for community and understandings of the self.

For a fictional definition of selfhood in social terms, we may look to what stands as the novelistic analogue of Emersonian individualism in antebellum literature, James Fenimore Cooper's Leatherstocking tales. The somewhat obsessive treatment of the Leatherstocking character during the 1950s and 1960s is well exemplified by R.W.B. Lewis's declaration, "If there was a fictional Adamic hero unambiguously treated—celebrated in his very Adamism—it was the hero of Cooper's *The Deerslayer*: a self-reliant young man who does seem to have sprung from nowhere."[22] Recent criticism has turned away from the purportedly representative personality of Leatherstocking and toward important questions of history, in particular those involving race and gender.[23] The value of these correctives notwithstanding, I would suggest that the dynamics of Cooper's most famous character in his most well-known novel, *The Last of the Mohicans*, bear review; but rather than approach selfhood directly, a turn toward history is first appropriate.

The Last of the Mohicans presents itself in its subtitle as *A Narrative of 1757*, that is, as a historical fiction. Cooper reinforces this claim in the 1826 preface when he instructs his reader that "an imaginary and romantic picture of things which never had an existence" does not lie ahead.[24] But Cooper's novel, if read not as a history but historically, as a commentary on his contemporaries, reveals a profound anxiety about the pos-

sibility of social dissolution. This in itself is not news; Cooper's conservative, antidemocratic politics are well-known.[25] Although he may have
looked abroad to Luddite agitation between 1817 and 1819, the particular
goad to his conservatism was no doubt the political and social turmoil of
the 1820s, a period in which political and labor violence grew increasingly
common. As social historian Paul Boyer notes, the changes in the population of the cities, the increasing number of laborers, immigrants, and the
poor, led to changes in the electoral process. Boyer describes it as a "period
when an older political order based on deference to elite figures gave way
to a system based on the manipulation of a mass electorate."[26] Accordingly, it was a time when political bosses, regarded by their opponents as
unprincipled, grew in strength: in Philadelphia, Joel Barlow Sutherland
rose in power; in New York, Tammany Hall would increasingly dominate
the local scene; and in Boston, the change in status from town to city in
1822 brought about a mayoral election that led to the installation of, in
Emerson's words, "a parcel of demagogues."[27]

In *The Last of the Mohicans,* we can see how Cooper's fear of
demagogues and distrust of democracy shape the narrative. The great vil-
lain of the novel is Magua, the deceitful Huron who successively betrays
friendly whites, captures Cora and Alice Munro, commands the Fort William Henry massacre, captures Cora and Alice yet again, and kills Uncas.
Cooper is less interested in the origins of Magua's animosity toward the
whites and their Native American friends than he is in the source of
Magua's power: the ability to sway Native American listeners through persuasive speech. Magua's masterful oratory is repeatedly presented throughout the novel—first during the Munro sisters' initial captivity, then several
times during the arguments in the Native American settlements. Cooper
asks us to marvel at Magua's skill:

> He commenced by flattering the self-love of his auditors; a never-
> failing method of commanding attention. When he had enumerated
> the many different occasions on which the Hurons had exhibited their
> courage and prowess, in the punishment of insults, he digressed in a
> high encomium on the virtue of wisdom. He painted the quality, as
> forming the great point of difference between the beaver and other
> brutes; between brutes and men; and, finally, between the Hurons, in
> particular, and the rest of the human race. . . . He spoke openly of
> the fruits of their wisdom, which he boldly pronounced would be
> a complete and final triumph over their enemies. . . . In short, he
> so blended the warlike with the artful, the obvious with the obscure,
> as to flatter the propensities of both parties, and to leave to each sub-
> ject of hope, while neither could say, it clearly comprehended his
> intentions.

The orator, or the politician, who can produce such a state of things, is commonly popular with his contemporaries, however he may be treated by posterity. All perceived that more was meant than was uttered, and each one believed that the hidden meaning was precisely such as his own faculties enabled him to understand, or his own wishes led him to anticipate. [797-98]

Magua's appeal to his audience is presented in a way that encourages an ironic perspective on speakers who praise their audiences for their abilities to reason. The demagogic Magua uses flattery to motivate his audience, as he had in an earlier episode, but here Cooper adds to Magua's arsenal skill at conveying vague promises. With this weapon, Magua thus becomes the equivalent of the politician "in a more advanced state of society," in which Magua would have "the reputation of a skilful diplomatist" (807). Lest the reader possibly interpret the political analogy as flattering, Cooper presents an unambiguously damning image: "It would not have been difficult to have fancied the dusky savage the Prince of Darkness" (799).[28]

The great irony of the action here is that "the Prince of Darkness" and those who follow his lead behave in what can only be described as a democratic manner, one that may logically be associated with the inclusion in the electorate of lower-class white males during the 1820s. By contrast, Hawkeye, Chingachgook, and their compatriots work within either the restrictions of military life (as in the case of Major Heyward and Colonel Munro) or those of aristocratic Mohican descent (as evidenced when the prisoner Uncas stuns his captors by revealing the tattoo of a blue tortoise, the primal clan). Cooper sets into play against each other two styles of government, the one extremely orderly and associated with inherited virtue, the other an almost anarchic democracy devoid of virtue. The conflict between order and disorder is not fully resolved by the end of the novel; rather, it is only momentarily paused, though the end of the conflict is by implication the destruction of the dominant Native American culture in *The Last of the Mohicans*, that culture associated with Magua. This projected end serves to contain and counteract anxiety over the possible breakdown of social order in Jacksonian America, an anxiety that is transposed backwards onto the image of bloodthirsty Native Americans. What links together 1820s America and the events of 1757 are the destructive capacities of demagogues. Their destructiveness can be held in check by one thing only: the regulation of desire. The ability of characters to regulate desire in *The Last of the Mohicans* is crucial to the action, and it conveys the idea that selfhood may not be so much the site of freedom as the occasion for internalized social control.

The story may largely be understood as the integration of Cooper's national concerns about the nature of democracy with the principles of individual action. When people are unable to regulate their feelings, they are susceptible to the machinations of demagogues—in other words, you can't cheat an honest man. One whose desires are regulated according to the dictates of virtue cannot be seduced by desire, whatever form it takes. Self-control is the distinguishing mark of Cooper's hero, and an early episode in the novel offers an illustration of Hawkeye's attribute. In the action that leads up to and includes the first fight with Magua's band, we can see how Cooper associates self-control with maturity. For example, restraint is emblematized by the proper use of gunpowder, as when Hawkeye repeatedly chastises Uncas: "You are wasteful of your powder, and the kick of the rifle disconcerts your aim!" (547); and, again, "Uncas, boy, you waste the kernels by overcharging; and a kicking rifle never carries a true bullet" (552-53). Control over the flow of powder serves as a metaphor for control over the flow of feelings: effective action follows only if one governs one's emotions. Hawkeye must also restrain the youthful and excessively compassionate Heyward: "The first generous impulse of Duncan, was to rush to the rescue of the hapless wretch, but he felt himself bound to the spot, by the iron grasp of the immoveable scout" (548). And shortly afterwards, Cooper presents a different though equally effective intervention: "Heyward felt a burning desire to rush forward to meet them, so intense was the delirious anxiety of the moment, but he was restrained by the deliberate examples of the scout and Uncas" (549). Uncas here shows his comparatively greater combat experience, though both he and Heyward require the counsel of an elder to develop self-mastery.

There are other moments when self-restraint (or its absence) is dramatized, such as the scene in which Magua's unruly band partakes of a "revolting meal," consuming a freshly killed fawn "without any aid from the science of cookery" (584), but none are so vital to the plot as the attack that culminates in the deaths of Cora Munro, Uncas, and Magua.[29] While chasing after Magua and the captive Cora, the impetuous Uncas unnecessarily exposes himself to danger: "In his eagerness to expedite the pursuit, Uncas had left himself nearly alone. . . . and reckless of the disparity in their numbers, he rushed upon his enemy" (859). Hawkeye warns him "in vain" to look after himself, but Uncas advances, joined by Heyward: "Uncas abandoned his rifle, and leaped forward with headlong precipitation. Heyward rashly imitated his example, though both were, a moment afterwards, admonished of its madness, by hearing the bellowing of a piece, that the Hurons found time to discharge" (861). By approaching the fleeing Magua, Uncas brings about the confrontation between captors and captive which leads to Cora's death. And the weaponless Uncas, maddened by her death, leaps "frantically," but he arrives on the scene too late to do any good and unable to effectively defend himself. By contrast, retribution against Magua results from Hawkeye's self-mastery: "the agitated weapon of the scout was drawn to his shoulder. The surrounding rocks, themselves, were not steadier than the piece became for the single instant that it poured out its contents" (864). Despite witnessing the death of his close companion Uncas, Hawkeye maintains a heroic composure, thus modeling Cooper's ideal of selfhood.

Hawkeye would seem to be Cooper's model citizen except for his famed social aversiveness. In what perhaps remains the most well-known work of criticism on the novel, Leslie Fiedler labels Hawkeye "the hunter and enemy of cities," and it is hard not to believe that this trait, this counterbalancing remainder that cannot be subsumed by the forces of regulation and social control, has contributed to Hawkeye's endurance in American culture.[30] An important aspect of Hawkeye's selfhood remains radically unknowable and irreducible—one might even be tempted to label this aspect, as did Henry Nash Smith, Hawkeye's "subversive impulses."[31] Yet it is not order that seems to most disturb Cooper, but disorder. Cooper, as well as Hawkeye, may be understood to be an "enemy of cities," if we presume cities were the places where demagogues ruled and civic order was most notable by its lapses. Cooper, like Emerson, expresses in *The Last of the Mohicans* impulses traditionally understood as individualistic alongside an overwhelming desire for social order. The presence of this desire leads to a question about the writing of American literary history: When even the nineteenth-century writers most closely identified with individualistic characters and arguments display so powerful a concern about the integrity and cohesion of society, why has the critical characterization of the period focused on individualism as its distinguishing feature? I propose that there are two overlapping sets of reasons for this critical tendency, one institutional, the other methodological.

From the perspective of institutional history, the position of Americanist literary scholars, like that of all engaged in the liberal arts, has been difficult. In large part their problems have resulted from populist anti-intellectualism and the hostility of a scientistically oriented society toward aesthetic studies. Because of these common attitudes, the professor of literature is in an embattled position in which many college freshmen feel perfectly comfortable expressing skepticism toward the seemingly random methodologies of literary studies, the absence of clearly definable results from these methods, and even the very worth of the discipline. Amidst such feelings, literary theorists have spent much time and energy formulating defenses for the discipline. One characteristic defense has been that offered by I.A. Richards, who in 1926 claimed that technology without the humanities is a soulless, empty pursuit. The other traditional justification, best embodied by E.D. Hirsch's *Cultural Literacy*, responds to the threat of philistinism with the assertion that knowledge of the humanities is useful to the individual who wants to get ahead in the world.[32] Despite these ethical and practical arguments for the importance of literary studies, the small budgets of English departments reflect the prevalent societal attitude.

In addition to this primary alienation of the literary scholar, Americanists have had to battle to establish a place for themselves within literature departments dominated by English literary studies. This domination has been reflected and reinforced by the continued numerical superiority of English literature specialists in English departments.[33] Much like early nineteenth-century cultural nationalists, the Americanist scholar has routinely had to assert the value of American literature. The first English language literary studies in the years after the Civil War exclusively treated English literature. This focus continued through the 1800s, and at the turn of the century the two dominant methodologies were philological and impressionistic criticism. Obviously, American literature could not compete with Old and Middle English in the sphere of philological studies. But impressionistic criticism, though a response to dry and nonemotional philological criticism, was equally biased toward British literature; only a few American authors, such as Longfellow, Lowell, and Holmes, were acceptable to genteel academic tastes. According to contemporary standards, American literature was second-rate, and it was commonly understood that no Americans could compete with Shakespeare and other British luminaries on aesthetic grounds.[34]

By the end of World War I, Americanists had begun to advance an alternative theoretical and methodological basis for their work: cultural criticism and a historicist method. The programmatic title of Van Wyck Brooks's "On Creating a Usable Past" suggested that literary studies be justified in terms of its cultural relevance: "The real task for the American literary historian, then, is not to seek for masterpieces—the few masterpieces are all too obvious—but for tendencies."[35] Having abandoned the attempt to justify American literature on the basis of aesthetic value, Brooks demanded a historical analysis of culture. The work that answered Brooks's call and established the academic respectability of American literary studies was Vernon Parrington's *Main Currents in American Thought*. Parrington, using Santayana's phrase "the genteel tradition" to describe the aesthetic orientation he was to eschew, surveyed the history of American literature and found American culture to be an ongoing struggle between conservative and liberal political tendencies.[36] Defining political conservatism as in principle contrary to the American democratic ideal—his description of Alexander Hamilton as "one to whom our industrialization owes a very great debt, but from whom our democratic liberalism has received nothing" typifies his assessments—Parrington claimed that the natural and social environment had created "an American liberalism, frankly and vigorously individualistic."[37] Parrington's endorsement of individualism may now seem strange in view of his reputation. Marxist literary historians during the 1930s, no advocates of individualism, claimed Parrington's work as a predecessor to their own, and this critical genealogy was affirmed, though with less approval and more ultimate effect, by Lionel Trilling in 1940.

Trilling, struggling to assert a more complex treatment of aesthetic issues within a cultural context, characterized Parrington's approach as overly reliant on questionable dichotomies and as ultimately reductive: "Parrington's was not a great mind. . . . Separate Parrington from his informing idea of the economic and social determination of thought and what is left is a simple intelligence."[38] Trilling's portrayal of Parrington's work highlighted the economic determinism further developed by Hicks and Calverton, among others, during the 1930s. Yet Parrington's vision of progressive individualism, understandably rejected by those Marxist historicist critics whom Parrington represented for Trilling, established the tenor (if not the methodology) of American literary scholarship: liberal political individualism was upheld as the best expression of American culture. This American expression of individualism, which contained within it an implicit protest against the conservative anglophilism of the academy, legitimized the posture of cultural critic assumed by Americanist scholars.

For Americanist literary scholars, the appeal of the symbol of the individual has been especially profound. The image of the embattled individual, struggling against an unappreciative, conformist society, routinely has been advanced by critics as a proper focus for disciplinary study. With the exception of Emerson, the central figures of the American Renaissance have been characterized as alienated from an unmindful society. We have therefore inherited the images of Thoreau in the wilderness, Melville on the brink of madness, Whitman struggling to defend his art against censors, Hawthorne isolated in his study, and the still more cloistered Dickinson. In these heroic figures, Americanist critics could find ideals analogous to their own tenuous positions. Marginalized by a society uninterested in literary pursuits, and further belittled within anglophilic English departments, the Americanist could look to these earlier social critics and, proclaiming the poetry of Whitman to a sleepy afternoon class of philistines, feel a symbolic elevation in the knowledge of a noble intellectual lineage.

This stance of alienated aesthetic individualism has its basis in literary modernism. Modernist thought advanced two ideas that were to be of particular significance to literary theorists: the notion of individual alienation from society, and the priority of individual experience. The idea of individual alienation from society seems so natural now as to be taken for granted. Marxist theories of alienation, the Freudian emphasis on individual analysis, the philosophical interest in ontological rather than strictly epistemological issues—all these fed into modernist ideas about individualism. An analysis by one critic who could hardly be said to champion individualism may best express the modernist literary outlook. In his discussion of the development of the novel, Georg Lukács asserted that the modern world generated a literary form that concentrates on the individual: "The epic individual, the hero of the novel, is the product of estrangement from the outside world. When the world is internally homogenous, men do not differ qualitatively from one another."[39] Lukács thereby accounted for novelistic expressions of individualism while he nostalgically looked back to the "integrated civilizations" that did not promote alienated individualistic differentiation.[40] Despairing of the possibility of integrated civilizations and preferring attention to immediate experience over the abstractions of historical theories, modernism sought new beginnings in the individual. Given the modernist penchant for dualisms, the individual was quite naturally perceived to be in opposition to society. The critical method that emerged from this desire for the integrity of the individual aesthetic imagination was the New Criticism.[41]

New Critical aesthetic formalism may be understood as a moral reaction to the emphasis on economic value characteristic of modern industrialist society. Kenneth Burke noted this in his contemporary response to the Agrarian agenda when he commented that the doctrine of "art for art's sake," an outgrowth of Kantian aesthetics, ultimately sought to subsume ethics under aesthetics.[42] Burke sharply criticized I'll Take My Stand, taking issue with the reactionary Agrarian vision, but he also understood that their vision of the aesthetic realm was an attempt to be "the corrective of the practical."[43] Advocates of this correction, though, uncritically adopted a central feature of the practical realm. The New Critics, while objecting to the dominance of science, used the privileged methodology of scientism: a repudiation of impressionism, exclusive attention to the object at hand, and the hope for a method that would yield reproducible results. Because New Critics were so successful, it is easy to overlook the compensatory nature of their project. Their exaltation of art was in large part a defensive response to an ungrateful world.

Most significant to the development of American literary history and criticism was the New Critical opposition of the individual to the community. Against a society that prized rational, scientistic, conformist thought, this critical method assumed an adversarial stance, one that promoted emotion, introspection, and a nonconformist individualism. This perspective eventually altered the meaning of earlier American literature: writers who had criticized contemporary social conventions became proto-modernists. Earlier American forms of individualism—individualisms understood by Parrington to be expressions of political liberalism and opposition—fused with the modernist outlook to produce a powerful symbol of the individual in opposition to society. It is no surprise, given this outlook, that critical tastes should change and that the novels of Howells, for example, with their close attention to social interaction, should fall into disrepute while Henry James's ironies and formal innovations with respect to narrative consciousness should find favor. Similarly, Parrington's rejection of Hawthorne's value, because of his purported inattention to the social realm with a resultant "intellectual poverty,"[44] seemed hopelessly old-fashioned to those later critics for whom an aesthetic orientation provided insights into the ways that historical knowledge of culture is mediated by symbolic systems. Seeking a balance between historicist and aestheticist approaches in his "History of a Literary Radical," Randolph Bourne had prophesied a critical method that would account for literary form and cultural history as well. A little more than twenty years later, F.O. Matthiessen's *American Renaissance* appeared to answer this call.

The importance of Matthiessen's attempt to accommodate antagonistic historicist and New Critical methods in *American Renaissance* is difficult to overestimate. His introductory chapter describes his approach and defends his attention to those writers committed to providing "a culture commensurate with America's political opportunity."[45] The unintended irony of this statement almost leaps off the page at the reader because, despite his clear statement of political allegiances, his book is strikingly inattentive to the issues of slavery and race relations. Similarly, for Matthiessen to speak of "the possibilities of democracy" (ix) and then two pages later cite Ezra Pound when justifying his choice of "past masterpieces" (vii) now appears to be an astonishing juxtaposition. His canon-making decision to deal only with writers who were northeastern males of Anglo-Saxon origin seems equally at odds with his politics. Perhaps most significant, as Myra Jehlen notes, was Matthiessen's recasting of political problems as aesthetic ones.[46]

Yet it is exactly Matthiessen's conflation of aesthetics and politics that made his work so influential to later Americanist critics. Whatever his theoretical inconsistencies or failures, Matthiessen managed to establish

American literary "masterpieces" as equivalent to their English counterparts. The subordination of history to aesthetics was an act that served to free Americanists from the need to constantly defend their field on the grounds of historical relevance. Not that Matthiessen neglected to cite the importance of culture: "Any artist's use of language is the most sensitive index to cultural history, since a man can articulate only what he is, and what he has been made by the society of which he is a willing or an unwilling part" (xv). The aesthetic approach thus justified on cultural grounds, Matthiessen only occasionally needed to touch on political issues to make his point. For instance, he understood Ahab to be Melville's depiction of those "strong-willed individuals who seized the land and gutted the forests and built the railroads" (459). This interpretation conformed to his socialist politics and must have appeared as a particularly timely reference to the personality cults of contemporary international politics.

By adapting a historicist interpretation of culture to the modernist aestheticism of the New Criticism, *American Renaissance* set the scene for Americanists to claim to be furnishing culturally relevant observations while primarily performing close readings of relatively few literary texts. Despite the success of *American Renaissance,* Matthiessen, as William Cain observes, was in fact unable to reconcile his conflicting allegiances to socialism, historicism, and the New Criticism. It is hard to disagree with Cain, given the theoretical inconsistencies of *American Renaissance;* there is no reasonable way to account for Matthiessen's neglect of mid-nineteenth-century race relations unless one sees it as the victory of a totalizing aesthetic vision over historical specificity. Yet the fact that at the time Matthiessen *appeared* to be successful in his book reveals much about Americanist literary criticism. Earlier historicist scholars had drawn on the image of American individualism either to criticize American culture, as Marxists like Calverton and Hicks had done, or to point hopefully to the possibilities for social change through individual action, as Parrington did with his claim of an American tradition of a progressive, Jeffersonian individualism. In their discussions of literary form, some later critics, such as Leslie Fiedler, continued to criticize individualism as an essentially delusory and ultimately unproductive protest against society. Most critics, however, followed Parrington's lead while they simultaneously claimed to escape his tendencies toward deterministic interpretations of literature. To these critics, the purportedly free individual imagination was an invaluable attribute of American literature.

American Renaissance exhibits both sets of attitudes toward individualism. Matthiessen was wary of the excesses of individualism, which, he remarked, could be heard in "the voice of Hitler's megalomania" (546). His comments about Ahab illustrate this wariness, as does his preliminary

justification of his choice of writers according to their "one common de-
nominator . . . their devotion to the possibilities of democracy" (ix). This
interest in democracy even led Matthiessen to defend Emerson from the
potential charge of "the extremes of rugged Emersonianism" (8) with the
argument that Emerson was by nature democratic. But Matthiessen's appropriation of the New Critical methodology, in which a few solitary
artists stand in for the culture as a whole, ultimately would overwhelm his
suggestion that individualism needs to be tempered. The New Critical
transformation of culture into a remote aesthetic realm further naturalized
the attention to individualism as a central feature of American literature.
And the modernist opposition of the individual to society established the
priority of the individual at both ends in the transmission of literature. The
mind of the author was acclaimed as supremely capable of appreciating
the aesthetic unity of the literary work, while the ideal reader's mind was
similarly understood as a corresponding site of authentic experience. The
aesthetic realm, situated in refined modes of consciousness, defensively offered an ethical alternative to the horrors of the modern world. With the
arrival of the New Criticism, the celebration of American individualism
appeared to lead quite naturally into a celebration of aesthetics. The individual, in the liberal spirit of Parrington's *Main Currents,* could be reliably
credited with the ability to work for social change in the world. The battle
over the symbol of the individual thus was largely resolved: champions of
aesthetics and advocates of social change could claim the individual for
their own. And, ironically, Leftist critics of American economic individualism relied on an individualistic methodology to argue their claims.

Despite the fact that after Matthiessen nineteenth-century American literature had acquired canonical status, American literary studies continued
to be warranted on the grounds of cultural relevance. Major thematic
treatments of American literature during the 1950s and 1960s, such as
R.W.B. Lewis's *The American Adam,* Richard Chase's *The American
Novel and Its Tradition,* and even Richard Poirier's *A World Elsewhere,*
however much they depended on aesthetic standards for their choices of
works to discuss and their methodologies, offered as their justification the
elucidation of significant cultural tendencies or conflicts. Their interpretations of American culture concur on the following crucial points: the
individual and society have a necessarily antagonistic relationship, and the
individual merits the critic's allegiance. Even more historically oriented
critics, such as Henry Nash Smith, cited individualism as a distinctive
characteristic of American culture. The important feature of this claim
about individualism was its value as part of an oppositional stance against
a conformist society. With few exceptions, critics, such as the ones men-

tioned above, situated themselves alongside their subjects, characterizing opponents as essentially conformist, while they and their cohorts stood for the spirit of the free individual or its artistic analogue, the imaginative realm. This is not to suggest that these critics, viewed from a more skeptical 1980s perspective as the developers of a "Cold War consensus," were less than sincere when they attempted to use this individualistic rhetorical tradition to advocate social change.[47] Yet their protests against the dominant order were apparently subverted by their reliance on the spatial metaphor of insiders versus outsiders.

The casting of complex social, intellectual, and literary problems in polarities remains a problem for any criticism that identifies itself as resisting or oppositional. Sacvan Bercovitch, in *The American Jeremiad,* describes how oppositional rhetoric has shaped American literary history, but he could equally have been describing the history of American literary scholarship. In both sets of situations, the boundaries between the inside and the outside become blurred as each category penetrates the other or, one might say, as the theoretically opposed categories deconstruct themselves. The loss of categorical purity is not, though, what really matters in terms of literary scholarship. Rather, the difficulty is one of dialectical dynamics—the kind of dialectical process we see at work in Emerson's *Nature,* which, unlike the later, more decidedly unresolved tensions of *Representative Men, Society and Solitude,* and even "The Transcendentalist," repeatedly preserves a version of the self capable of transcending the conflicts between the "NOT ME" (8) and an increasingly refined essence of selfhood. Selfhood as a distinct subject matter may no longer generate the same resonances among literary and cultural scholars as it once did; yet the dialectical role of the self, often in the persons of critics who oppose potentially overwhelming, frequently oppressive social forces as well as corollary literary or historical figures, has been preserved in the disciplinary debate. In the wake of the New Historicism, cultural critics face a situation in which the problematics of selfhood are further complicated by the now prevalent awareness of how history has been either ignored or textualized in literary studies. This set of difficulties is raised with revealing results in Eric Sundquist's *To Wake the Nations: Race in the Making of American Literature.*

From the perspective of a disciplinary historian, *To Wake the Nations* may be understood as the recovery of a cultural history overlooked—or suppressed—by Matthiessen's *American Renaissance* and the works that followed in that vein. Sundquist insists on the importance of race in the United States, yet he avoids characterizing his work as a displacement of an outmoded literary history. Sundquist accordingly maintains that he is not offering a "new genealogy of American authorship."[48] In refraining from this claim, he does not specify theoretical skepticism at the possibility of such a narrative of descent, nor does he interrogate the function of textual structures within historical accounts. Rather, he identifies his goal as the act of "verification" of African American experience; in effect, he moves from more strictly disciplinary concerns to a broader social sphere.[49] This move, in which textual analysis is set off against a larger disciplinary (and extradisciplinary) vision, raises questions about historicist textual analysis.

In the climactic reading within *To Wake the Nations,* Sundquist turns his attention to *The Souls of Black Folk,* an attention that serves as a necessary corrective to a history of academic neglect: "Perhaps no other book of such stature, such beautiful accomplishment and influence, is so little appreciated even today by a general scholarly audience, let alone a literate public."[50] Sundquist reads Du Bois as a kind of dialectician, one who fully fathoms and explores the antitheses between white and black and between elite and folk cultures. Du Bois, despite his own elitist notion of a talented tenth in which would inhere the best hope of African American culture, recovers a scorned folk culture in *The Souls of Black Folk.* Or, more precisely, Du Bois alludes to black spirituals, using brief musical excerpts to preface each chapter and leaving to the scholar the task of fully fleshing out the unspoken—or unsung—language of the text. According to Sundquist, Du Bois effectively transcends the opposition of folk and elite cultures by the close of his book. As evidence, he offers the "concluding song of *The Souls of Black Folk,* the only one . . . in which music and text coexist."[51] Du Bois's inclusion of words suggests the recovery of voice and a renewed ability to articulate tensions in a self-conscious and self-possessed manner. Hence, it "brings the metaphor of the journey to a conclusion and functions as an envoy for the book as well as Du Bois's message to the modern world."[52] But this act of textual resolution is followed by an additional, textually unsettling, rhetorical appeal.

The Souls of Black Folk ends with a section called "The Afterthought," in which Du Bois asks "O God, the Reader" to make certain that his book "not fall still-born into the world wilderness."[53] With this direct appeal to the reader, Du Bois points out the textuality of the text. He is concerned that his book be an effective attempt at social action, that it generate "vigor of thought and thougtful deed" in pursuit of "righteousness." And he concludes by asking that "these crooked marks on a fragile leaf be not indeed THE END."[54] The text itself thereby indicates its own incompleteness. This sense of its incompleteness, in effect, complements the sense of textual—and musical—closure analyzed by Sundquist. My point here is not that a sense of textual openness displaces closure; rather, it is to note the persistent tendency toward closure in historicist criticism, a stabilizing tendency that can accompany the attempt to locate formal, textual solutions to cultural problems.

The critical penchant for textual and interpretive solutions to cultural problems may be conceived as an unwitting inclination to legitimize or naturalize power relations. Wai-Chee Dimock addresses this when she distinguishes between feminists and New Historicists, whose "universalization of power and blurring of genders have struck many feminists as nothing short of reactionary."[55] Dimock, like Sundquist, defines her reading self in terms of an interplay between cultural politics and poetics. But she delineates her own subject position in a movement away from a male-dominated New Historicism, which has been preoccupied with "the sociocultural field at the text's moment of production," and toward a feminist historicism that reinscribes the reader in the arena of cultural production.[56] As she programmatically asserts, "the interplay between production and reception," an interplay that historicizes reading, is "crucial, I think, to any historical criticism."[57] Dimock's rejection of the totalizing— and demoralizing—tendency of the New Historicism has been voiced by various critics.[58] But the obvious alternative, a return to a kind of advocacy position that insists on critical activity as the site of cultural agency, involves a risk that Gayatri Spivak identifies as "the fraud at the heart of identity politics."[59] Spivak's cautionary remarks are worth noting: "The ethnic American—who is the nonethnic American?—has her face turned back *and* front."[60] In effect, Spivak suggests that *all* critics may make some claim to marginality as a way of situating themselves as readers, not unlike the claim of Bercovitch's Jeremiahs, and the risk is a return to a selfhood that is purportedly cognizant of the poststructuralist critique of subjectivity but which behaves as if this critique has itself been transcended.

The most sustained recent exploration of the problematic engagements between selfhood, interpretation, and historicism in American literature may be found in Sacvan Bercovitch's *The Office of the Scarlet Letter*. In this study, Bercovitch inquires into a selfhood that derives its significance from the symbology of America, and he thus expands on his earlier work in *The Puritan Origins of the American Self* and *The American Jeremiad*. By attending to the problem of Hawthorne's silence about Hester Prynne's return to New England in the final chapter of *The Scarlet Letter*, Bercovitch opens up for discussion two distinct issues that bear heavily on each other. These two issues are the relationship between ambiguity and what he identifies as "the principles of liberal exegesis," and the ways by which the reader is implicated in the exegetical process.[61] The underlying questions here are quite similar to the ones that shape Sundquist's and Dimock's discussions of nineteenth-century American literature: How are we to understand the workings of cultural power, and how are we to situate ourselves as readers in relation to its operations? Bercovitch, more than the others, stresses the subtly cooptational capacities of American liberal ideology. He initially presents the problem as a textual one—"*The Scarlet Letter* is a story of socialization in which the point of socialization is not to conform, but to consent"[62]—but it is plain that there are disciplinary ramifications to his account of a culture in which speech constitutes both the ends of social action and the simultaneous affirmation of the status quo.

This situation resists easy answers. Simple assertions of oppositional stances readily fall under the heading of "the fraud at the heart of identity politics," and the discourse of resistance may engage the critic in the logic of "liberal exegesis." By assuming oppositional postures, critics risk unconsciously replicating the cultural work of earlier generations or, more dubiously, engaging in what Cornel West calls the "self-serving careerism" of those who espouse the "rhetoric of oppositional politics of little seriousness and integrity."[63] The alternative, though, as Emily Miller Budick warns, is a deathly silence, and her suggestion that one may articulate "an aversive relation with America" is made with cognizance of potential theoretical pitfalls.[64] With the awareness that no simple remedy or cautionary strategy is available, and with the hope of balancing the competing impulses to see texts as sites of repression as opposed to their value as sources of criticism, I approach the problem by maintaining a historicist skepticism toward the smooth translation into universalist terms of nineteenth-century narratives and theories. As Steven Mailloux suggests, interpretation "should move from theory to history as quickly as possible."[65]

One potential problem of a historicist approach is that when foregrounded the cultural contexts of the works being studied may threaten to either overwhelm or undermine relevant late-twentieth-century disciplinary and cultural concerns. When Sundquist encloses his reading of Du Bois within a disciplinary framework, he effectively responds to this potential difficulty. By contrast, the approaches suggested by Bercovitch and Budick, for example, while attentive to issues of form and aesthetics, avoid presupposing the centrality of literary studies and thus manage to suggest engagement in a wide cultural arena. The price to be paid for this relative openness is the loss of the certainty of ending that often accompanies the reinstatement of disciplinary boundaries. When these critics, along with Sundquist, return to questions of the interpretive functions of selfhood, it is with a desire to shift the critical discourse of selfhood toward the ethical and the interpersonal realm. While my own work on the self is aimed in this same direction, a direction that amounts to a corrective to either a humanist self-aggrandizement or a poststructuralist self-denigration, I also see this critical tendency as substantially continuous with the theoretical and ethical dimensions of the nineteenth-century writings to be discussed in the chapters that follow.

2

Hawthorne's Drama of the Self

Antebellum Psychology and Sociality

The generation to which he belonged, that generation which grew up with the century, witnessed during a period of fifty years the immense, uninterrupted material development of the young Republic; and when one thinks of the scale on which it took place, of the prosperity that walked in its train and waited on its course, of the hopes it fostered and the blessings it conferred, of the broad morning sunshine, in a word, in which it all went forward, there seems to be little room for surprise that it should have implanted a kind of superstitious faith in the grandeur of the country, its duration, its immunity from the usual troubles of earthly empire. This faith was a simple and uncritical one, enlivened with an element of genial optimism.

—Henry James, *Hawthorne*[1]

When, in his 1879 essay on Hawthorne, Henry James offered this assessment of Hawthorne's generation, he looked back nostalgically to the antebellum United States and the political and societal simplicity—"the broad morning sunshine"—he associated with it. James believed, of course, that this simplicity exacted a price; earlier in the essay he had made his famous assertion that "the flower of art blooms only where the soil is deep, that it takes a great deal of history to produce a little literature" (320). A local, provincial, limited knowledge of the world and its intricacies may have posed, according to James's criteria, aesthetic obstacles to Hawthorne as a member of an "earlier and simpler generation," but Hawthorne appeared to have transcended his limitations through his astute observations of "the deeper psychology" (427, 368). James thus introduced a pair of characterizations that would prove enduring in the history of Hawthorne criticism: the relative naïveté of Hawthorne's generation (accompanied by his corresponding lack of interest in contemporary affairs), and, turning his loss into gain, Hawthorne's acumen as a student of human psychology.

Hawthorne's relationship to contemporary psychological thought and its importance to interpretations of his work will be the primary focus here. Contemporary psychology, utterly dominated by Common Sense philosophy, offered behavioral prescriptions, for which it is best remembered, but it also was more than a compendium of moralisms. As I argued in the preceding chapter, antebellum thought about the nature of the individual responded to increased societal complexities and perceived threats of social upheaval. An awareness of these things is necessary for a balanced assessment of antebellum psychology. Before discussing Common Sense thought, therefore, I think it useful to more fully appreciate how James's profoundly influential characterization of Hawthorne and his time may have been colored by late-nineteenth-century concerns, while concerns that preoccupied Hawthorne escaped James's notice.

James's estimation of the comparative simplicity of Hawthorne's time is best discussed in late-nineteenth-century terms. The Civil War and its aftermath appeared to furnish one demanding set of problems unknown to Hawthorne's era; by comparison, the antebellum debate over abolition seemed to James to have been rather limited. Of even greater immediate importance to James as a sign of the difference between early- and late-nineteenth-century American society was the issue of immigration. Hawthorne's era, according to James, was marked by an absence of immigrants, and this absence would create the insular outlook that informs James's Hawthorne. James characteristically maintained, "Forty years ago the tide of foreign immigration had scarcely begun to break upon the rural strongholds of the New England race; it had at most begun to splash them with the salt Hibernian spray. . . . It is very possible, however, that at this period there was not an Irishman in Concord; the place would have been a village community operating in excellent conditions" (389). Henry James, himself the grandson of an Irish immigrant, here overlooks the transatlantic origins of his forebear, and he treats the threat posed by immigration to his sense of social cohesion purely as a concern of his generation.

The mythically simple and stable New England village past that James describes in *Hawthorne* achieves salience when it is juxtaposed against the complexities and cultural instability characteristic of James's time. James does not speak directly to the issue of late-nineteenth-century immigration in *Hawthorne* or most of his other writings, but one may find pertinent observations in *The American Scene*. The cosmopolitan narrator of this account, devoting considerable attention to immigration, reflects on the presence of "the representatives of the races we have nothing 'in common', with."[2] The narrator looks with suspicion on immigrants while, with the ironic tone James so often used to satirize the upper class, he simultaneously distances himself from those who might constitute themselves as the *we* who lack the common grounds necessary to establish a coherent, unified social body with the conspicuously alien Jewish and Italian immigrant populations. In contrast to this later scene of cosmopolitan social disintegration, in *Hawthorne* James presents a New England that "must have been an even better specimen than to-day—more homo-geneous, more indigenous, more absolutely democratic" (389). In this instance, James condescendingly dismisses provincial antebellum culture while concurrently evoking a time before the arrival of newer immigrants, an era when democracy was unthreatened and a secure feeling of commu-nity prevailed. James's precise allegiances in these two separate, ironically ambiguous statements matter less than the typically nineteenth-century anxiety to which he gives voice: Is American society losing its cohesion in the face of pressures from inside and outside?[3]

Concerns about community were not, however, exclusive to Henry James and the late nineteenth century. These concerns can readily be traced at least as far as the world of eighteenth-century mercantile capital-ism, a time when older, more stable social and political forms appeared increasingly remote and philosophers like Shaftesbury and Adam Smith at-tempted to develop new rationales for community cohesion. Psychology as an inquiry into selfhood and social bonds began to assume prominence as a discipline at this time, and we can find the roots of the dominant psy-chology of Hawthorne's era in late- eighteenth-century Scottish Common Sense moral philosophy.[4] Members of Hawthorne's own generation, de-spite Henry James's view that theirs was a simpler time, also experienced a desire for social cohesion in the face of the threats to stability posed by economic expansion, increased industrialization, the associated growth of immigration and an urban working class, and the corresponding antebel-lum problems posed by regional differences. An attempt at a coherent theoretical response to these threats against community stability was pro-vided by contemporary psychologists, as a close look at their writings will reveal. It is therefore no accident that the interest in psychology displayed by Hawthorne and his contemporaries thus arose simultaneously with anxieties over the loss of social cohesion in antebellum New England.

Early-nineteenth-century social instability and change in New En-gland largely resulted from the transformation of a primarily rural and maritime economy to one dominated by water-powered manufacture and associated industry. This rapid development radically altered the economic bases of the region and induced corresponding changes in politics and mo-rality, such as the introduction of the new industrial morality, generally identified as the "Puritan" work ethic, which reverenced such behaviors as punctuality and abstinence from alcohol and, in addition, the notion that work is valuable for its own sake.[5] Resistance to this industrial morality often took the form of mass action, the kinds of behaviors abhorred by Emerson and Cooper. As Charles Sellers notes, in Jacksonian America, "The crowd in the streets was the ultimate working class weapon. Tradi-tionally enforcing the preindustrial moral economy, it was invoked more frequently and coercively in strikes."[6] For example, episodes of collective objections to low wages in Massachusetts took place in the summer of 1831, when 227 shoebinders of Reading and surrounding towns formed a "Society of Shoebinders" to obtain a uniform wage scale, and in 1833, when more than 750 women organized in Lynn and Saugus to protest a wage cut.[7]

Although Hawthorne did not dramatize so clearly as did Cooper concern about mob action, the prominence of group violence in "My Kinsman, Major Molineux" and "Earth's Holocaust" suggests that civility and social stability were not taken for granted. Hawthorne's descriptions of the countrymen of William James, grandfather of Henry, in "Sketches from Memory" pointedly raise questions about the potential loss of civility: "Nothing struck me more, in Burlington, than the great number of Irish emigrants. They have filled the British provinces to the brim, and still continue to ascend the St. Lawrence, in infinite tribes, overflowing by every outlet into the States. At Burlington, they swarm in huts and mean dwellings near the lake, lounge about the wharves, and elbow the native citizens entirely out of competition in their own line."[8] Hawthorne's account of these immigrants to American cities who lack a developed sense of civility is augmented by the conventional claim that "a glass of whiskey" is "doubtless their first necessity of life"; he further amplifies this when he compares a group of "wild Irish" to "devils" (*Snow-Image*, 299, 305). These "wandering hordes" concisely symbolize the threat to social stability that population migration was understood to pose.

Such direct portrayals of potential disruptions to the older bases of social stability are relatively infrequent in Hawthorne's work. Nevertheless, as this chapter will maintain, fear of such threats to social stability informs Hawthorne's work. And this returns us to Henry James's description of Hawthorne as someone who studied human nature while avoiding the study of his own times. Michael Colacurcio has contended that James's Hawthorne, the Hawthorne obsessed with questions of literary form and psychology, is himself a work of fiction. Colacurcio's attention to the historical bases of Hawthorne's fiction largely restored history and historicism to Hawthorne studies during the early 1980s, thus serving to counterbalance the contemporary critical preoccupation with formal or phenomenological issues. Nevertheless, despite Colacurcio's strenuous attempt to rescue Hawthorne studies from what he perceived as the debilitating effects of Henry James's influence, he essentially accepted the terms James established, that history and psychology form the opposing poles in Hawthorne studies and that the critic must choose between them.[9]

It may well be more useful to conceive Hawthorne's psychology in a manner contrary to that of both James and Colacurcio and more in accord with the way Hawthorne's contemporaries understood the discipline, that is, as a way of responding to contemporary society. My argument is that the conflict between psychologically and historically oriented critiques of Hawthorne recedes when we understand the ways Hawthorne interpreted contemporary psychology, transformed these interpretations into aesthetic terms, and made salient latent tensions within this psychology. Thus, in effect, Hawthorne's work suggests an alternative perspective on the moral, psychological, and metaphysical conventions of his time, conventions that informed Common Sense thought.[10] This is particularly true of Hawthorne's novels, along with those shorter works that have engendered the greatest critical commentary. But in such sketches and short stories as "The Great Stone Face," "Egotism; or, The Bosom-Serpent," and "The Haunted Mind," for example, Hawthorne's relatively uncritical reliance on conventional psychological—and metaphysical—thought to generate plots and characters is, I will be arguing, quite apparent. Before discussing these and other fictions, I will turn to the writings of Thomas C. Upham, a Common Sense psychologist whose prominence extended from the 1830s through the 1860s and whose work was known by Hawthorne.[11] The Common Sense theoretical account of the individual's relationship to the community provided the basis for Hawthorne's depictions of individual psychology, but he did not consistently reflect contemporary thought as he did in the works mentioned above. Rather, in stories such as "Young Goodman Brown," which depicts a failed relationship between the individual and the community, Hawthorne began to explore tensions latent in Common Sense thought, thereby furnishing an equivocal response to contemporary metaphysics and opening onto the problematics of the interpreting self raised by Sacvan Bercovitch and Emily Miller Budick in their studies of Hawthorne.[12]

The association between Hawthorne and an intuitively Romantic, aestheticized individualism has rested on seemingly certain textual grounds. Perhaps most famously, the narrator's rejection of mundane affairs in "The Custom-House" as antithetical to art supports this association, and, more forthrightly, Hawthorne's description of himself and his surroundings in an 1840 letter to his fiancée, Sophia Peabody, evokes a similar perception: "This deserves to be called a haunted chamber, for thousands upon thousands of visions have appeared to me in it; and some few of them have become visible to the world. If ever I should have a biographer, he ought to make great mention of this chamber in my memoirs, because so much of my lonely youth was wasted here, and here my mind and character were formed."[13]

To those critics for whom Hawthorne emblematizes the socially isolated, alienated artist, this letter to Sophia Peabody, with its references to
his "lonely youth" and "visions" in his "haunted chamber," has indicated
an artistic and imaginative estrangement from his contemporaries. This
individualistic characterization of Hawthorne has proved remarkably enduring, and despite the efforts of biographers and critics such as James
Mellow, Arlin Turner, and Gloria Erlich to revise this attitude, the idea
that Hawthorne was a man immersed in his social surroundings often gen-
erates indifference, if not resistance. Thus a recent biography of Hawthorne, falling back on the older critical cliché, asserts, "No biographer
has failed to quote the [letter's] passage," drawing as its conclusion the idea
that the letter serves as evidence of Hawthorne's "lonely meditations and
self-imposed isolation."[14]

But Hawthorne's letter to Sophia continues, and as it does, the
earlier, more famous remarks are recontextualized in a way that significantly alters their meaning. The letter likens Sophia to a dove who draws
Hawthorne out of his seclusion, a detail revealing the earlier assertion of
isolation to have been in the service of a love letter's rhetorical strategy.
As historicist critics such as Michael Colacurcio, Lauren Berlant, and
T. Walter Herbert have shown, the image of Hawthorne as a champion of
the isolated artistic consciousness does not satisfactorily correspond to his
work.[15] Despite their corrective effects, however, critical arguments that
have demonstrated the historical and social bases for much of Hawthorne's
writings have not adequately accounted for his fascination—as evident in
his letter to Sophia—with psychological phenomena and the frequently
strange distortions of perception so often revealed in his work. To understand Hawthorne's engagement with psychology, we must turn our attention to the dominant system of antebellum psychology, that derived
from Scottish Common Sense philosophy.

The history of Common Sense psychology in the United States is not
unknown, yet its relation to Hawthorne's work has been obscured by the
tendency among Hawthorne's twentieth-century critics to describe his
concerns and attitudes as if they were directly opposed to those of the
prevalent antebellum school of psychology.[16] This school of psychology
gained its strongest purchase on academic discourse precisely during a time
when community values were perceived to be eroding. The philosophy of
Common Sense thus developed in the United States, depending on one's
view, as either a compensatory belief system, one that advocated commu-
nitarian social ethics while legitimating the politics and economics of
individualism, or, alternatively, as a sort of rearguard protest based in
Christian morality. As noted earlier, the study of psychology achieved a

new importance during the eighteenth century as one facet of the intellectual response to a changing political and economic milieu. The Scottish school of Common Sense philosophy, associated with Thomas Reid, Dugald Stewart, James Beattie, and Thomas Brown, emerged during the latter half of the eighteenth century as a refutation of the philosophies of Hume and Berkeley. Its importation into this country during colonial times was effected by John Witherspoon and Benjamin Rush. (It was Rush who claimed to have suggested the title *Common Sense* to Thomas Paine.) Rush, the founder of American psychiatry, expressed concern over the moral effects of physical and psychological phenomena; Witherspoon revealed his moral concerns in a religious conservatism associated with the Scottish philosophy. The overwhelming influence of Common Sense philosophy on nineteenth-century American thought is undisputed: from the start of the nineteenth century until the arrival of German physiology and British empiricism during the 1860s, the Common Sense dominance over American psychology was unchallenged, and its influence, albeit attenuated, endured through the remainder of the century. Pedagogical practices extended the influence of this thought throughout college curricula with the choice of Common Sense textbooks, such as the extended supplements to the *Encyclopaedia Britannica,* a project designed and overseen by Dugald Stewart. At Yale, the standard texts in Intellectual Philosophy were those of Reid, Stewart, Beattie, and Brown.[17]

The dominance of Common Sense realism in the nineteenth century accorded well with the moralizing aspects of popular sentimental fiction. It is thus no surprise that twentieth-century critics who have found fault with the one should have discredited the other.[18] The impression that Hawthorne chose the path of individualism in order to counter the prevalent mode of conformity is, however, problematic for several reasons. On the level of social analysis, it necessitates a disregard of the idea that individualism in the United States itself has constituted a mode of conformity. Further, and more significantly, the notion that the imagination was regarded as suspect by those who subscribed to Common Sense psychology is based on an ahistorical and uncritical reading of late-nineteenth-century opponents of Common Sense thought; denunciations by these reform-minded psychologists are best understood as part of an ongoing disciplinary argument (and thus as prone to the exaggerations and distortions typical of such argumentation).[19] It is necessary to note that not all Common Sense philosophers agreed on all points. One important example of disagreement is provided by Thomas Reid's attack on the theory of association of ideas; when understood in terms of the contemporary philosophical debate, Reid's attack appears situational, and Reid's successors, apparently taking this into account, generally departed from him on this point.[20] If we actually return to the works of the period without use of the oversimplifying dichotomy posited by advocates of the idea that Hawthorne simply was a Romantic opponent of Common Sense thought, a more complex understanding of the relationship between the individual and society will emerge.

The intricacies of the relationship between the individual and society preoccupied Common Sense theorists.[21] In keeping with their preoccupation, their theoretical discourse was not the exclusive province of an academic elite. Rather, the ideas of Common Sense thought were broadly disseminated through the use of textbooks, designed for high-school and college students, that closely followed Scottish models. Such texts as Thomas C. Upham's *Elements of Intellectual Philosophy* (1827), Francis Wayland's *Moral Philosophy* (1835), and Laurens Perseus Hickok's *Empirical Psychology* (1854) were popular in college curricula even after the Civil War.[22] Upham's *Elements* is particularly noteworthy because it represented the first American attempt to offer a system of psychology for students. Upham's *Elements of Intellectual Philosophy* was combined with the later *Elements of Mental Philosophy* (1831) and *The Philosophical and Practical Treatise on the Will* (1834) in his *Abridgement of Mental Philosophy* (1861). This compilation is important in part because it displays a friendlier attitude toward literature and imagination than is usually attributed to the American followers of the Scottish realists. In addition, it reveals significant epistemological and methodological assumptions that shaped Hawthorne's approach to individual psychology.

The works of Thomas C. Upham are useful now precisely because of their status as textbooks. Their perspectives were relatively conventional; moreover, their specific purpose as textbooks was to indoctrinate high-school and college students into the prevalent belief system of the time. Upham himself graduated from Dartmouth in 1818, prepared for the ministry, and served as a pastor for one year before going to Bowdoin College. Hawthorne studied mental and moral philosophy with Upham during his senior year (1824-25); during this year Hawthorne read Dugald Stewart's *Elements of the Philosophy of the Human Mind*.[23] It is plausible that Upham's direct influence on Hawthorne, then completing his studies at Bowdoin, extended as well to Upham's advocacy of an American literature based in American experience.[24] Upham's most complete work, the *Abridgement of Mental Philosophy*, essentially recapitulates the range of his earlier works. It will accordingly provide the focus for our inquiry here, to which will be added an occasional reference to his *Outlines of Imperfect and Disordered Mental Action* (1840), the first American text on abnormal psychology.[25]

Two aspects of Upham's *Abridgement* are especially relevant to a consideration of the way it organizes psychological discourse: the establishment of the field of knowledge and the method of inquiry. Upham's Common Sense method of psychological inquiry will form an important feature of this discussion because of the way it delineated the theoretical boundaries that Hawthorne was to test. More striking, though, to those for whom twentieth-century psychological discourses are the norm, is the relationship between rational and emotional processes that constitute the field of Common Sense psychological knowledge. In the *Abridgement,* Upham divided mental operations into three parts: (1) the intellect, a category that includes sensation, perception, and internal mental processes such as dreaming, memory, and association; (2) the sensibilities, inclusive of various emotions, desires, and the moral senses; and (3) the will, or volitional states of mind.[26] The prescriptively rationalist orientation of Common Sense thought has made an easy target for those who might scrap it along with the rest of pre-Freudian psychology. So conditioned are we to a psychology of nonrational drives that earlier attention to the conscious mind appears embarrassingly positivistic and simplistic. But aside from its importance as a precursor to pragmatist philosophy and its conceptions of the human mind, Upham's Common Sense psychology cannot be so easily dismissed. Its comparatively mechanistic application of faculties and categories can lull the modern reader into ignoring the fact that it treated with some subtlety the relationship of individuals to their natural and social environments.

The intellectual functions cited by Upham were basically of two types, external and internal. The external has to do with sensory input, knowledge of things of external origin, the material world. Thus, unlike the psychoanalytic emphasis on personal history, realist psychology maintained as essential the idea of ongoing contact between the perceiving individual and the world. Upham justified this ordering scheme by citing human development: "Far the greater of the mind's acts during [the early period of life] can be traced to a material source."[27] He clearly relied on individual memory, an internalization of the external, for his rationale. The description of internal mental states that follows posited a structure of self-evident ideas, such as time, personal identity, space, power, and concepts of right and wrong. There is a consequent interplay between empirical facts acquired through sensory perception and the workings of structures of consciousness.

Upham presented consciousness as the second source of knowledge after sensory perception. Consciousness as the object of its own inquiry, a basis of Common Sense psychology, rendered introspection the preferred methodology for psychological exploration. Dugald Stewart, whose *Elements* was closely followed by Upham, explained the importance of introspection by analogy: "As all our knowledge of the material world rests ultimately on facts ascertained by observation, so our knowledge of the human mind rests ultimately on facts for which we have the evidence of our own consciousness."[28] The self-conscious methodology, fully practiced by Upham, leads to a classification of various "intellectual states of internal origin" (as opposed to those based in perception), such as memory, association, and reasoning. Among those states Upham treats is the imagination.[29]

The imagination is a central issue in Hawthorne criticism, and the prescriptive, rationalist orientation of Common Sense thought has suggested the idea that Hawthorne's interest in the imagination is, if not unique in its own time, at least a conscious challenge to Common Sense hegemony. A close look at what a Common Sense psychologist like Upham actually said, however, reveals the shortcoming in this thinking. Upham discussed the imagination in the *Abridgement,* and his discussion is hardly the material from which anti-imaginative biases may be constructed. Upham did review disorders of the imagination in *Outlines of Imperfect and Disordered Mental Action,* but he specified at the start that "great Imagination does not necessarily imply a disordered or insane action of the Mind."[30] One of the disorders of imagination cited by Upham is a *lack* of imagination, of which he remarks, "Can there well be a greater mental defect than this?"[31] His statements on the imagination in the *Abridgement* more closely resemble paeans than condemnations.

The crucial point for Upham is the ultimate source of the imaginative faculty. As far as Upham was concerned, the imagination would not exist unless "the Creator had some design or purpose in furnishing men with it, since we find universally that he does nothing in vain" (228). He cited as examples of imagination the books of the Prophets in the Bible:

> If it be said that those venerable writers were inspired, it will still remain true that this was the faculty of the mind which inspiration especially honoured by the use which was made of it. . . . Many an hour it has beguiled by the new situations it has depicted, and the new views of human nature it has disclosed; many a pang of the heart it has subdued, either by introducing us to greater woes which others have suffered, or by intoxicating the memory with its luxuriance and lulling it into a forgetfulness of ourselves; many a good resolution it has cherished and subtended, as it were, a new and wider horizon around the intellectual being, has filled the soul with higher conceptions, and inspired it with higher hopes . . . the soul enters with joy into those new and lofty creations which it is the prerogative of the imagination to form; and they seem to it a congenial residence. (228-29)

Imagination is here associated with the Bible, the highest source of truth to Upham, a writer imbued with a sense of moral certainty based on his belief in Christianity. And Upham's discussion of art was certainly a congenial one, albeit based on a definition of the artistic enterprise that highlighted its social value—here largely in terms of its use as a means of moralistic self-improvement or as relief for the grieving—rather than its expressive qualities.

The question of the source and uses of the imagination is central to an understanding of Hawthorne's psychology and his ideas about the proper relationship between the individual and the community. The imagination, valorized in Romantic rhetoric and in the tradition of American literary scholarship that has perceived artistic antagonism toward society (and vice versa), need not be regarded as an avenue of individual protest against community consensus. Hawthorne may not have explicitly endorsed the theological origins of the imagination claimed by Upham, but when he talks of the imagination, he does so in a way that recalls the individual's social network. Hawthorne's most well known account of the imagination, in "The Custom-House," conveys this notion when describing the "neutral territory . . . where the Actual and the Imaginary may meet."[32] The successful writer of the romance, according to Hawthorne, must be able to add the interpersonal warmth of "a heart and sensibilities of human tenderness to the forms which fancy summons up." Only the presence of such emotional attachments "converts" the fanciful forms "from snow-images into men and women."

Hawthorne appreciates the artistic imagination's social aspects—a sociality that informs not only his description of the proper workings of the imagination but also his interest in the artist's ability to communicate with an audience—and this appreciation is most consistent with Upham's Common Sense account of the imagination. The sources of imaginative truth may possibly differ as far as the two are concerned, but their assumptions about its effects as well as their methods of testing their ideas are identical. For Upham, the only way to verify claims to truth, understood to be objective and absolute, was by way of social consensus, and this was in accord with Hawthorne's interest in the sympathetic reader.[33] Upham did not arbitrarily begin his study of the intellect with a discussion of sensory perception: by definition, objects of perception were real and their presence was revealed by the senses. The internal faculties (i.e., mental categories and processes such as imagination) were similarly real, and they were revealed, in a manner analogous to the workings of the senses, by the introspective method. Sensory perception and introspection thereby formed the methodological bases of a psychology that revealed to us our common sense. And this common sense, when functioning normally in the individual, would be able to verify truths through their common or social recognition.

What is problematic in Upham's psychology, from the perspective of American cultural studies, is less the metaphysical origins of his epistemology than the relationship between his epistemology and the introspective methodology associated with Scottish realism. The basis of Upham's psychological explorations was the analysis of mental phenomena by reflection. The introspective method works insofar as there are common mental faculties that function reliably to confirm the truth about the world. The problem with this methodology is not unlike the discrepancy revealed by analyses of Puritan culture between, on the one hand, the idea of the individual as the source of religious truth and, on the other, the Puritan community as the agent that confirms this truth. Once the source of truth is believed to reside in the individual, then the paradox arises that an authentic reliance on individual insight or interpretation invalidates the community's claim to confirmation of that insight, and antinomianism logically follows.

This tension would subtend Scottish Common Sense philosophy and, even more sharply, Upham's psychology, which was eclectic and open to ideas identified with Romanticism. A case in point is Reid's rejection of association of ideas because it denoted an arbitrariness within mental functions that could result in solipsism. Upham, following the lead of Dugald Stewart, found no such problem with the idea of association and did not consider as potentially unsettling the implications of a division between the perceiving mind and the world.

The fact that Upham could overlook the tension between an introspective methodology and a way of affirming epistemological data through the social affirmation of introspective insights may indeed be the result of an American context that, from the Puritans onwards, had institutionalized the individual as the source of theological truth. So, when discussing the sensibilities, Upham relied on individualist assumptions to prove the moral emotions to be of a higher order than the "natural": "There is obviously a sort of graduation in the feelings of regard and honour which we attach to different parts of the mind. We at once, as it were instinctively, regard some as higher than others. We may not be able always to tell why it is so; but such is the fact" (264). This passage, chosen because it is typical, shows the premises latent within Upham's rhetoric. The *we*, himself and the audience of students empowered by their inclusion into the author's community of reasonable adults, functioned to legitimate the conclusion that there is a hierarchy of emotional states. This order was affirmed through what is "obviously" apparent, what we "instinctively" see. To perceive this truth, though, the *we* had to decompose into introspecting individuals who were then presumed to reconstitute themselves as a community in order to affirm this truth. But, in the disintegration of community to individuals, the radical disjuncture between an objective confirmation of truth and individual discovery of proof becomes manifest. Once the introspecting individual is credited with the power to find truth, there is no easy turning back to an objective truth claim. This conceptual gap would provide the space for Hawthorne to begin his literary explorations of selfhood.

The acuity of Hawthorne's psychological observations in his sketches and tales often led critics during the 1950s through the 1970s to apply Freudian and other psychoanalytic approaches. Hawthorne scholars during those decades seem to have been trying to rescue Hawthorne from the earlier critical characterization of him as a kind of latter-day Puritan, itself an attempt to lend intellectual and moral weight to a writer who had been dismissed by Parrington because of his "intellectual poverty."[34] The more recent revival of historicist methodologies among Hawthorne critics has shifted the terms of debate by focusing on Hawthorne's historical milieu and sources.[35] As a way of mediating between historicist and psychological approaches to Hawthorne's work, I will raise questions about the functions of consciousness in terms of Common Sense tensions between its introspective methodology and its socially oriented epistemology. Hawthorne's use of an introspective method, his interest in the imagination, and his preoccupation with the power of benevolence—all explicitly discussed in Upham's text as well as in the writings of the Scottish philosophers—emerge in certain tales and sketches, and they may be comprehended as explorations of contemporary psychological tenets.

Rather than approach consciousness within Hawthorne's writing in a direct manner, I will look at the way it arises as a function or response to problems in narrative. To this end, I propose that in his tales and sketches Hawthorne repeatedly dramatizes travel, often using it as a way to enter into discussions of the individual consciousness. Certain depictions of travel and its consequences may at times evoke contemporary, antebellum concerns about social stability and the effects of migration. These depictions include the boat trip in "Sketches from Memory," with its derogation of immigrants, or the account in "My Kinsman, Major Molineux," in which young Robin's migration from countryside to the city coincides with the apparently unrelated mob uprising. Against these associations of travel with social disorder, Hawthorne repeatedly suggests the positive value of home. One instance of this is the action in "The Great Stone Face" (1850), a story that illustrates the way a departure from home may offer relatively few benefits to the aspiring self.

"The Great Stone Face" dramatizes a presumably instructive comparison between Ernest, who remains in the valley overlooked by a mountainside called the Great Stone Face, and a series of more ambitious natives who had left the rural settlement to gain prominence in the world. Each of the first three returnees is greeted by the locals as the fulfiller of the prophecy that one whose visage resembles the Great Stone Face will come and will be "the greatest and noblest personage of his time" (*Snow-Image*, 28). By contrast with the simple and virtuous homebody Ernest, each of these three—a wealthy businessman, a celebrated general, and a former candidate for president—is in turn hailed by the deluded crowd as the prophesied one. But all three worldly and shallow men are false fulfillments of the prophecy. The withered, barely human old businessman merely scatters with his "yellow claw" a few gold coins to beggars; the general's face displays an utter lack of "deep, broad, tender sympathies"; and the statesman's life is revealed to be "vague and empty, because no high purpose had endowed it with reality" (*Snow-Image*, 32, 37, 41). Only the last arrival, an acclaimed poet, is sufficiently virtuous to acknowledge bluntly that he is not the awaited one. In contrast to his predecessors, all of whom gained worldly distinction without displaying or acquiring wisdom, the returning poet announces that it is, in fact, Ernest who resembles the Great Stone Face and thus is the most noble of all.

The revelation here that virtue attaches itself to one who has not left his rural home amplifies the lesson that worldly success is no guarantee of character. The conventional wisdom that there is no place like home would not be worthy of comment were it not for the fact that it frequently arises in Hawthorne's short works. Repeatedly, Hawthorne presents stories in which a departure from home is associated with danger. Perhaps the simplest of these is "Little Annie's Ramble," in which little Annie "feels that impulse to go strolling away—that longing after the mystery of the great world—which many children feel, and which I felt in my childhood."[36] To biographers of Hawthorne, this account of a child leaving "her father's doorsteps" who then returns after being reported lost might seem an inversion of the story of how Hawthorne's seafaring father died abroad when young Nathaniel was not yet four years old.[37] Without reducing little Annie's successful return home, which accompanies the narrator's celebration of the effects of children on adults ("the pure breath of children revives the life of aged men" [*Tales*, 129]), into a wish-fulfillment fantasy of family reunion, we may still note how cultural anxieties about wandering populations intersect with Hawthorne's personal history and how this plot of departure and return is one that sustained Hawthorne's interest.

A departure and return home, for the sake of dramatic action, often is problematic, and problems in Hawthorne's fiction frequently lead to representations of mental processes. Even in a pair of early sketches in which the departure and return is relatively void of dramatic conflict, Hawthorne displays his interest in introspection as well as his commitment to sociality. In "The Haunted Mind" almost nothing really seems to occur. Despite the ominous word *haunted,* which recalls the "haunted chamber" of the letter to Sophia that, too, would lead away from possible intimations of the gothic and toward ordinary experience, the minimalist action of the story is the chronicle of confused, random thoughts that arise in those minutes during the middle of the night when one has awakened between stretches of sleep. The other noteworthy feature of this sketch is the unusual second-person mode of narrative address:

> What a singular moment is the first one, when you have hardly begun to recollect yourself, after starting from midnight slumber! By unclosing your eyes so suddenly, you seem to have surprised the personages of your dream in full convocation round your bed, and catch one broad glance at them before they can flit into obscurity. Or, to vary the metaphor, you find yourself, for a single instant, wide awake in that realm of illusions, whither sleep has been the passport, and behold its ghostly inhabitants and wondrous scenery, with a perception of their strangeness, such as you never attain while the dream is undisturbed. (*Tales,* 304)

Both tone and imagery make clear that the narrator speaks from personal experience; the sketch's very nature is so decidedly idiosyncratic and personal that no other possibility is tenable. But the ascription of the experience to another implies universality, that despite the highly personal nature of the narrative the basic experience is commonly shared. This foundation in common experience accompanies the idea of the mind as subject (narrator) and object ("you") of psychological inquiry. The introspective methodology of Upham's Common Sense psychology demands this split in which the self becomes its own object of study. The embedded narratee, the "you," resultantly assumes its two functions as an imagined reader who has had analogous experiences and as the subject for inquiry. This reenacts the methodological basis of Upham's psychology, in which introspection reveals the operation of common faculties.

The thoughts and observations recounted in this sketch attain the status of action only when a metaphor, the "train" of association, is imposed on mental activity. Hawthorne implies the possibility of a meaningful link between what might otherwise appear to be random thoughts, observations, or perceptions. The metaphor of travel is presented at the start of the sketch with the use of the terms *passport* and *scenery.* Hawthorne plainly refers to the idea of the "train of association," a commonplace of association psychology, when he states, "Ah! that idea has brought a hideous one in its train" (*Tales,* 306). The function of the associative train is then described: "In an hour like this, when the mind has a passive sensibility, but no active strength; when the imagination is a mirror, imparting vividness to all ideas, without the power of selecting or controlling them." The salient feature of the associative process is its passivity, its openness to the unknown.

Some critics have cited Hawthorne's reliance on association psychology as indicative of a Romantic vision of the mind and creativity.[38] Certainly it is true that "The Haunted Mind" presents a vision of the "intermediate space" (*Tales*, 305) that has been identified as a basic component in Hawthorne's concept of creativity. Hawthorne's foregrounding of the metaphor of travel ("Or, to vary the metaphor") bespeaks a very conscious use of the theory of association and its impled metaphor. Despite this appearance, an analysis of the action of the sketch shows that, instead of a simple association psychology, Hawthorne presents an interplay of willed thought and sensory perception with association. Along with mundane perceptions of the bells of a church clock, the frosty air, or the light of a star, a decision is made to defer thought on the analogy between the frozen windowpanes and dreams: "There will be time enough to trace out the analogy, while waiting the summons to breakfast" (*Tales*, 305). Elsewhere, in an attempt to escape a series of gloomy thoughts, "You start upright, breaking from a sort of conscious sleep" (*Tales*, 307), and then "Your eye searches for whatever may remind you of the living world" (*Tales*, 308).

This alternation of willed thought and unwilled association depicts quite well the imaginative process as described by Upham: "Whatever a person wills, or, rather, professes to will to imagine, he has, in fact, already imagined; and consequently, there can be no such things as imaginations which are exclusively the result of direct acts of will. So that the powers of invention, although the influence and subordinate action of the will may be considerable, must be aroused and quickened to their efforts in some other way" (226). Upham took for granted the relationship between the imagination and the will, as indicated by his use of the word *exclusively*. Upham, though, stressed the importance of unwilled association in order to distinguish himself from Thomas Reid, who excluded association from his psychology. Reid's attack on association, or "the theory of ideas," was part of his attempt to champion the cause of reason over what he saw as the threat of radical subjectivity.[39] Upham, following the lead of Dugald Stewart, saw no problem with the concept of the imagination as a combination of associated and willed thought together with sensory input. Moreover, Upham presumed that the operation of the imagination followed the same basic rules as those governing the powers of reason (221-22). Like Upham in the *Abridgement*, Hawthorne asserts no priority between willed and unwilled thought in "The Haunted Mind." The play between the two creates the "intermediate space" associated by critics with creativity. This unusual mental state is sustained during this sketch only so long as the subject remains awake. Once sleep arrives, association dominates, willed thought and sensory perception recede, and the story is over: "Your spirit has departed, and strays like a free citizen, among the people of a shadowy world, beholding strange sights, yet without wonder or dismay. So calm, perhaps, will be the final change; so undisturbed, as if among familiar things, the entrance of the soul to its Eternal home!" (Tales, 309).

This conclusion, a return to a metaphysical "home," recalls the ending to "Night Sketches." The narrator of "Night Sketches" presents a play between perception and fantasy during an evening walk. The sketch closes with an image similar to that of "The Haunted Mind": "If we bear the lamp of Faith, enkindled at a celestial fire, it will surely lead us home to that Heaven whence its radiance was borrowed" (Tales, 432). Because of their openness to fantasy and the unconscious, these two sketches might appear to support readings that emphasize the gothic, the frightening impulses suppressed in normal, rational, quotidian consciousness. But despite their foreboding titles, both "The Haunted Mind" and "Night Sketches" present images of balanced mental action in terms appropriate to the psychology of Hawthorne's contemporaries. The key is that so long as mentation is guided by the Common Sense principles of attention to external stimuli and rational thought kept in balance with association then all is well. But Hawthorne's most popular descriptions of mental action tend to be those of disordered thought. In these situations, the focus on the individual mind is a focus on deviance, and the mental states explored are not offered as exemplary. A work in which such deviance is associated with narratives of departure from home is "Egotism; or, The Bosom-Serpent," an account of a successful return to normalcy following a period of alienation.

The bulk of comment on "Egotism" has been confined to explication of the footnote Hawthorne appended to the title: "The physical fact, to which it is here attempted to give a moral signification, has been known to occur in more than one instance."[40] Critics have found sources for the image of the bosom serpent in classical literature, Puritan tracts, medical texts, and journalistic reports, none of which really help to explain this apparently simple story.[41] The brief comments Hawthorne recorded in his notebooks, which presumably were the origins of the tale, are limited in their value to the reader, because they focus primarily on the significance of symbol: "A type of envy or some other evil passion"; "a cherished sin."[42] The symbol and its significance become apparent not through an analysis of sources but through attention to the relationship between the plot dynamics of this highly moralized story and the protagonist's nature.

The story is about Roderick Elliston's domination by delusions and hallucinations, in particular tactile hallucinations that lead to his belief in an indwelling snake. Elliston generalizes his case and exhibits the egotism of the title, the "cherished sin," when he accuses others of the same condition and posits it as the normal human state. Despite the tale's ambiguity (the etiological speculations on Elliston's malady as possibly sorrow, physical disease, guilt, or even dyspepsia), Elliston's misery is afforded a legitimacy based on its real effects on his mental state, and the narrator sympathetically offers information about Elliston in a manner consonant with the eventual plot resolution. The uncertainty of the narrative account, however, is significant. In the end, we are offered an interpretation of Roderick Elliston's problem, but the narrator has access to information the reader does not and displays this access prominently. References to things beyond the reader's knowledge abound at the start, such as George Herkimer's comment on Rosina, identified several paragraphs later as the one whose life is "indissolubly interwoven" with Elliston (*Mosses,* 270). A proleptic reference is found in an early description of Elliston: "Herkimer remarked that his complexion had a greenish tinge over its sickly white, reminding him of a species of marble out of which he had once wrought a head of Envy, with her snaky locks" (*Mosses,* 269). More significantly, vital information is given the reader, embedded in a subordinate clause: "Shortly after Elliston's separation from his wife . . ." (*Mosses,* 270). The earlier set of associations, likening Elliston's complexion to marble from which Herkimer created an image of envy, becomes comprehensible to the reader at the end of the tale when the sculptor announces the moral: "A tremendous Egotism—manifesting itself, in your case, in the form of jealousy—is as fearful a fiend as ever stole into the human heart" (*Mosses,* 283). Likewise, the offhand reference to Elliston's marital separation is rendered significant only at the end when we see that marital reconciliation drives out the serpent.

These instances of prolepsis, though they create a sense of ambiguity, are relatively standard devices to promote suspense as well as to indicate narrative control. But finally the process of reference transcends narrative control when we are told, during a seemingly unimportant anecdote of Elliston's crazy behavior, that one of Elliston's victims "was, in fact, the very ship-master whom George Herkimer had encountered, under such singular circumstances, in the Grecian Archipelago" (*Mosses,* 277). The knowledge claimed by the narrator points to his identity as Herkimer, the artist who rendered the image of envy. This identity is no surprise, for the shape of the narrative is not that of Elliston's mental degeneration but rather the course of Herkimer's progressive discovery of Elliston's illness. The excess of detail offered here, the "singular circumstances" of which we hear no more, manifests the artifice of the story, the fact that it is a piece of narrative art, reaffirming the footnote at the start, which claims that this is a moralized version of some event whose truth is common knowledge. This break in the text, in which both too much and not enough information is given, does not stand by itself. Instead, there are other questions raised by the text, references insufficiently elucidated, that point toward the conflict underlying "Egotism."

The action of the story, the reconstruction of the course of Elliston's illness by Herkimer, runs a smooth course, but the cause of Elliston's problems, the impetus for the narrative itself, ultimately remains enigmatic. By the close, we are left with the following information: that Rosina left Elliston, presumably because of his jealousy; that over the course of their four-year separation Elliston suffered from the belief he harbored a snake; that he harassed the townspeople, proclaiming they suffered as he did; and, finally, that Rosina decided to return to Elliston, and her return drove out the snake. The moral announces a formal ending, yet the springs of the tale's action remain as obscure as at the start. Even though it is suggested that Rosina left because of Elliston's jealousy, we are never told any more than that. Nor are we to know why Rosina chose to return when she did or even why she chose to return at all. The narrative only points toward causative events without adequately explicating them. In order to show sufficient grounds for the narrative action, it is necessary to return to the conflict between the individualistic method of introspection and the idea of social validation of truth.

In the case of "Egotism," the composite image of home and wife furnishes social validation. When the woman leaves home, hallucinations, delusions, and the loss of a feeling of relationship with the community follow. Domestic relations thus serve to figure an entire social network, as the woman is aligned with the idea of social stability. Hawthorne's letter to Sophia Peabody, cited earlier, makes this association quite clear. Imprisoned in his "lonely chamber," Hawthorne's "escape into the world" was made possible by his relationship with Sophia.[43] The identification of the wife with the home and with society in general follows a cultural pattern common to Hawthorne's day and our own. When there is a threat to the relationship with the primary female figure in Hawthorne's stories, the sense of self begins to break down, and all social relations are problematized. In terms of the conflict implicit to Common Sense psychology, when social validation of individual insight is gone, mental disorders result.

Hawthorne's position on the conflict between individual insight and social validation resists simple classification by allegiance because it is impossible to disentangle the one from the other. This entanglement is reflected by the terms Hawthorne uses to describe the social relationships lost by Elliston. To return to the introduction of Rosina's relationship with Elliston, the narrator claims her life was "interwoven" with Elliston's

(*Mosses*, 270). But very shortly thereafter, this same domestic image is problematized when Elliston's pain is described: "The unfortunate man clutched both hands upon his breast, as if an intolerable sting or torture impelled him to rend it open, and let out the living mischief, even were it *intertwined* [my emphasis] with his own life." This time the imagery of weaving refers to a destructive influence, quite the opposite of the salvation offered by Rosina. Still more equivocal is the narrator's assertion that all who suffer chronic mental or physical diseases become obsessed with themselves, whatever the cause, "whether it be sin, sorrow, or merely the more tolerable calamity of some endless pain, or mischief among the cords of mortal life" (*Mosses*, 273). These "cords," reminiscent of "the magnetic chain of humanity" abandoned by Ethan Brand (*Snow-Image*, 99), may serve two purposes simultaneously, that of interconnection and that of bondage. Hawthorne's equivocation dramatizes a basic conflict between individual introspection and a reliance on social validation of truth claims.[44]

Roderick Elliston is rescued from isolation by Rosina's return to the household, and by the time of "The Christmas Banquet," the story that follows "Egotism" in *Mosses from an Old Manse* (both subtitled "From the Unpublished 'Allegories of the Heart'"), Elliston has been sufficiently rehabilitated to become the artist who himself narrates the tale. Rehabilitation does not, however, necessarily follow domestic reunion. "Wakefield," a story perhaps most notable for its highly qualified narrative speculations, presents a departure and reunion without such a promise. Wakefield himself is the subject of some narrative questioning, but the absence of a narrative resolution to the question of *why* Wakefield behaves as he does suggests the counterbalancing importance of the basic plot form.[45] Conforming to the moral associated with the plot of departure and return, the conclusion presents a powerful vision of the necessity of—and tenuousness of—sociality: "Amid the seeming confusion of our mysterious world, individuals are so nicely adjusted to a system, and systems to one another, and to a whole, that, by stepping aside for a moment, a man exposes himself to a fearful risk of losing his place forever. Like Wakefield, he may become, as it were, the Outcast of the Universe" (*Tales*, 140).

The emphasis here on social bonds may be understood as ironic, but Hawthorne's placement of the tale directly after "Little Annie's Ramble" in *Twice-Told Tales* suggests a thematic continuity, albeit with deepening complexity. This complexity fully emerges in Hawthorne's more acclaimed short story "Young Goodman Brown." Having seen the way Common Sense thought provided a theoretical structure of selfhood in relationship to sociality, and with an awareness of how Hawthorne's narratives of departures and return home explore different aspects of this relationship, we are in a position to observe how Hawthorne's problematic depiction of selfhood in "Young Goodman Brown" probes the limits of Common Sense thought by foregrounding the tension between the "opposing forces of social and personal intentionality."[46]

The implications of introspection and individual psychology in Hawthorne's work are best understood when they are situated against the socializing concept of benevolence, an eighteenth-century commonplace that was still an active force in nineteenth-century psychology and moral thought. Despite the predominance of individualistic economics, the idea of benevolence maintained a hold on the American imagination, as typified by the popularity of the sentimental novel and the social criticism of the day. For example, one labor union president explicitly acknowledged the doctrine of self-interest at the heart of American laissez-faire economics, but he simultaneously based his argument in defense of unions on an appeal to his audience's feelings of benevolence: "In order to mitigate the evils that ever flow from inordinate desire and unrestricted selfishness, to restrain and chastise unlawful ambition, to protect the weak against the strong, and to establish an equilibrium of power among nations and individuals, conventional compacts [i.e., labor unions] were formed."[47] The notable attribute of this address is its presumed audience: not workers, whose motivation would be self-interest, but those uninvolved in the labor struggle, for whom the only operative force would be sympathy. The speaker continued: "We have the consolation of knowing that all good men, all who love their country, and rejoice in the improvement of the condition of their fellow men, will acknowledge the policy of our views and the purity of our motives."[48] The appeal here is toward a collective view of society in which mutual support would prevail.

Straightforward expressions of the importance of benevolence constituted a large part of antebellum discourse. For example, they formed much of the basis of popular sentimental novels. Whether or not one agrees that these novels articulated a fully developed critique and alternative to the prevalent nineteenth-century laissez-faire ideology, the appeal of novels grounded in sentimental principles was unquestionably powerful, and their power no doubt drew in part from the fact that the doctrines they espoused were a common part of the academic curriculum.

The records of Hawthorne's formal education and his readings are consistent with common practice—they indicate his familiarity with the moral writings of Adam Smith (*The Theory of Moral Sentiments*), Thomas Brown (*Lectures on the Philosophy of the Human Mind*), and Francis Hutcheson (who acknowledged Shaftesbury's influence on the title page of *An Inquiry into the Original of Our Ideas of Beauty and Virtue*).[49]

These works on moral philosophy, in conjunction with Upham's psychology, employed the same basic terms and approaches Hawthorne adopted when discussing benevolence and its social significance. The operation of benevolence apparently was understood to counterbalance economic individualism; the power of "irresistible compassion" was posited as "an automatic mechanism for social good, not simply an intellectual option."[50] Adam Smith accordingly described benevolence as a "social passion," a way we are moved almost mechanically to feeling through an act of imaginary identification with the suffering (or pleasure) of another.[51] Hutcheson similarly described an "Instinct toward Benevolence" and further declared that "the ordinary Springs of Vice among Men, must then be suppos'd to be a mistaken Self-Love, made too violent, so as to overcome Benevolence."[52] And, as Thomas Brown insisted, "[Nature] has given us a *benevolence* that desires the good of all."[53] These affirmations of benevolence became prescriptive moral statements in Thomas Upham's psychology. Upham understood mutual love to be the general rule, as opposed to the alternatives of indifference or, worse, mutual hostility. Nevertheless, he did not think all instances of benevolence expressed moral significance. The introspective Common Sense method led him to believe that parental, filial, or fraternal concerns tended to be instinctual rather than volitional; hence, the exercise of these faculties did not convey the same moral value as did expressions of disinterested concern.

Despite questions as to precisely which expressions of benevolence were instinctual and which were volitional, Upham agreed with Smith and Hutcheson that domestic relations furnished important indices of benevolence. Disturbances in domestic relations were considered manifestations of what Upham termed "perversions of the benevolent affections" (473). Upham, illustrating the effects of this problem, recalled a case history, originally offered by Benjamin Rush, of "a citizen of Philadelphia, who was remarkable for his strong affection for his wife and children when his mind was in a sound state, who was occasionally afflicted with this apathy, and, when under its influence, lost his affection for them all so entirely, that he said he could see them butchered before his eyes without feeling any distress, or even inclination to rise from his chair to protect them" (474). This description of a severe depressive state is noteworthy because it illustrates, through the horror the reader was expected to feel, the primary, instinctual form of benevolence that was understood to exist within the family. The more general desire for good to all was thus an attenuated form of the familial bond, and it was accordingly taken to be volitional rather than instinctual.[54]

The relationship between the individual and society within Hawthorne's stories frequently reveals an interplay between two important sets of problems inherent to Common Sense thought: (1) the tension between the introspecting individual and the community that affirms the reality of the individual's inquiry; and (2) the question of how the force that ensures social cohesion, benevolence (along with its originating site, the family), is to be understood in relation to the introspecting individual. Although introspection itself does not automatically create a hazard, when the process takes place within a character whose commitment to social bonds is suspect, the individual faces the epistemological crisis that ensues when one's knowledge differs from the conventional and, in addition, the social difficulty of reintegration into the community. This related pair of problems arises in "Young Goodman Brown."

As does "The Haunted Mind," "Young Goodman Brown" presents the reader with a simple course of action within the framework of a strange, hallucinatory narrative: Brown leaves home in the middle of the night, walks about in the forest, and then returns home. The return home, hardly so peaceful as in the preceding stories and sketches, is shaped by the significance of Brown's perceptions while in the forest, perceptions that seemingly relate to Brown's unstated motivation for his midnight journey. This motivation has spurred much critical debate. From the historicist point of view, Brown appears to be acting out the guilt and anxieties of third-generation American Puritans.[55] The more prevalent discussions of "Young Goodman Brown" have emphasized psychological terms insofar as they are presumed to indicate Hawthorne's individualistic protest against the strictures of a conformist community.[56] Advocates of the historicist approach—most notably Colacurcio, who admonishes, "We must psychologize with caution"—object to interpretations of "Young Goodman Brown" that universalize the psychological experience instead of situating it in the historical circumstances of late-seventeenth-century Puritan New England.[57] But a reading of "Young Goodman Brown" within the context of nineteenth-century psychology accounts for Brown's actions and also obviates antagonism between historical and psychological interpretations.

The nature of Brown's experience, whether regarded as a distorted initiation ritual or as an immature test of his own faith, reveals multiple levels of psychological disorder. The most obvious is Brown's dream experience or, alternately, his hallucinations and delusions in the forest. The ambiguity of the narrative is most strikingly illustrated by the "something" that fluttered down through the air, which Brown "beheld" as a pink ribbon (*Mosses,* 83). By contrast, Hawthorne signals an answer to his question, "Had Goodman Brown fallen asleep in the forest, and only dreamed a wild dream of a witch-meeting?" when he states in the following paragraph that "it was a dream of evil omen for young Goodman Brown," later referring to "the night of that fearful dream" (*Mosses*, 89). Brown's "dream," whatever its relationship to late-Puritan guilt feelings, illustrates what Upham would call a disordered intellectual action.

Upham discussed hallucinations of the visual, auditory, and tactile variety in his descriptions of disordered intellectual action. As his tripartite psychology indicated, the disorders of the intellect logically would precede those problems of sensibility, or emotion, and of will. Because of the intellect's primacy, its problems were most closely associated with the physical bases of many disorders, and Upham relied on this association to cite a variety of physical causes for hallucinations or "excited conceptions and apparitions" (232). These physical causes included retinal sensitivity, neglect of periodic blood-letting, febrile states, and cerebral "inflammations" brought on by such things as excessive alcohol consumption. Most pertinent to Brown's problem is the "melancholy imagination" described by Upham: "[These cases of melancholy imagination] in general attract but little notice, although sources of exquisite misery to the subjects of them. But such are the extravagant dreams in which they indulge; such are the wrong views of the character and actions of men, which their busy and melancholy imaginations are apt to form, that they cannot be reckoned persons of truly sound minds" (255). This account of melancholy is of interest because of how its stress differs from that of present-day descriptions of depression, which emphasize the sufferer's intractable dysphoric mood and associated physical disorders. The pivotal moments in Upham's description of "the melancholy imagination" are the "extravagant dreams" that reveal "wrong views" of the people around them. Upham's description of this socially and emotionally isolated state sounds almost diagnostic of Brown.

Brown's melancholy is revealed after his forest experience: "A stern, a sad, a darkly meditative, a distrustful, if not a desperate man, did he become, from the night of that fearful dream" (*Mosses*, 89). But this melancholy, this final indication of Brown's disorder, is signaled at the beginning by his overwhelming desire to go off into the woods to witness for himself the imagined actions of witches. Hawthorne, recalling the obsession of the witchcraft trials with empirical and spectral evidence, places Brown within a culturally sanctioned Puritan tradition of witnessing for oneself. When translated into the context of nineteenth-century American psychology, an implicit critique of the Puritan tradition emerges because, according to Upham, Brown's need to see for himself indicates a kind of insanity. Of the three types of associated disorders of belief classified by Upham, the first bears directly on the opening to "Young Goodman

Brown": "The first class are those who seem incapable of believing any-thing which they are required to receive on the testimony of others. They must see it with their own eyes" (256). Brown's desire to test his Puritan faith, as well as Faith's trust in him, is already symptomatic.

Hawthorne dramatizes Brown's self-imposed solitude by presenting Brown's trial of faith as subsequent to his rejection of Faith's attempt to dissuade him from the journey. The sense of isolation Brown presumably felt prior to his experience, his presumptive motivation, is amplified by his isolation in the forest. Brown's fantasy that all his neighbors, and even his forebears, were involved in a grand conspiracy he somehow managed to uncover is confirmed by his identification of neighbors and family mem-bers at the witches' convocation. But Brown's madness is signaled from the very start. The narrator suggests that Brown's perceptions are disordered when, at the beginning of Brown's walk on the narrow forest path, it is stated that there was "*this peculiarity in such a solitude,* that the traveller knows not who may be concealed by the innumerable trunks and the thick boughs overhead" (*Mosses,* 75; my emphasis). The steady equivocation of the narrator would seem an attempt to replicate in the reader the un-certainty of Brown in the forest. Thus Brown sees his companion's staff writhe like a snake, though the narrator reports that his vision could "have been an ocular deception, assisted by the uncertain light" (*Mosses,* 76); al-though Goody Cloyse seems to appear, for example, the narrator is care-ful to state that it was *Brown* who "recognized" her (*Mosses,* 78); the voices of the old minister and Deacon Gookin are heard, but, despite his best efforts, Goodman Brown, "pulling aside the branches, and thrusting forth his head as far as he durst," was unable to discern "so much as a shadow" (*Mosses,* 81); and, though Brown suspects he hears the voices of his townspeople, the narrator reports that it may have been "the murmur of the old forest" (*Mosses,* 82).

Brown's perceptual difficulties are both complicated and motivated by his sense of himself as radically disenfranchised from his community. His alienation from his community may be described in Common Sense terms as based in the sentiment of malevolence or, alternatively, a lack of benevo-lence. These terms, *malevolence* and *benevolence,* are important because they directly address the question of the individual's relationship with the community. Brown's perceptions lead to his feeling alienated from his com-munity. But Hawthorne has indicated in "The Haunted Mind" and "Night Sketches" that such alienation does not automatically spring from intro-spection and association. The complicating factor in "Young Goodman Brown" is Brown's basic emotional response to those around him: fear.

The overwhelming feeling projected by the narrative of Brown's ex-perience in the forest is that of fear. Fear, in Upham's psychology, fell under the general heading of benevolence and malevolence; these constituted two primary passions, with fear a category of the latter:

> The passion of Fear like the other passions or affections that have passed under examination, embraces both a simple emotion of pain aroused by some object which we anticipate will be injurious to us, and also additional to the painful emotion, the desire of avoiding such object or its injurious effects. . . . the fact that we experience pain in viewing the object feared, accompanied by the desire of avoiding it, seems very clearly to involve the idea that it is an object of greater or less aversion. In other words, that we have more or less ill will towards it . . . .
>   It is a state of mind of great power, and one which will not bear to be trifled with. It may serve as a profitable hint to remark, that there have been persons thrown into a fright suddenly, and perhaps in mere sport, which has immediately resulted in a most distressing and permanent mental disorganization.—In cases where the anticipated evil is very great, and there is no hope of avoiding it in any way, the mind exists in that state which is called DESPAIR. [370]

The congruence of Upham's description of fear and Brown's mental degeneration is striking. Brown's fear of his neighbors manifests itself in his initial distrust and his need to test his faith. Those same neighbors whom he is later unable to trust are likewise fear-inspiring in the forest. Brown's experienced lack of social engagement culminates in the despair that persists throughout his life, so that "his dying hour was gloom" (*Mosses*, 90).

But Hawthorne's rendering of fear as Brown's motivation and his final state deserves a closer look since, despite the course of narrative action, the only change within Brown is the making salient of psychological features that had been latent from the beginning. To appreciate the complexity of Brown's fear, we need to recall both the plot conventions within Hawthorne's stories of departure from home and subsequent return, and the semiotics of the sentimental formula as described by Fred G. See: "The rules of this [sentimental] fiction develop the possibility of a natural return, through maternal intervention, to that absent unity. Maternal intervention becomes the matrix . . . at which we are gazing, and through which we may return to an original myth of infancy: *infans*, without speech, without need for language but replete with intention and understanding."[58] See correlates the function of return with what antebellum thinkers routinely presented as the site of benevolence—home and family—itself most sharply denoted in the mother-child relationship. This return arrives with both promise and threat. The promise is the fulfillment of primal desire and the

recovery of that which is absent. But the threat may indeed be more significant to the narrative function within "Young Goodman Brown": the loss
of language and, with the loss of language, the abandonment of interpretation. This threatened loss of language is overwhelming, particularly when
the self arises through the course of narration, as it does when
Hawthorne translates Common Sense ideas of selfhood into a mode of
narration.

    The crises of Hawthorne's narratives of departure and return reach
their most highly developed state in "Young Goodman Brown." Throughout these stories and sketches, the self arises as a structure that makes
narration not only possible but necessary as a means of situating the
self within a social milieu. When the self seeks fulfillment in sociality, the
narrative of its ventures into the world charts the varied deferrals of such
fulfillment, even when the self's travels are as modest as little Annie's
ramble and the motivations are as simple as her "longing after the mystery
of the great world." The operation of narrative deferral reaches its fullest
form in accounts of individual withdrawal, such as Goodman Brown's.
In purely psychological terms, Brown's withdrawal suggests a lack of sympathy. It simultaneously suggests, however, in a manner concordant with
Common Sense psychology, that the self has a resource with which to defer
engagement with the community (or family). This resource, introspection,
becomes the necessary ground for narrative, and the disengagement of the
self from the social realm, a disengagement characterized by the silences of
Wakefield and Goodman Brown, is displaced by the artist's rhetorical
engagement with an audience. In the case of a relatively simple story like
"Egotism," which, like "Young Goodman Brown," presents interpretive
crises, questions about language use are foreclosed with the plot resolution
and the rendering of the protagonist's problems as a symptomatic embodiment of moral and psychological difficulties. In "Young Goodman
Brown," however, the problematic epistemological questions of the knowing, introspecting self readily suggest additional questions about the
significance of interpretation, or, to use Budick's phrasing, "the process of
meaning making," and the social regulation of interpretation.[59]

    Brown creates meaning when interpreting his natural and social envi-
ronment, and the reader makes meaning interpreting Brown's dilemma.
The obvious analogy here is one that, I think, may well be worth resisting
or at least deferring, for "Young Goodman Brown" presents more than a
simple allegory of reading. Instead, interpretation, a necessary function of
selfhood within Common Sense thought, works in Hawthorne's short
works to define the self as stable and social or, alternatively, to reveal problems of sociality when the self is fixated by the interpretive process and
seduced by the prospects of some original knowledge. The play between

the dangers of solipsism and the demands for interpretation provides the basis for Hawthorne's other, more complex depictions of the interpreting self, such as that offered in *The Scarlet Letter,* in which Hawthorne poses the problem of how introspecting, interpreting selves that require sociality must create or find meaning within a tainted cultural framework.

3

"But the Past Was Not Dead"

Aesthetics, History, and Community in
Grandfather's Chair and *The Scarlet Letter*

In "Young Goodman Brown," "Egotism; or, The Bosom-Serpent," and the other short works discussed in the preceding chapter, Hawthorne highlights the value of domestic stability and the dangers enveloping those who attempt explorations of themselves or their social environments without a firm domestic grounding. Hawthorne's warning, repeated in so many of his writings, bears emphasis: although the individual consciousness may provide the site for psychological exploration by way of introspective processes, any individual claims to knowledge of the truth must stand the social test of reproducibility. If others cannot ultimately confirm individual insights, those insights are depicted by Hawthorne as at best suspect and potentially delusory, and at worst dangerous. Such an epistemological assertion seems, however, more appropriate to the sciences than to aesthetic works, and it even threatens to violate the spirit of Hawthorne's representations of individual psychological experiences. These representations often lead Hawthorne's readers to find in his writings accounts of the individual consciousness as outposts of resistance against a society that rewards those in power with wealth and, of greater ultimate consequence, with the (frequently self-serving) guardianship of popular truth. It is difficult to align this understanding of Hawthorne with the Common Sense claim that epistemological certainty is properly the province of a relatively complacent society rather than the potentially subversive individual. The Hawthorne who exposes the Pyncheons' crude acquisitiveness in *The House of the Seven Gables*, the creator of arguably the strongest female character of nineteenth-century fiction in *The Scarlet Letter*—how is he to be reconciled with such deeply conformist ideas and ideals as those present in "Egotism," "Sunday at Home," and other, less frequently anthologized, conventionally sentimental, and moralizing works?

This is the problem that Nina Baym identified when she speculated that an epistemological break separates the romances of the 1850s from Hawthorne's earlier works.[1] The problem that Baym discussed is one that Hawthorne's interpreters still must come to terms with, particularly because a consequence of presuming with Baym a radical epistemological break is the allied presumption that Hawthorne anticipates decidedly twentieth-century concerns. A recent explication of "The Minister's Black Veil," offered by the distinctly antihistoricist J. Hillis Miller as representing all of Hawthorne's writings, shows one consequence of this type of thinking. Miller, attentive to those things that Hawthorne leaves unsaid and therefore ambiguous, asserts that "the lifting of a veil only reveals another veil behind, as Hawthorne's story 'shows.'"[2] Because the chain of signification allows for no specifiable end, Hawthorne's meaning, Miller insists, is violated when subjected to methods that make claims to interpretive specificity. Miller's remarks about Hawthorne are noteworthy because they convey the power Hawthorne's ironic and multivalent style has held for generations of critics.[3]

With the exceptions of Emerson and Melville, no other antebellum writer so consistently made demands on readers to adopt new interpretive modes, and Hawthorne's formal innovations, while proving a continuing inspiration and challenge to critics, have played a large role in sustaining scholarly interest in his work. Critics during the 1950s and 1960s established the modernist reading of Hawthorne's ambiguities, one in which an aesthetics of ambiguity meshed with meaning in Hawthorne's romances so as to convey a radical skepticism about social authority when it is challenged by the individual consciousness. Critics since that time who have, like Miller, adopted a deconstructive approach have found in Hawthorne's works an analogously postmodern design, one in which problems of formal uncertainty lead the perceptive reader toward the thematic considerations of epistemological and existential uncertainties.[4] The demands that Hawthorne places on his readers cannot be dismissed; the reader must adapt to uncomfortable doubts and equivocations about characters' motivations and events within Hawthorne's stories. But, in the face of Hawthorne's fictions of sociality, it is difficult to conclude that Hawthorne's writings display a postmodern indeterminacy. And, given the earlier criticisms of communal verification of truth, as in "Young Goodman Brown" (1835), and later endorsements of sociality, like those of "Ethan Brand" and "The Great Stone Face" (both 1850), as well as *Tanglewood Tales* (1853), a precise shift in Hawthorne's allegiances seems obscure. A challenge to the reader of Hawthorne thus emerges: How are Hawthorne's epistemologically certain and moralistic writings to be reconciled with his deeply ironic and ambiguously multivalent works, such as his romances and stories like "Young Goodman Brown"?

To respond to this question, this chapter will juxtapose Hawthorne's most radical social critique, *The Scarlet Letter*, in terms of its aesthetic, historiographic, and psychological bases, against his highly moralistic children's history, *The Whole History of Grandfather's Chair*. *Grandfather's Chair*, like all of Hawthorne's writings for children, poses a dilemma for scholars. It is difficult to correlate a strictly antiauthoritarian interpretation of *The Scarlet Letter* with a reading of Hawthorne's conventionally moral children's literature. Scholars generally have sought to deal with this problem in one of three ways: (1) most popularly, by totally ignoring the children's literature; (2) by pronouncing it decidedly inferior "hackwork," unfit for sustained scholarly attention; or, most recently, (3) by finding beneath the surface of the children's literature "alternative realities, worlds of magic, alchemy, and disguise, that encourage an escape from the hegemony within and without the stories."[5] The discussion of *The Whole History of Grandfather's Chair* to be offered here will take a different route, one informed by attention to the antebellum debate over American history and, more significantly, to early-nineteenth-century thinking about aesthetics.

Antebellum ideas about aesthetics are closely related on several levels to the psychology discussed in the preceding chapter. Both were guided by the precepts of the prevalent Common Sense moral philosophy, and frequently their objects of inquiry overlapped. The overlap is not surprising, given the fact that aesthetic responses combine those intellectual actions necessary for interpretation with the readers' affective reactions. Psychological faculties were necessarily understood to be involved in interpretation and in the creation of the work of art, as Thomas Upham's descriptions of the imagination indicated. Upham was himself a published poet, and, along with many others of his time, he advocated a national literature. The desire for a national literature and a postcolonial artistic identity is not to be lightly taken. The preceding chapter advanced the argument that when Hawthorne's depictions of individual psychology are understood in the context of antebellum psychology he, like many of his contemporaries, emerges as an advocate of domestic and social stability. Antebellum literary nationalism may be similarly understood to have been, like Common Sense psychology, a response to the threats against community cohesion experienced by Hawthorne and his middle-class contemporaries.

Hawthorne's commitment to social cohesion creates, as in "Young Goodman Brown," the potential for tension between it and the value his writings ascribe to individual experience and consciousness. The place where consciousness and social cohesion must meet, in Common Sense terms, is in the social corroboration of individual insights. When the introspecting individual cannot corroborate insights socially, then the dilemma of young Goodman Brown—or, in *The Scarlet Letter,* those of Hester Prynne and Arthur Dimmesdale—arises. But Brown's situation also raises a troubling question: When social judgments are themselves suspect, on what bases are individual insights to be validated? Obviously, the Puritan community that had been engaged in witch-hunts compromised its own claim to epistemological certainty, particularly according to the values of nineteenth-century "liberal culture," as Bercovitch designates it in *The Office of the Scarlet Letter*. This epistemological problem, one left unresolved by "Young Goodman Brown," remains prominent in *The Scarlet Letter*. With *The Scarlet Letter*, Hawthorne was able to deliver a narrative solution to this problem, and perhaps it is because of this resolution that in Hawthorne's subsequent work the problem never recurs so strongly. Within *The Scarlet Letter*, Hawthorne poses a number of other concerns and formulations that arose in his other writings, most notably the confrontation with the found object that requires the artist's intervention for it to communicate and thus be available for an audience's interpretations. As I will argue, the foregrounding of interpretation does more than simply recapitulate certain Common Sense empiricist tendencies; it also translates the issue of the self's confrontation with its social and material milieus into the realm of semiotics and language. It is through the social power of language that Hawthorne will resolve the tensions of *The Scarlet Letter*, and it is because of this social power that Hawthorne's contemporaries understood aesthetics to be important.

The moral and psychological preoccupations that shaped Hawthorne's aesthetics reflect the Common Sense outlook, one that looked backwards toward an imagined time when individual and communal allegiances maintained a balance with each other. The aesthetic principles that correlate with this balance are distinctly eighteenth-century, and we may look to Dr. Johnson's "Preface to Shakespeare" (1765) for an articulation of this position. Johnson defended the value of individual genius against those who would attack the individual genius—in this case, Shakespeare—for not adhering to conventions of aesthetic unity: "The work of a correct and regular writer is a garden accurately formed and diligently planted, varied with shades, and scented with flowers; the composition of Shakespeare is a forest . . . filling the eye with awful pomp and gratifying the mind with endless diversity."[6] This organic metaphor dramatizes Johnson's claim that Shakespeare's genius was a "natural" attribute, one which transcended the "minute and slender" criticism for not attending to dramatic rules posed by French neoclassical critics.[7]

But, as Johnson pointed out at the start of his essay, this defense of Shakespeare ultimately relies on common experience as the means to validate the truth of artistic judgments:

> To works, however, of which the excellence is not absolute and definite, but gradual and comparative; to works not raised upon principles demonstrative and scientifick, but appealing wholly to observation

and experience, no other test can be applied than length of duration
and continuance of esteem. What mankind have long possessed they
have often examined and compared; and if they persist to value the
possession, it is because frequent comparisons have confirmed opinion
in its favour. . . .

The reverence due to writings that have long subsisted arises
therefore not from any credulous confidence in the superior wisdom
of past ages, or gloomy persuasion of the degeneracy of mankind, but
is the consequence of acknowledged and indubitable positions, that
what has been longest known has been most considered, and what is
most considered is best understood.[8]

Much as Common Sense psychology espoused the social ratification of individual insights, Johnson's defense of Shakespeare was framed by a social
orientation toward aesthetic valuation. Johnson was, of course, no twentieth-century social constructivist, and his claims about the value of common responses were not complicated by ideological criticism. Societal
responses here came as close as possible to duplicating the "demonstrative
and scientifick" methods of empiricist disciplines; they provided the most
reliable access to truth. And, in a similar fashion, early-nineteenth-century
American critics discussed and defended literature's value in social terms,
terms that presumed ultimate ideas about stable and universal truths.

A coherent body of critical thought prevailed in the United States
during Hawthorne's time, one described by William Charvat in his study
of early-nineteenth-century aesthetics as "the work of a practically homo-
geneous upper class which felt itself competent to legislate, culturally, for
other classes."[9] Critics tended to be "men of the world—lawyers, legis-
lators, ministers, physicians, and teachers," rather than academicians or
journalists.[10] Certain basic principles guided their evaluations of literature:
opposition to rebellion against the existing order, conformity to religious
and moral standards, a desire for philosophical optimism, intelligibility,
and a social rather than egocentric outlook. Their politically conservative
program further promoted the notion of didactics as an appropriate literary function.[11] The prescriptive concept, that literary presentation of an
ideal social behavior inculcated virtue, formed the basis of the neoclassical
defense of literature's social function. Along these lines, Hawthorne's
fiction itself was accorded praise for its "fine moral tone."[12] One contemporary critic who found reason to question "the mental and moral influence of the most faultless novels and tales of the fashion now current"
instead preferred Hawthorne's "higher fiction," which "breathes into
[things] a vital glow, writes upon them the image of the unseen and spiritual, and robes them in a softer light, a richer charm, a purer beauty."[13]

This praise for Hawthorne's imaginative fiction involved not mere recognition of its technical virtues but satisfaction over its presumed social effects. Even those who have been identified as precursors to Emerson, such as William Ellery Channing and William Cullen Bryant, affirm concepts congruent with the theories advanced by explicitly hegemonic critics.[14]

Bryant's "Lectures on Poetry" (1825-26) furnish a valuable example of how a desire for social stability could merge in aesthetic theory with an affirmation of individual expression. The "Lectures" initially convey the expressivist idea that "the great spring of poetry is emotion."[15] Bryant aligned individual emotion with ideas reminiscent of didactic criticism when he suggested that the mind instinctively would recognize truths: "Do we not know that poetry delights in inspiring compassion, the parent of all kind offices? Does it not glory in sentiments of fortitude and magnanimity, the fountain of disinterested sacrifices? It cherishes patriotism, the incitement to vigorous toils endured for the welfare of communities. It luxuriates among the natural affections, the springs of all the gentle charities of domestic life. . . ."[16] The distinctly social orientation, the affirmation of domesticity and patriotism, and the condemnation of self-interest were all values common to sentimental fiction and worthy of the approval of most of the critics Charvat designates as spokesmen for "their own homogenous patrician society." William Ellery Channing, in his "Remarks on National Literature" (1823), argued along similar lines that literature "is plainly among the most powerful methods of exalting the character of a nation, of forming a better race of men; in truth, we apprehend that it may claim the first rank among the means of improvement. We know nothing so fitted to the advancement of society as to bring its higher minds to bear upon the multitude."[17] The social value of literature is here restated amid a general call for literature as an expression of national character. The desire for a postcolonial national identity when combined with a strong sense of community-based recognition of truth provided an aesthetic counterpart to Common Sense ideas about individual psychology. Admittedly, the notions of national identity and an innate ability to recognize truth may be identified with Romantic values. Nevertheless, it is important to understand these statements not simply as precursors to Transcendentalism but as expressions of a fully developed belief system in its own right.

The theoretical basis for this approach to literature found its most complete statement in Archibald Alison's extremely influential *Essays on the Nature and Principles of Taste*.[18] Like Upham's *Abridgement of Mental Philosophy*, Alison's work presented the inherent contradiction of Common Sense thought that simultaneously relied on a socially oriented, realist epistemology and a potentially subjective, introspective methodology.

Alison's central concept, association, reflects this inherent tension. Association, generally taken to be an attribute of an individualist epistemology, was definitively grounded in the social realm by Alison. Alison's method was basically that of reader response—he attempted an empirical approach to works of art when he stated that "repeated Experiments" are necessary to judge accurately the effects of aesthetic phenomena.[19] The effects of these phenomena, the semiotic process by which associative trains are formed, are predicated by two types of signs, the natural and the conventional.

The natural sign provided the basis for his theory of universal response to aesthetic phenomena. Thus, he commented on autumn: "Who is there, who, at this season, does not feel his mind impressed with a sentiment of melancholy?" (Essays, 17). The train of association that began with the sensory signs of autumn universally would lead to the specific feeling of melancholy. Similarly, Alison argued that numerous "material signs" (Essays, 181) engendered specific emotional responses: "The Strength of the Oak, the delicacy of the Myrtle, the boldness of a Rock, the modesty of the Violet, etc. are expressions common in all languages, and so common, that they are scarcely in any, considered as figurative. . . . How much the effect of descriptions of natural scenery arises from that personification, which is founded upon such associations, I believe there is no man of common taste who must not often have been sensible" (Essays, 183-84). Alison treated a variety of visual, auditory, and other sensory phenomena in what essentially comprises a catalog of aesthetic responses. These were understood to be universal responses based in common taste; although Alison did acknowledge unique individual associations, the most noteworthy are those which were shared. The word common was of strategic value to Alison, for he opposed what he refers to as "philosophy" against the "common opinion [which] is by much the most defensible" (Essays, 316). Alison argued here that philosophical explanations of aesthetics were secondary to explanations based on experience, specifically common experience. Thus, he followed Dugald Stewart's lead of grounding association theory within a social context.[20]

Alison could appropriate the theory of association to social rather than individual ends because he took as axiomatic the empirical validation of aesthetic judgments. He proceeded from traditional responses to natural signs onward to various responses to conventional signs. Thus, historical associations would enhance the effect of natural scenes: "The majesty of the Alps themselves is increased by the remembrance of Hannibal's march over them; and who is there, that could stand on the banks of the Rubicon, without feeling his imagination kindle, and his heart beat high?" (Essays, 27). Alison noted as one product of "national associations" the "effect of the celebrated national song, which is said to overpower the Swiss soldier in a foreign land with melancholy and despair" (*Essays*, 35). Further conventional responses might be found among people who share an occupation; conditioned to regard the world from a specific point of view, they would value certain things while rejecting others as worthless (*Essays*, 87-89). In short, common mental habits were crucial to Alison's aesthetics.

A focus on history and tradition as the bases for conventional signification fully accords with the didactic emphasis of so much early-nineteenth-century criticism, for without a shared tradition the attempt of the artist to evoke certain associated responses would have been futile. Within the American context, the attempt to invent a new tradition still had as its theoretical basis Alison's sign theory and a concomitant reliance on social validation. The artist's work in the new tradition was twofold: to use traditional associations in the production of aesthetic effects, and to revise the traditional at the same time so as to make it more relevant to American conditions. This artistic task largely shaped Hawthorne's use of history in his children's writings.

Hawthorne's writings for children were not confined to histories—before he wrote *The Whole History of Grandfather's Chair* and *Biographical Stories for Children*, Hawthorne had achieved sufficient recognition for his children's fiction to encourage continued production for this audience.[21] *The Whole History of Grandfather's Chair*, his most substantial nonfiction juvenile project, first appeared in three separate volumes: *Grandfather's Chair*, completed in late 1840, treated the history of the Puritans up until the witchcraft trials of 1692; the two subsequent volumes, *Famous Old People* and *Liberty Tree*, published in early 1841, gave an anecdotal history through the American Revolution. Hawthorne expressed his didactic goal most directly in the preface to a book that appeared the following year, *Biographical Stories for Children*: "This small volume, and others of a similar character, from the same hand, have not been composed without a deep sense of responsibility. The author regards children as sacred, and would not, for the world, cast anything into the fountain of a young heart, that might embitter and pollute its waters."[22] The biographical stories that follow, set within a fairly perfunctory narrative frame of a family with three children, promote conventional values. So, for example, when the children fight, they are told the story of Dr. Johnson, who, as a boy, refused his gravely ill father's request that young Sam work in his stead selling books at the public market in Uttoxeter. Johnson's refusal left him so greatly stricken with remorse that fifty years later he went out on market-day to Uttoxeter to perform silent public penance. The narrator concludes, "My dear children, if you have grieved—I will not say, your parents—but, if you have grieved the heart of any human being, who has a claim upon your love, then think of Samuel Johnson's penance!" (*True Stories*, 248).

This manipulative tale with its message of filial piety conveys the moral tone Hawthorne typically assumes with children. The imaginative quality we customarily associate with children's literature is absent here, as well as from Hawthorne's specifically fictional writings for youth; Hawthorne's attempt to "revolutionize" children's literature primarily involved "purifying and preaching."[23] The contents as well as the stated intent of Hawthorne's *Biographical Stories* and *The Whole History* fully conform to the standard defense of literature's value as a device to promote conventional social morality. And *The Whole History of Grandfather's Chair* accords with the interest of his contemporaries in national literature.[24] The work promotes a vision of life in which the individual is always caught up within a social network, and the Common Sense emphasis on sociality thereby converges with Alison's ideas of a national semiotics. The literary artist's task becomes that of creating a set of associations that anchor the individual within a community and establish community continuity by envisioning the present moment as the continuation and culmination of past traditions.

The literary conceit on which Hawthorne relies in *The Whole History of Grandfather's Chair* is one that is quite familiar to students of Hawthorne: the silent object that stands in need of interpretation. The object itself forms a physical link between the present and the past, and the work of its interpreter becomes that of elaborating this link through story telling. The most famous instance of reliance on a physical object is the found package in the Salem customhouse, but Hawthorne also uses this narrative device elsewhere, as in, for example, "The Antique Ring," "A Book of Autographs," and the "Legends of the Province-House." In these stories, the artists interpret the materials at hand, and through the transmission of these interpretations, they create within the narratives a sense of community. In the series of sketches, generally about prominent historical figures, that comprise *The Whole History*, the social function of the artist is similarly incorporated into the story. Four children surround Grandfather, listen to his stories, and respond to his commentaries, drawing from him additional reflections and interpretations. The narrative frame for the individual stories is designed to create for its auditors—whether the grandchildren or the readers—a sense of membership within a national community. In addition, the physical device of Grandfather's old oak chair, which seems to have witnessed many important events in early American history, reinforces the notion of history's immanence and strengthens the idea of connection between past and present.[25]

The first volume of *The Whole History of Grandfather's Chair*, with its focus on the Puritans, is most relevant to *The Scarlet Letter* in its treatment of Puritan history. Puritan history was itself troublesome in Hawthorne's time, and the problem of legitimizing a sense of continuity and community colors its presentation. Toward the beginning, Grandfather tells a story that dramatizes a basic tension in Hawthorne's Puritan histories. The gentle, highly cultured Lady Arbella, "too pale and feeble to endure the hardships of the wilderness" environment "fit only for rough and hardy people," is contrasted with the figure of John Endicott, whose "heart was as bold and resolute as iron" (*True Stories*, 15-17). While she withers away and dies, Endicott thrives in the harsh American wilderness. The children are moved to tears at Lady Arbella's death, and Hawthorne transmits the message that, of necessity, the Puritans placed little value on the more refined civilized qualities associated with England.[26]

Grandfather's Chair thus conveys early-nineteenth-century ambivalence toward the Puritans. As Lawrence Buell notes, the period's histories of Puritan times were "enlivened by perpetual conflict between filiopietistic and critical instincts."[27] On the one hand, historians expressed an allegiance to Puritan ideals of piety and civil liberty; Bancroft's history specifically praises the Puritan people (as opposed to their leadership) for embodying these ideals. At the same time, however, a critical instinct emerged as "liberal historians declared a semiindependence from [the Puritan leadership's] authority through their urbanity and their sympathy, however patronizing, with the heretic."[28] In retrospect, this conflict between filiopietism and criticism seems inevitable. The theological vision of history that actuated the Puritan mission in the New World was transformed into a secular vision of human progress: a teleology without telos. This popular belief in the inevitably progressive course of United States history conflicted with the desire to ground history in the ideals of the Founding Fathers, Puritan and revolutionary. Political oratory of the 1830s and 1840s emphasized this conflict; we have the example of one conservative politician of the period who expressed typical sentiments when he declared that "the political history of the country . . . is, in a word, the history of a struggle, more or less remitted as the power of the opposition has increased or declined, to maintain in their purity the original principles on which the government is founded."[29] This fear of falling away from original principles is consistent with the rhetoric of social crisis so typical of nineteenth-century political discourse. Yet the idealization of the past coincided with a sense of evolutionary development, and it generated a powerful intellectual tension in Hawthorne's time.[30]

A sense of progress, a projection of community endurance into the future, was fueled by criticisms of the past, while idealization of the

Founding Fathers affirmed a sense of communal coherence and continuity. Thus, although Grandfather praises Puritan accomplishment, he has an eye to their faults; accordingly, he commends Bancroft's history to the children (*True Stories*, 33).[31] But the approbation accorded the Puritans in *Grandfather's Chair* is also consistent with an antebellum vision of American history. As progenitors, they provided the values that would flourish as the American Revolution. The desire to flee religious persecution, accompanied by the tenacity with which they held to their beliefs, provided the basic positive values asserted by Grandfather. This quality is most clearly embodied in the figure of John Endicott.

Hawthorne's treatment of Endicott in *Grandfather's Chair* is enlightening. On the one hand, Grandfather expresses his approval of Endicott as a precursor of the revolution: "A sense of the independence of his adopted country, must have been in that bold man's heart" (*True Stories*, 24). The character of the country itself as naturally "independent" is conveyed, and Endicott's act of cutting the cross out of the flag in protest against "Popish idolatry" emerges as "a very strong expression of Puritan character" (*True Stories*, 24-25). But by the dramatic juxtaposition of Lady Arbella's death against Endicott's hardiness, *Grandfather's Chair* obliquely criticizes the narrowness of Puritan concerns. This criticism is not nearly so pronounced as is the depiction of Puritan intolerance in "Endicott and the Red Cross"—the narrative procession of those who had their ears cropped, cheeks branded, and noses slit in punishment—yet the ultimate point is the same. Whether Hawthorne wrote for children or adults, the nineteenth-century conflict between filiopietism and the instinct to criticize the nation's progenitors informs his historical vision. *Grandfather's Chair* is no aberration: its didactic purpose accords fully with both Alison's semiotics and a conventionally progressive view of history, and the values it promotes are consistent with those of the tales and romances. These values are most clearly evident in Hawthorne's treatments of Quaker persecution in *Grandfather's Chair* and "The Gentle Boy."

Grandfather briefly describes the Quaker persecution of 1656-59: "The children were amazed to hear, that, the more the Quakers were scourged, and imprisoned, and banished, the more did the sect increase, both by the influx of strangers, and by converts from among the Puritans. But Grandfather told them, that God had put something into the soul of man, which always turned the cruelties of the persecutor to nought" (*True Stories*, 40). Grandfather appropriates the Quaker experience to serve the later values of the Revolution, and he thereby generalizes the struggle against unjust authority. As if to emphasize the point, the children find this the most moving story they have yet heard. But unlike its depiction in *Grandfather's Chair*, in "The Gentle Boy" the Quaker persecution is attributed to the "pious forefathers" *and* the Quakers themselves, whose desire to come to New England manifested an "enthusiasm, heightened almost to madness by the treatment which they received, [that] produced actions contrary to the rules of decency."[32] Quaker indecency is embodied by Ilbrahim's mother, who, "neglectful of the holiest trust which can be committed to a woman," gives him up for adoption in order to pursue her religious fanaticism, itself an expression of her "disordered" imagination.[33] This most reprehensible of religious enthusiasts stands as a dramatic counterbalance to Puritan intolerance, and her preference for religious commitment over her maternal role renders her actions the moral equivalent of unjust Puritan authority.

Although *Grandfather's Chair* refrains from such harsh judgment of Quakers, it, too, promotes the social values of benevolence, sympathy, and compassion. What makes the children's history noteworthy is less its advocacy of particular values, themselves common to Hawthorne's writings, than the way it situates these values with reference to the inherent conflict of antebellum historiography and also the work of the writer as creator of a set of national associations. The overlap of these artistic tasks, the advocacy of such transcendent values as domesticity and national progress, the apparent subject matter of the storyteller in *Grandfather's Chair,* in effect forestalls the conveyance of these values. In place of uncomplicated advocacy, questions about the legitimacy of social authority as the adjudicator of morality and experience simultaneously arise alongside the articulation of conventional values. Antebellum historiography, aesthetics, and psychology intersect within this children's book, and their inherent tensions are momentarily obscured when problems of national identity and communal relations are collapsed into the story propelled by the narrative frame, one of family cohesion and continuity. But when Hawthorne reverses this process in *The Scarlet Letter,* when he projects a story of the *failure* of domesticity onto the backdrop of national formation, a strikingly different narrative strategy emerges.

Among Hawthorne's writings, *The Scarlet Letter* offers the most sustained attempt to resolve problems in the relationship between history, community, and the individual consciousness. In effect, the historiographic and aesthetic concerns treated in *Grandfather's Chair* are further complicated by the psychological and narrative problematics of "Young Goodman Brown." The vexed relationship between social authority and the individual conscience is reflected by the ethical questions the novel raises: When our historical traditions are tainted by the actions of unjust authority, how are we to constitute our present sense of communal tradition? When social judgments are suspect, on what grounds are individual insights to be corroborated? Although these questions pose challenges to antebellum psychological and aesthetic theories, I would argue that a Common Sense outlook nevertheless shapes the novel's responses and that, while a critique of Puritan social authority is maintained, the range of Hester Prynne's rebellion is circumscribed.[34]

• • •

"But the past was not dead."

Emily Miller Budick suggests the ethical and political dimensions of Hawthorne's turn to history when she asserts that "Hawthorne restores to conscious memory a history that the dominant culture has repressed."[35] History returns, then, not as the force which substantiates contemporary political and social authority but which instead threatens to overturn it. Nowhere in the body of Hawthorne's writings is there stronger evidence for this view of his use of history than in *The Scarlet Letter*. Its repeated, almost obsessional, turns to the past are introduced in "The Custom-House" by encounters with physical objects. Most notable is the encounter with Surveyor Pue's manuscript and the scarlet letter itself, which seemed to communicate "some deep meaning . . . most worthy of interpretation."[36] Hawthorne here provides a physical link between the narrative frame and the story within while he also introduces a pair of demands on the reader's sensibilities: the understanding that the past is always present, and the idea that despite its presence the past does not speak for itself but rather requires elaboration and interpretation. It is the job of the narrator, as in *Grandfather's Chair*, to present and interpret events, but in "The Custom-House" the narrator's own position predisposes him toward the goal of restoration and complication described by Budick.

The story of Hawthorne's political appointment to the Salem customhouse and his equally political dismissal from that position upon the election of Zachary Taylor's Whig administration in 1848 is too well known to need repetition.[37] Certainly "The Custom-House" presents the attitude that "the delicate harvest of fancy and sensibility" (34), the transfer to the more subtle and significant work of writing, required his removal from office. But his rendering of the episode is marked by a series of narrative transitions that signal a reluctance to speak directly about political matters. Hawthorne opens the sketch with a description of the Salem customhouse that concludes with a reference to himself as surveyor: "The besom of reform has swept him out of office; and a worthier successor wears his dignity and pockets his emoluments" (8). This remark, which would seem to promise a political exposé, is promptly deflected by the initial gesture toward the past: "The old town of Salem . . . possesses, or did possess, a hold on my affections." Hawthorne's later musings on the surveyorship and the use of his name in an official capacity to mark merchandise, which "carried [his name] where it had never been before, and, I hope, will never go again" (27), likewise immediately precede his statement that "the past was not dead." And, finally, after speculations on the differences between Democratic and Whig handling of political appointments, Hawthorne retreats into "the lucubrations of my ancient predecessor, Mr. Surveyor Pue" (43), the story that Hawthorne converts into the succeeding narrative, "The Scarlet Letter."

These three moments in the narrative provide clues to the relationship between present and past. Initially, the present appears to be more or less simply predicated by the past, as Hawthorne suggests in his mildly comic depictions of quaint local scenes. The "old gentlemen" who populate the customhouse, the "dilapidated wharf" on which rests the customhouse, with its view of "old salts," its "old paint," and an "old pine desk" within—all these could attest to an innocuous relationship between past and present (7). Even the image of Hawthorne himself as the "topmost bough" of "the old trunk of the family tree," haunted by the "old dry bones" of his Puritan forebears (9-10), at first seems sufficiently fanciful to support the idea that he is merely conveying local color. But the more Hawthorne describes the presence of the past, the more oppressive it becomes. The wood of the old wharf might appear venerable when it is recalled as once living, when it is juxtaposed against the image of a family tree. But when situated against "the phosphorescent glow of decaying wood" (16), the metaphor with which Hawthorne condemns what remains of intellect within the old customhouse men, the past becomes a burden that threatens to utterly obscure the present moment. And so the past returns to the narrative whenever the history of the present, that of the political intrigue surrounding the Salem customhouse, impends. The present moment may be characterized as one dominated by unjust political authority; accordingly, Hawthorne disingenuously protests in his "Preface to the Second Edition" that his treatment of the old men is not satirical but rather reflects an attitude of "frank and genuine good-humor," and he claims that "the unprecedented excitement in the respectable community immediately around him" and "the public disapprobation" resulted from a misapprehension of his intentions (1).[38]

But the return of the past does not simply shift attention from a corrupt present in which "wearisome old souls, who had gathered nothing worth preservation from their varied experience of life" (16) set the intellectual standard. It also raises questions about the uses of tradition during a time when community authority is threatened—not only from without, as when nineteenth-century writers agonize over immigration, but from within, as a result of moral decay. This concern over contemporary decay is hardly unique to Hawthorne: the opening sentences in Emerson's *Nature* decry the obsession with "the sepulchres of the fathers" and "the dry bones of the past."[39] Emerson's tone may be more dramatic than Hawthorne's, but he, too, is haunted by ancestral "dry bones." Emerson's solution to the problem of a "retrospective" age, his famed insistence that we "demand our own works and laws and worship," is both more radical and more in the tradition of an American rhetoric of freedom than Hawthorne's. Hawthorne instead makes the decidedly non-Emersonian suggestion that a preoccupation with the past would constitute an evasion of the present, *except* for the point made by Budick, that this history is itself one which the "dominant culture has repressed." Thus, as Evan Carton points out when reading "But the past was not dead," we are turned "toward Hawthorne's literary future as it returns to the past, drawing both into the life of the present."[40] The rewriting of Surveyor Pue's brief manuscript thereby points to the past, to the future, and, most importantly, to a present preoccupied with concerns over the proper basis for community cohesion.[41]

The two related sets of concerns raised by "The Custom-House" that shape the presentation of Hester Prynne's story are the interpretive functions associated with the artist's work and the social implications of history writing. In the case of *The Scarlet Letter,* Hawthorne reveals a conflicted attitude toward the function of history as warrantor of tradition. Hester Prynne's story evokes at the very least a skepticism over the legitimacy of social authority. Yet the act of redacting the found manuscript indicates a conception of the past much like that displayed by *Grandfather's Chair,* in which the telling of stories about the past reflects a desire for historical continuity and a belief in consistent national character and ambition. Hawthorne's insistence on the need for community stability demands a mediation of the present by the past—he would reject the Emersonian dichotomy between "a poetry and philosophy of insight" as opposed to one "of tradition"[42]—but the process is not closed to Hawthorne, who, as the narrator of *The Scarlet Letter,* inserts himself into the historical process by assuming the historian's role. By presenting the kind of traditional associations that Alison described as a foundation of common thought, Hawthorne recovers the past, and his interpretive involvement revitalizes American historical associations. And in terms of narrative structure, "The Custom-House" narrator's writing of history redeems a potentially alienated character through his return into the social realm, a pattern of return familiar from Hawthorne's shorter works.

The historical problem of American political and social authority is introduced almost immediately in the first chapter of Hester Prynne's story. The opening sentences carry forth from "The Custom-House" a critical attitude toward the past, citing the establishment of cemeteries and prisons as the first tasks in establishing the colony and quickly following with the conventional attributions of Puritan narrow-mindedness. Descriptions of "the grim rigidity that petrified the bearded physiognomies of these good people" as indicative of "that early severity of the Puritan character" implicitly convey a sense of historical progress (49). This belief in progress is thereafter made explicit:

> Morally, as well as materially, there was a coarser fibre in those wives and maidens of old English birth and breeding, than in their fair descendants, separated from them by a series of six or seven generations; for, throughout that chain of ancestry, every successive mother has transmitted to her child a fainter bloom, a more delicate and briefer beauty, and a slighter physical frame, if not a character of less force and solidity, than her own. The women, who were now standing about the prison-door, stood within less than half a century of the period when the man-like Elizabeth had been the not altogether unsuitable representative of the sex. [50]

But even within this portrayal of coarse, "man-like" women, Hawthorne, in a filiopietistic gesture, suggests a falling away from the strength and tenacity of the Puritans. This vacillation, which recurs throughout *The Scarlet Letter*, typifies Hawthorne's interpretation of the past. When he notes the change from the "ponderous sobriety" of the Puritan "primitive statesmen," along with the evolution of the people, he comments, "The change may be for good or ill, and is partly, perhaps, for both" (237-38).[43] Hawthorne thus begins the story of Hester Prynne by holding in suspension the same polarization of filiopietism and progressivist criticism found in *Grandfather's Chair*.

Suspicions about the legitimacy of social authority quickly grow with the account of Hester's punishment and ostracism. The remarks on Governor Bellingham and the assembled Puritan authorities are to the point: "They were, doubtless, good men, just, and sage. But, out of the whole human family, it would not have been easy to select the same number of wise and virtuous persons, who should be less capable of sitting in judgment on an erring woman's heart" (64). This as well as subsequent responses to Hester, particularly by the Puritan leadership, suggest criticisms of forebears and the idea that American history is progressive. At the same time, however, Hawthorne does not neglect to label Hester as "erring," and he thus maintains a skeptical attitude toward experience outside the bounds of community sanction, even when the community is Puritan. A Common Sense perspective mandates such skepticism about acts that cut oneself off from communal validation, the only reliable source of psychological stability. When communal validation is undermined by an illegitimate social authority, then dissenting or nonconforming characters are left the task of replicating this validating psychological function. And when Hawthorne refers to "the whole human family," he suggests where the possible solution to this problem might be found. In the characters of Hester Prynne and Arthur Dimmesdale, we can see the results of their differing attitudes toward the human family.

• • •

"The past is gone!"

The forest meeting between Hester and Dimmesdale provides a vital transition as the two attempt to redefine their relationships with the community—hence Hester's pronouncement, "The past is gone!" (202). At this point, her personal history understandably provokes Hester's desire for escape, and communal history, the recollection of Puritan authority, approximates the deadening force prevalent in "The Custom-House." Hester, her autonomous tendencies intensified by the scarlet letter, "her passport into regions where other women dared not tread" (199), accordingly musters her resolve in defiance against an oppressive Puritan community. The image of oppressive Puritan rigidity in *The Scarlet Letter* drew its strength from the embarrassment of nineteenth-century American historians over Puritan persecution of heretics, a feeling Hawthorne reveals through his mention in "The Custom-House" of his forebears' "cruelties" (9). Similarly, *Grandfather's Chair* summons up the image of "the iron race of Puritans" (*True Stories*, 71), a characterization that was already a cliché by Hawthorne's time. Contemporary reviews of *The Scarlet Letter* casually spoke of a "sterner Puritan aspect," "the cold and rigid Puritan," and "those stern old Popery-haters."[44] Ambivalence toward the Puritans was thus apparent not only in histories but in more popular literature as well, and the tendency in Hawthorne's time to typecast Puritans exhibits itself in the characterizations and actions of *The Scarlet Letter.*

It is important, however, when recalling the crisis of the forest meeting to distinguish this dramatized historiographic conflict—that between filiopietism against criticism of the Puritans—from the theoretical opposition within contemporary psychological theory at work here—that of the introspecting individual against community validation of truth. Appropriate as it may seem to collapse these two separate oppositions by creating the analogy between introspection and criticism of the Puritans on the one hand, and filiopietism and a social orientation on the other, interpretive specificity may be retained only when these registers are kept separate; this is necessary even though there are moments when the narrative logic of

Hester Prynne's story strongly gestures toward such an alignment. Despite this logic, Hawthorne's shorter works show how a simple affirmation of individual consciousness—even, as in "Young Goodman Brown," against questionable authority—may lead the individual toward a perilous isolation.

Isolation in *The Scarlet Letter* is most prominently associated with Roger Chillingworth, the figure who consciously severs emotional ties. The assertion that "he chose to withdraw his name from the roll of mankind" ominously indicates how Chillingworth could subsequently generate his vengeful plot, his "new purpose; dark, it is true, if not guilty" (118-19). The cumulative effect of isolation on Chillingworth's character was to create a moral revolution. The results of this revolution furnished "striking evidence of man's faculty of transforming himself into a devil, if he will only, for a reasonable space of time, undertake a devil's office" (170). Chillingworth's forfeiture of human sympathy provides a dramatic caveat, but in terms of Hester's and Pearl's fates it is Dimmesdale's deficiency that is the more significant.[45]

A lack of sympathy governs Dimmesdale's actions and attitudes, and the results are twofold: as a minister he embodies the debilitating Puritan sovereignty that has victimized Hester, and he lies by not acknowledging his relationships with Hester and Pearl. One does not need to recall the young Hawthorne's loss of his father to interpret Dimmesdale's abandonment of his paternal obligations as paramount. By evading parental obligations while retaining his position of ministerial authority, Dimmesdale personifies both the fanaticism that leads Ilbrahim's mother to reject conventional maternal obligations and that of the Puritans who persecuted Quakers. His inattention to Pearl may be, from Hawthorne's perspective, the worst of his sins, but he expresses an egotism specific to Puritanism as well. While in the forest, Dimmesdale conveys his misery to Hester, and she responds by pointing out the social value of his work: "Your present life is not less holy, in very truth, than it seems in people's eyes. Is there no reality in the penitence thus sealed and witnessed by good works? And wherefore should it not bring you peace?" (191). This statement sharply reveals the difference between Hester's and Dimmesdale's characters. Her appreciation of sociality gives Hester a firmer psychological foundation. This feature of her character emerges in her fight to keep Pearl, her desire to remain in Boston to be near Dimmesdale, and even her choice to keep Chillingworth's identity secret because of spousal loyalty. It is thus no surprise that she should regard Dimmesdale's good works in a more typically nineteenth-century Arminian manner as primary. Correspondingly, Dimmesdale's idealistic faith mirrors that of the Puritan hierarchy and its diminution of the value of earthly sympathy and social bonds. Because of his skewed and unsympathetic outlook, Dimmesdale can lament of his "good works" to Hester, insisting "There is no substance in it!" (192). He further signals his lack of benevolent impulses by refusing to respond to Pearl's incisive question, "Will he go back with us, hand in hand, we three together, into the town?" (212). Much as Ethan Brand resists the "magnetic chain of humanity," Dimmesdale cuts himself off from the "electric chain" (153) the three formed the night they stood together on the scaffold.[46] But yet more specific evidence of his psychological state is provided by his disordered perceptions.

When Dimmesdale first encountered Hester in the forest, "he knew not whether it were a woman or a shadow. It may be, that his pathway through life was haunted thus, by a spectre that had stolen out from among his thoughts" (189). Such a question about his perception might seem relatively innocuous or simply in keeping with Hawthorne's penchant for ambiguity. But perceptual ambiguity is less a stylistic feature here than it is a moral indicator, as suggested by Dimmesdale's history of fasting vigils, of "constant introspection wherewith he tortured, but could not purify, himself. In these lengthened vigils, his brain often reeled, and visions seemed to flit before him" (145). Dimmesdale's bizarre practices lead him to delusions, and the presence of delusions reinforces the isolation that makes it possible for him to resist acknowledging Pearl as his daughter. This crucial moral deficiency and his associated solipsism are most dramatically signaled by the way he sees and interprets the letter A in the sky: "We impute it, therefore, solely to the disease in his own eye and heart, that the minister, looking upward to the zenith, beheld there the appearance of an immense letter,—the letter A,—marked out in lines of dull red light" (155). Dimmesdale's disordered imagination leads him to discover "a revelation, addressed to himself alone," and this is evidence of his "highly disordered mental state" (155). Because of his perceptual difficulties—according to Common Sense psychology, unimpaired perception is the basis of proper mental functions—from that point on, it is appropriate for the reader to regard Dimmesdale's mental processes as suspect.

The following morning, when Dimmesdale hears from the sexton of "a great red letter in the sky,—the letter A,—which we interpret to stand for Angel" (158) in celestial recognition of Governor Winthrop's death, a multifaceted understanding is suggested. As the "head of the social system, as the clergymen of that day stood" (200), Dimmesdale's disorder represents not simply an individual aberration but also a cultural problem. In his comment that Dimmesdale "thus typified the constant introspection wherewith he tortured, but could not purify, himself," Hawthorne makes more explicit his criticism. The individual, glorified in the independent ability to interpret scripture, is made solitary, even insane, by an excess of that same freedom. Individual independence, sanctioned by Puritan theology, potentially leads to the kind of isolation that engenders disordered perceptions.[47] If we return to the situation of Goodman Brown, another victim of the Puritan dilemma—and in another story told with ambiguity—a significant parallel comes into view. As with Brown's return from his forest journey, all has changed on Dimmesdale's return to town. Dimmesdale "took an impression of change from the series of familiar objects that presented themselves" (216). Unable to account for the change that extended to all the townspeople, he felt himself to be a new person. This transformation was "nothing short of a total change of dynasty and moral code . . . At every step he was incited to do some strange, wild, wicked thing or other, with a sense that it would be at once involuntary and intentional" (217). Dimmesdale's wishes to whisper blasphemies to the deacon and teach obscenities to the children may themselves have seemed involuntary, but the originating acts, those that separated him from Pearl and Hester, were intentional.

Although Hester Prynne does not share Dimmesdale's disorder, Hawthorne states that "her imagination was somewhat affected, and, had she been of a softer moral and intellectual fibre, would have been still more so, by the strange and solitary anguish of her life" (86). The prospect of possible relief from "solitary anguish" leads to her speculations in the forest with Dimmesdale. When she says that their adultery "had a consecration of its own" (195), Hester affirms the priority of individual experience, even when it defies a repressive Puritan authority. But Hester's use of a religious term, *consecration*, grounds her argument in the social unity of the church; her attempt to legitimize their relationship by an appropriation of theological discourse is subverted by the language's cultural associations. Hawthorne further questions Hester's understanding when he expounds on the scarlet letter's impact: "The scarlet letter was her passport into regions where other women dared not tread. Shame, Despair, Solitude! These had been her teachers,—stern and wild ones,—and they had made her strong, but taught her much amiss" (199-200). The indication that Hester had been taught amiss is her statement "The past is gone" (202), an assertion that defies the lesson of "The Custom-House."[48] Her similarly problematic attempt to free herself from the past by throwing off the scarlet letter leads to Pearl's rejection, the refusal to recognize Hester without it.

Pearl's demand that Hester resume wearing the scarlet letter underscores the strength that social authority wields in determining personal identity, particularly within the most intimate of relations. Pearl's act thereby subverts Hester's attempt to create a present moment unmediated by either history or social demands. Hester's desire for newness is based on her own strength of character, and it testifies to the false lessons learned from the scarlet letter. While the Puritan authority that mandated her social isolation is criticized, Hester's excessive desire for action without regard for the past indicates the troublesome results of isolation. Hester, ostracized by the community, nevertheless maintains social contact from her dwelling on the border between the town and the wilderness. The location of her cottage reinforces Hawthorne's description of the struggle between, on the one hand, "the wildness of her nature," her passionate nature (to which Hawthorne repeatedly refers), and her freethinking, and, on the other, "the chain that bound her" to the town, her gregariousness (79-80).

The question of Hester's passions and their relationship to both sociality and legal authority is raised by Janet Gabler-Hover when she comments on the priority of ethics over law: "In *The Scarlet Letter,* passion is seen to be complicit with law, and just as in the Custom-House, characters who relinquish self-regulation for the substitutive regulation of the law remain stagnant."[49] Legal authority and psychology interpenetrate each other, and the inception of passion, an emotional category, coincides with the legalities associated with self-regulation. The earlier discussion of *The Last of the Mohicans* describes how the psychological processes of self-regulation may be aligned with visions of political and social order. In *The Scarlet Letter,* though, Hawthorne raises questions about the political metaphor embedded in the term *self-regulation* that Cooper and others would take for granted. As Gabler-Hover suggests, to Hawthorne the double bind created by the "powerful dialectic of passion and law" may be circumvented through attention to the ethical realm.[50] The emergence of ethical action and the turn away from individual selfishness and unethical social authority in *The Scarlet Letter* will finally be associated with the return of Hester Prynne to the Puritan community, an act reminiscent of Hawthorne's shorter narratives portraying the redemptive power of return. What may be most strange about the emergence of the ethical in *The Scarlet Letter,* however, is the way it is introduced by the most destructive character.

When Chillingworth discovers Dimmesdale's secret, he finds that knowledge of Pearl's paternity leads to a new desire: "To make himself the one trusted friend, to whom should be confided all the fear, the remorse, the agony, the ineffectual repentance, the backward rush of sinful thoughts, expelled in vain! . . . All that dark treasure to be lavished on the very man, to whom nothing else could so adequately pay the debt of vengeance!" (139). The flaw in Chillingworth's thinking here is not new. When during his visit with Hester in the jail he self-mockingly recalls the fantasies of domesticity that led to their marriage, he exposes an inability to perceive the difference between his self-involved abstractions and the less tractable interpersonal realm. This perceptual obtuseness shapes his plan to become Dimmesdale's confessor and is disclosed by a double substitution. He reifies his desire for vengeance by identifying the process of confession with economic exchange, regarding the anticipated disclosure by Dimmesdale as a "treasure" that "could so adequately pay the debt." This reification falsely grounds a fantasy that itself displaces what is for Hawthorne a more psychologically and ethically proper understanding of interpersonal communication. Chillingworth may here exhibit an inverted set of values, and his dramatic situation with respect to Dimmesdale may demand his prejudice and tenacity, but he nevertheless introduces the idea of a confession as a dyadic, interpersonal process.

This interpersonal communication serves as a contrast to the demand by Puritan authorities for Hester Prynne's *public* confession that is the springboard for the action of the novel. An adulterous liaison creates the situation in which Hester Prynne's confession is ordered, but the action of the novel originates in her refusal to abide by Puritan notions of justice. By transposing confession from the realm of public authority to that of the interpersonal, Chillingworth's desire marks an important narrative movement. Chillingworth's obvious shortcoming is that a lack of sympathy makes it impossible for him to understand confession as communication rather than exchange, and he thus reveals how in this important respect his thinking parallels that of the Puritan authorities. The lesson of the scarlet letter will emerge only during moments at the novel's conclusion when confession is reinstated within the interpersonal realm from the legal and contractual, and when sympathy is restored to the confessional process.[51]

•   •   •

"And Hester Prynne had returned, and taken up her long-forsaken shame."

In *The Scarlet Letter,* Hawthorne presents as a basic moral error any vision of the world in which sympathy is overcome by an idealism, whether religious or secular. This issue is not unique to *The Scarlet Letter:* the same tension largely informs *The Blithedale Romance,* and "The Gentle Boy" levels Quaker and Puritan ideologies in favor of characters motivated by compassion and sympathy.[52] The opposition between idealism and sympathy in *The Scarlet Letter* interacts with Hawthorne's illustration of the Common Sense psychology tension between the introspecting individual as the source of truth and communal validation of truth claims. All three main characters in *The Scarlet Letter* are led by introspection to commit transgressions, and these transgressions threaten to cut them off from their social relationships, thereby invalidating their insights. For example,

Hester's isolation "had made her strong, but taught her much amiss"; Dimmesdale's hermitical excesses lead to disordered thought; and Chillingworth, who like so many of Hawthorne's scientists is motivated by a too highly abstracted interest in the human condition, manifests a secular idealism, which Hawthorne suggests prevented many physicians or scientists from joining the Puritan venture: "They seldom, it would appear, partook of the religious zeal that brought other emigrants across the Atlantic. In their researches into the human frame, it may be that the higher and more subtle faculties of such men were materialized, and that they lost the spiritual view of existence amid the intricacies of that wondrous mechanism" (119). This "spiritual view of existence" recalled by Hawthorne is consistent with Common Sense Christian metaphysics. Hawthorne may not have displayed much interest in the Christian theology supported by Common Sense thinkers, but he was willing to extract from the prevalent theology ethical principles.

The basic ethical principle at work in the conclusion of *The Scarlet Letter* is that of sympathy, and its reemergence is understood to supply a more constructive basis for social cohesion than did the legalistic Puritan demand for justice. The source of sympathy, in Common Sense thought, is the home, and it is through the operation of domesticity that the most dramatic transformation of the novel may be understood. Pearl's metamorphosis from demon child to a young woman who would become a wealthy heiress and then, after an apparent marriage into Old World nobility, a mother herself becomes possible only after she has been claimed by her two fathers. The more important paternal acknowledgment is Dimmesdale's; his claim comes during the final scaffold scene when he asks to be kissed, though not by Hester: "Pearl kissed his lips. A spell was broken. The great scene of grief, in which the wild infant bore a part, had developed all her sympathies; and as her tears fell upon her father's cheek, they were the pledge that she would grow up amid human joy and sorrow, nor for ever do battle with the world, but be a woman in it" (256). The breaking of Pearl's "spell" and her subsequent restoration progresses from the parent-child relationship Dimmesdale had previously evaded. His public acknowledgment of their bond is precisely what Pearl repeatedly demanded during both the midnight scaffold scene and the forest meeting, and, when Dimmesdale equivocated, Pearl's response was to "show no favor to the clergyman" (212). Dimmesdale's public confession restores Pearl, although, unlike Hester's consistent commitment to parental responsibility, it is too little and too late to redeem him. It also represents a dramatic inversion of his demand, on Hester's initial emergence from the jail, for her confession. The public response to Dimmesdale displays a shift from a problematic Puritan social authority based on belief in justice to an authority that expresses sympathy. That this sympathetic regard for Dimmesdale is both present and yet incomplete is shown by the narrative remarks following the townspeople's interpretations of his death: "We must be allowed to consider this version of Mr. Dimmesdale's story as only an instance of that stubborn fidelity with which a man's friends—and especially a clergyman's—will sometimes uphold his character" (259). However welcome their expression of sympathy may be, it is deficient insofar as it fails to represent a general principle of social authority. The emergence of a community in which sympathy serves as a more general interpretive principle does not come until Hester Prynne's return in the final chapter.

Hester Prynne's return is an annoying mystery to those who, like Lawrence Buell, discover in *The Scarlet Letter* a defense of individualism. To Buell, Hester's return "imitates Dimmesdale's submission to the rites of the community," but she engages in this imitation only "nominally," and thus she represents a principle of individual resistance against social authority.[53] But even critics like Sacvan Bercovitch and Emily Miller Budick, who do not perceive in it an endorsement of individualism, are intrigued by the conclusion. Bercovitch, explicitly citing the question of her return, asserts that in the novel dissent is effectively drained of potentially revolutionary impact and that Hester's return dramatizes a ritual of liberal consensus. And Budick, by turning attention to the appearance of letters within the novel—Hester's *A* and the words on her tombstone—finds in the return a renewed insistence on interpretation. Although these critics do not concur in their readings, there is a common ground: they all are drawn toward discussions of the novel's conclusion in terms of a vision of community. Hawthorne's vision of community here is complicated by his argument against repressive social authority; but, whatever antiauthoritarian implications the novel may at times suggest, it finally restates its understanding of individualism and sociality in terms that are in significant respects consistent with conventional antebellum thought.

The two especially conventional aspects of the conclusion are its assertions of the value of sympathy and the related narrative form evident in his short works, the plot of departure and return home. In *The Scarlet Letter*, like "Egotism," the return to the social realm follows an obscure initial event that causes isolation. Unlike "Young Goodman Brown," however, which similarly offers a critique of Puritan social authority, *The Scarlet Letter* shows Hester successfully reintegrating herself into the community. The difference between *The Scarlet Letter* and "Young Goodman Brown" reflects a complex narrative strategy that takes into account the social significance of interpretation.

Hester's return and final fate collapse associated conceptual problems while resolving certain remaining plot issues. Chillingworth is dispensed of, but not before he has undertaken a paternal role by bequeathing his fortune to Pearl. Not only does Pearl abandon her social role as outcast, but it is suggested that she enters the world of European society, "married, and happy, and mindful of her mother" (262). Pearl's happy domesticity— "Hester was seen embroidering a baby-garment" (262)—restates the Common Sense and sentimental formula, but it also bears on Hester's stance. Her return to New England and her resumption of the symbol come with her new function as a counselor to women. This is accompanied by her assumption of a prophetic role, and she announces the advent of "the destined prophetess," at which point, "when the world should have grown ripe for it, in Heaven's own time, a new truth would be revealed, in order to establish the whole relation between man and woman on a surer ground of mutual happiness" (263). Hester's prophecy follows Common Sense thought in aligning social harmony with domestic happiness, and it simultaneously resolves the historiographic conflict of *Grandfather's Chair*, that of filiopietism versus criticism, by suggesting the availability of an alternative historical tradition. Hawthorne thus manages to displace the image of Puritan Founding Fathers with one of Hester Prynne in a revisionist gesture of filiopiety.

In place of a Puritan community marked by intolerance, legalism, and a lack of sympathy, Hawthorne creates a new community constituted by people with "all their sorrows and perplexities" seeking out Hester Prynne, who "comforted and counselled them, as best she might" (263). The basis of this community is the voluntary confession of problems that elicits a sympathetic response. Thus the trajectory of confession within *The Scarlet Letter*, begun with Hester's and Dimmesdale's differing acts of resistance against the compulsion of confession, is coterminous with the emergence of sympathy as a principle of social organization that would displace traditional authority. By thus displacing an illegitimate social authority, the psychological and social problems of the novel are resolved through a process of verbal communication, and Hawthorne presents the Common Sense image of a community in which the insights of the introspecting individual may be validated by a proper social authority. He thereby manages to resolve the problem of "Young Goodman Brown" from within a Common Sense framework. What is especially noteworthy about Hawthorne's resolution of these narrative and ideational conflicts, however, aside from its economy, is the way it leads to a consideration of the relationship between interpretation and community.

Hester Prynne's community is constituted through an interpretive commitment to provide sympathy, and it is worth recalling this when reading Hawthorne's earlier remarks about changes in gender relations. Hester, inclined to "freedom of speculation," often found herself considering the "dark question" about "the whole race of womanhood. Was existence worth accepting, even to the happiest among them?" (164-65). Hawthorne goes on to describe the processes and costs of such speculation:

> As a first step, the whole system of society is to be torn down, and built up anew. Then, the very nature of the opposite sex, or its long hereditary habit, which has become like nature, is to be essentially modified, before woman can be allowed to assume what seems a fair and suitable position. Finally, all other difficulties being obviated, woman cannot take advantage of these preliminary reforms, until she herself shall have undergone a still mightier change; in which, perhaps, the ethereal essence, wherein she has her truest life, will be found to have evaporated. A woman never overcomes these problems by any exercise of thought. They are not to be solved, or only in one way. If her heart chance to come uppermost, they vanish. [165-66]

The novel's conclusion demonstrates that Hester had taken the path prescribed by Hawthorne and fully recognized the preeminence of sympathy. Sympathy performs several critical operations here. It orients the individual toward self-regulation and away from potentially destructive isolation by displacing the dangerous effects of passion. And, in the novel's conclusion, sympathy guides the process of interpersonal communication, a process governed by Common Sense ideas of social legitimation and bound by a historical sense of cohesion that stretches backward in time to Hester Prynne and forward to "the destined prophetess." The sympathetic community of interpreters is created by the work of the artist, whether it is the narrator of "The Custom-House" or Hester Prynne, and the community's work is preferable to that which might lead a woman's "truest life" to have "evaporated." *The Scarlet Letter* thus reflects a commitment to a normative hermeneutics, one with a basis in sympathy. Hawthorne here offers a radically Common Sense social ideal in place of either feminist or individualistic antiauthoritarianism. Hawthorne's social ideal may be, as Budick suggests, implicitly critical of the dominant culture and patriarchy, despite the apparently antifeminist slant to the passage on the "nature of the opposite sex." But what Hawthorne dramatizes is less an obsession with individual freedom than the possibility of a community in which social authority works to mediate between, rather than isolate, individuals who themselves have successfully internalized regulatory functions.

4

The Altrurian Romances

Evolution and Immigration in Howells's Utopia

Hawthorne's gesture toward the future at the conclusion of *The Scarlet Letter* conforms to an American rhetoric of progress, though Hawthorne's is a specifically moral progress, one implied by his vision of a relationship between men and women that someday would rest on a "surer ground of mutual happiness."[1] His ideal of "mutual happiness" not only serves to describe domestic harmony; it also offers a figure of the proper social order, an order that balances individual emotional and intellectual needs against demands for community cohesion. Hawthorne thus imaginatively shifts the popular early-nineteenth-century belief in American progress, based on a historical outlook that criticized the Puritans while it simultaneously preserved the Puritan ideal of America's special mission, toward a more distinctly interpersonal and ethical level.

A focus on ethics and the interpersonal realm similarly characterizes William Dean Howells's *A Traveler from Altruria* (1894) and its sequel, *Through the Eye of the Needle* (1907), and in this respect these works resemble Edward Bellamy's more famous *Looking Backward* as well as other utopian works published toward the end of the nineteenth century.[2] Instead of focusing on socioeconomic solutions to American problems, Howells primarily attends to questions of human nature. Howells uses this emphasis in his two Altrurian Romances to critique the individualist thought associated with late-nineteenth-century social Darwinism. Yet, despite Howells's forthright criticism of prevalent American attitudes, certain popular anxieties rather incongruously emerge from his utopian vision. The most prominent of these anxieties underlies the tension between Howells's social criticism and his ambivalence about immigration, an important political and social issue in the decades after the Civil War. The point of this discussion is not to deride Howells for being an unwitting purveyor of repressive attitudes or for a supposed superficiality in his treatment of social and psychological issues. Rather, the goal here is to use the Altrurian Romances to examine "how the critical and the symptomatic interact in a text or a work of art," because this interaction has sustained importance in American culture.[3]

The Altrurian Romances also suggest a certain dissatisfaction on Howells's part with realist literary conventions insofar as these writings differ markedly from Howells's prior novels that explicitly had treated social and economic conditions. *The Minister's Charge* (1887), *Annie Kilburn* (1889), and *A Hazard of New Fortunes* (1890), for example, deal with problems of the working poor and discuss ameliorative plans. Unlike these novels, which adhere to a realist avoidance of direct commentary, the Altrurian Romances are polemical, didactic, and even hortatory. Howells bases his moral argument on the idea that America has fulfilled neither its democratic political ideals nor its Christian ethical ideals. Yet, despite the insistent didacticism and a focus on grievances and censure worthy of a jeremiad, the plot and tone of the Altrurian Romances are surprisingly comic.[4] In addition to this inherent generic discord, the three successive narrators within the Altrurian Romances exhibit markedly distinct emotional and ethical outlooks. The differences between the narrators may be due in part to the textual history of the Altrurian Romances.

The first installment of Howells's essay series, "A Traveller from Altruria," was printed in the November 1892 issue of the *Cosmopolitan*.[5] Portions of "A Traveller" continued to appear on a monthly basis through October 1893; these were immediately followed by eleven "Letters of an Altrurian Traveller," from November 1893 through September 1894. *A Traveler from Altruria,* an edition of the first twelve essays, was published in 1894. Howells, after leaving his project untouched for more than a decade, returned to complete the second Altrurian Romance, *Through the Eye of the Needle.* Howells arranged the final six "Letters" into part 1 of *Through the Eye;* he then wrote part 2 in less than a month early in 1907. Possibly because of contemporary reviews that criticized his increasingly socialistic outlook and caustic social commentary, Howells never published a separate edition of the "Letters." In fact, the later addition, part 2 of *Through the Eye,* introduces a narrator who uses a far milder tone—a tone perhaps more appropriate to the setting, for only in this final section does Howells explore his utopian realm.[6]

The exiguous question of Altruria's authenticity propels the plot of the Altrurian Romances. Aristides Homos, the traveler from Altruria, and Mr. Twelvemough, the narrator, meet in a train station at the start of *A Traveler.* Twelvemough describes himself as "a writer of romantic fiction . . . occupied in manipulating the destinies of the good old-fashioned hero and heroine, and trying always to make them end in a happy marriage."[7] The sort of writer for whom Howells the realist had little respect, Twelvemough's humorous personality appeals mildly, though his narrative consciousness reverberates with bromides and clichés.[8]

By contrast, Homos, an immigrant from an unknown land, whose behavior seems designed from the start to defamiliarize everyday experience, challenges Twelvemough's—and the reader's—conventional views. For instance, Homos immediately embarrasses Twelvemough when he helps a porter unload the train's baggage. Twelvemough, attempting to dissuade Homos from an unseemly indulgence in manual labor, initiates an exchange:

> "We must make haste a little now . . . we shall not stand so good a chance for supper if we are not there pretty promptly."
> "No?" said the Altrurian. "Why?"
> "Well," I said, with evasive lightness, "first come, first served, you know. That's human nature."
> "Is it?" he returned, and he looked at me as one does who suspects another of joking. [9]

This dialogue raises questions about human nature, the principal issue of the Altrurian Romances. Howells himself notes the centrality of this question in his introductory comments to a proposed one-volume edition of the Altrurian Romances: "Human nature, which the individualists declare cannot be changed, has been constantly changed for the better" (4). For his utopian dream to appear viable, Howells must argue that a society based on a cooperative, rather than a competitive, vision of human nature is both reasonable and practical.

The dialogue also explicitly introduces the topic of comedy and jokes. Characteristic of debased human relations in a nonutopian society, Homos's and Twelvemough's distrust is revealed by the suspicion of "joking." This suspicion recurs throughout A *Traveler*, and, with an irony that increases as the story progresses, each considers the other somewhat barbaric. Because Homos helps waiters and other hotel workers, Twelvemough thinks Homos is deranged or, at best, devoid of good social taste. In turn, Twelvemough's ability to rationalize the economic inequities of American society in accord with his belief that social conditions reflect human nature seems to Homos inhumane and hypocritical. Despite the Altrurian's increasingly evident censure and the narrator's "cold doubt of something ironical in the man" (25), Twelvemough notes rather affectionately that all are amiably disposed toward Homos, whom he describes as a kind of "spiritual solvent, sent for the moment to precipitate whatever sincerity there was in us" (99). When Homos is introduced to several hotel guests—a banker, a minister, a lawyer, a doctor, a professor, and a retired manufacturer—they find they like him, even as they argue with him about America.

Homos's dialogues with these successful Americans, in which the hotel guests defend American ideals and practices, constitute a major portion of *A Traveler*. Homos early makes clear that he, along with all Altrurians, admires the American political ideals expressed in the Declaration of Independence. However, his belief that political egalitarianism should provide the model for social and economic relations is abhorrent to his listeners: "'Merely to conceive of its possibility is something that passes a joke; it is a kind of offence.' . . . 'I don't know,' the banker continued, 'how the notion of our social equality originated, but I think it has been fostered mainly by the expectation of foreigners, who argued it from our political equality'" (40). The banker, although more liberal than his peers, strikes a recurrent note with his comment that Homos, a foreigner, cannot truly understand the United States.

Howells uses Homos's posture of naïveté within a question-and-answer format to reveal the discrepancies between economic realities and political and ethical ideals. As Elsa Nettels comments, "Howells himself was keenly aware of the contradiction within American society, which affirmed the principles of equality and justice for all, yet perpetuated an economic system and a class structure that divided rich from poor, employers from laborers."[9] Nevertheless, a reaffirmation of political and ethical ideals forms the basis of the proposed evolutionary solution to America's economic problems. During the lengthy public lecture with which *A Traveler* concludes, Homos calls for working people to bring about socialism through the ballot. Homos, referring to the capitalists of Altruria's distant past as "the Accumulation," recounts Altruria's history in a prescriptive manner: "The Accumulation had no voters, except the few men at its head, and the creatures devoted to it by interest and ignorance. It seemed, at one moment, as if it would offer an armed resistance to the popular will, but, happily, that moment of madness passed. Our Evolution was accomplished without a drop of bloodshed" (154). In place of the violent class struggle associated with Marxism, altruism provides a socialist vision in which a change of human nature throughout all classes leads to utopia. For this reason, Homos rejects labor-union activity as simply one more expression of self-interested behavior. Rather, the unifying image of society as an extended family is posited as the basis for social change—"Altruria, I say again, is a family" (170)—and Homos thus appeals to what he treats as a latent force for social good in American life. Howells's analogy of the family and society derives from what Kermit Vanderbilt has called "an *idealized* utopian view of the Ohio village which he occasionally fancied as a psychological refuge from the urban-industrial complexities of the new Boston, and later of New York."[10] Accordingly, Homos discovers a realm of virtue in the Camp family, farmers who live near the resort hotel but whose moral outlook tellingly contrasts with that of the corrupt city-dwellers.

Although those who meet Homos are captivated by him, Twelve-mough notes in his concluding comments that "the more cultivated people" (179) were still uncertain about both Homos's authenticity and the existence of Altruria. With the start of Homos's narrative in "Letters of an Altrurian Traveller," his authenticity as an Altrurian is no longer a narrative issue. The change of narrator effects changes in setting and tone as well—Homos travels to the city, where he vents his frequently acerbic observations to his Altrurian correspondent. Like the preceding novel, the "Letters" are not motivated by much of a plot; rather they resemble the scattered observations of a tourist, somewhat on the order of Howells's *Atlantic* columns or his early successful travel book, *Venetian Life* (1866). From this estranged position, the narrator is free to comment on the dreariness of New York City—which he refers to as "Babylon"—and the comparative beauty of the 1893 Chicago Exposition's "White City." In the "Letters," Homos emphasizes Christian idealism in order to criticize the United States for not being "a Christian country, though it abounds in good people" (184). The focus on how Americans have fallen away from their Christian and democratic ideals gives Homos's narrative an urgency generally absent from *A Traveler*. Unlike Twelvemough's account, in which social criticism is indirectly conveyed by the foolishness and insensitivity of the narrator, Homos critiques American culture in a more straightforward manner.

Twelvemough, returning in the role of editor, provides an introductory comment to *Through the Eye of the Needle* that explains how he came to possess the manuscript, originally letters to and from Altruria that he has fashioned into narratives. The first part of *Through the Eye,* based on the later "Letters," continues to feature Homos as an observer of "the plutocratic mind" (277). Although Homos focuses in the early chapters on such material issues as urban housing, before long he becomes socially involved with a group of upper-class New Yorkers and then romantically involved with a wealthy widow, Eveleth Strange. Eveleth, displaying how even a rich person can transcend her environment, soon agrees to marry Homos. A romantic farce ensues in which the couple is faced with the unusual dilemma of how to handle Eveleth's unwanted wealth. After an argument in which Homos insists she give up all her property, he leaves, but Eveleth, with her reluctant mother in tow, catches up with Homos in England. They get married on the voyage to Altruria.

Eveleth, the narrator of *Through the Eye*'s second part, provides an account of Altruria from the perspective of a sympathetic American. Part 2 of *Through the Eye* is again characterized by minimal dramatic action. A peaceful mutiny by their ship's crew after landing provides an opportunity for evolutionary progress: the captain apologizes to the crew for their mistreatment, and, following a voyage back to the United States, he agrees to return with them to Altruria. The bulk of *Through the Eye* consists of the couple's desultory travels about Altruria to deliver talks on American life. Eveleth's repeated surprises and small difficulties with Altrurian life provide a bridge between the sympathetic reader and utopia while, like Homos's dialogues in *A Traveler,* it creates opportunities to discuss the differences between American and utopian practices. Some comic episodes result when a yacht bearing wealthy Americans is beached, and they with their crew are integrated, with resistance from both sides, into Altrurian society. The conclusion features the resolution of Eveleth's lingering doubts over Altruria's reality when the first ship returns as promised to Altruria.

In the absence of a unifying and compelling plot, the prevalent comic tone and the guiding issue of human nature provide coherence to the Altrurian Romances. Howells, like some literary theorists who were his contemporaries, reveals an awareness that comedy can serve as a means to socialize individuals and, conversely, that it can reflect individual discontent with societal strictures. For example, in his "Essay on Comedy" (1877), George Meredith identifies comedy's socially coercive purpose when he refers to its "vigilant sense of a collective supervision."[11] Similarly, in 1900 Henri Bergson noted that comedy's "function is to intimidate by humiliating."[12] Yet this conformist function—"a utilitarian aim of general improvement"—simultaneously coexists with an individualist impulse to undermine social order, particularly when the order is perceived as unresponsive to human need: "Rigidity is the comic, and laughter is its corrective."[13] Freud perhaps most sharply describes the "corrective" aspects of the comic when he identifies two basic types of jokes, the "*hostile*" joke (serving the purpose of aggressiveness, satire, or defence)" and the "*obscene* joke (serving the purpose of exposure)."[14]

Howells uses these two comic operations of hostility and exposure to delineate community boundaries in the Altrurian Romances. In *A Traveler,* one member of a group will frequently ridicule another's ideas in an attempt to argue a point; the hostility of the joke suggests that social interactions are too often characterized in our society by competition and aggression. Homos's repeated questions, which Twelvemough regards as suspiciously "ironical," are intended to expose something hidden—in particular, the true function of the social order. But these divisive aspects of comedy also serve a larger social function. As Freud points out, the need to share a joke is part of the comic process.[15] Thus, when Howells ridicules his narrator Twelvemough by showing him to be overly rigid, he shares an important joke with his readers.

Within the Altrurian Romances, this sharing process works to create a new sense of community, one ultimately based on altruistic values emerging steadily in the progression of consciousness in each successive narrator. The conclusion of *Through the Eye of the Needle,* with the absorption of the sailors into the Altrurian community, provides a dramatic enactment of the desired course of reading, in which the reader will ideally join the community of Altrurians.[16] Howells's wish to keep the available community as large as possible is reflected by Homos's description of a grotesquely abundant Thanksgiving dinner given by his wealthy New York hosts. Rather than dwell on the plight of the poor and hungry—and thereby convey a sense of bitterness—Homos calls attention to the absurdly rigid and ritualistic aspects of the affair. The upper-class characters, who adhere to social norms as if they were laws of nature, are "altruistically" displayed as foolishly mistaken, rather than evil, in their outlooks.

In addition to the use of comedy throughout the Altrurian Romances to enforce social cohesion, the issue of human nature also serves to link the three narratives. The distinctions between the three narrators on this issue are as enlightening as the similarities between them. Their comments on one another, mostly composed of Twelvemough's criticism of the Altrurian outlook, suggest their implicit differences, primarily on the issue of human nature. Twelvemough, along with most of his wealthy friends, complacently appeals to human nature to justify class and gender inequalities: "We do not expect to outlive [present economic conditions]. We regard them as final, and as indestructibly based in human nature itself" (16).

Throughout his travels, Homos argues against this static vision of human nature. According to Homos, the negative aspects of human behavior are the result of fear and want; it is also human nature to be concerned with the common good, as in Altruria. Homos, following realist tenets of social criticism, insists that the environment is critical in the creation of character. He notes with displeasure during his travels in New York the "malign change here that has transformed the Italians from the friendly folk we are told they are at home, to the surly race, and even savage race they mostly show themselves here: shrewd for their advancement in the material things, which seem the only good things to the Americanized aliens of all races, and fierce for their full share of the political pottage" (261). Homos's firm belief that environment shapes human nature is dramatized in the conflict between his outlook and that of Twelvemough: each, through his respective state of mind, reflects his environment of origin.

But when Eveleth emerges as a narrator, the simple correspondence between individual perspective and environment begins to break down. Instead, the progression of narrative altruistic consciousness, evident in the change from Twelvemough's to Homos's narrative, continues, and Eveleth provides a narrative outlook that is more tolerant and open-minded than those of her two predecessors. Although raised in "Egoria," the Altrurian name for the United States, she sees the world in a more accepting and hopeful manner than does Homos. Eveleth's ability to transcend her environment points out the underlying tension in Howells's treatment of human nature. In Howells's view, despite the formative quality of environment, something within human nature allows for individual variation. Howells's attempt to balance his more old-fashioned faith in the individual with a belief in environmental determinism gestures toward important contemporary treatments of the topic of human nature.

The antithetical positions of environmental determinism and free will defined the poles of the intellectual compass after the introduction of evolutionist theory.[17] This antithesis was considered crucial because deterministic theories threatened both orthodox religious views and the secular belief in the centrality of the individual. Although Darwin's ideas became well known in the United States after the publication of *On the Origin of Species,* it was Herbert Spencer who set the terms for intellectual debate in the latter decades of the 1800s. In addition to Spencer's own work, the writings of John Fiske, Spencer's great American popularizer, established the framework for Howells's treatment of human nature in the Altrurian Romances.

Spencer's theories of human behavior arrived at a time when Common Sense psychology appeared inadequate in the face of the empirical methodology of the new German physiological psychology. Its late-nineteenth-century defenders tried to preserve the older Common Sense approach to psychology, primarily because of its strong moral framework. But the Common Sense stress on universal human qualities, such as morality, appeared weak because it relied on introspection to verify—and to justify—its findings. Rather than scientific replicability, conformity to such underlying philosophical principles as universal morality prevailed. The Common Sense method of introspection can be said to have led logically to the next step, that of experimentation; but, as was evident in the work of Thomas Upham, a reliance on physiological data was merely an implicit possibility. With the late-nineteenth-century move toward physiology and laboratory experimentation, and away from moral philosophy, the discipline of psychology began to assume its modern form. The breakdown of the older moral philosophy was furthered by the advent of Herbert Spencer's universal theoretical framework.[18]

Evolutionary theory, particularly in the form of Spencer's social Darwinism, predominated during the 1870s and 1880s, and Darwin's own views on the social implications of his work were relatively insignificant at the time because most Americans learned about evolution from Spencer. In its subtitle, though, *On the Origin of Species* contributed the influential metaphor of "the struggle for life," a figure which conveyed the tragic vision of life that came to be associated with evolutionary theory.[19] Spencer further amplified this tragic cast with the phrase "survival of the fittest," and he generalized this outlook when using evolutionary theory as the universal rule for social sciences as well as for the physical and the biological. His vision of evolution was pre-Darwinian; he first published on the subject before *Origin*, and his theories reflected a belief in the Lamarckian notion of inheritance of acquired characteristics. According to Spencer, the ability to adapt to the environment was the primary measure of biological competence. A passage from an early work, *Social Statics* (1851), that may have been distressing to Spencer's American followers, reflects the importance of environment in the formation of character, both individual and cultural: "The barbarizing of colonists, who live under aboriginal conditions, is universally remarked. The back settlers of America, amongst whom un- avenged murders, rifle duels, and Lynch law prevail—or, better still, the trappers, who leading a savage life have descended to savage habits, to scalping, and occasionally even to cannibalism—sufficiently exemplify it."[20] The ease by which the colonists fall from the height of civilization when they live in primitive physical conditions indicates the importance of physical surroundings to moral character. In addition, Spencer's vague account reinforces the class bias that those who live in the greatest material ease will show the highest degree of moral refinement.

Despite a general attention to human behavior and his books on psychology and sociology, Spencer denigrates the social sciences as secondary pursuits. To Spencer, as to twentieth-century behaviorists, mental processes are epiphenomenal. And, on a larger level, the actions of social groups are simply regarded as reactions to natural conditions: "Life consists in the maintenance of inner actions corresponding with outer actions . . . the progress to life of higher and higher kinds essentially consists in a continual improvement of the adaptation between organic processes and processes which environ the organism."[21] According to Spencer, the social realm does not mediate between the individual and the natural universe; instead, each stands in a direct relationship with nature. Furthermore, because the community, like the individual, is reactive, it merely reflects the mechanisms of nature. As a result, the Spencerian vision naturalizes social constructs, and it extends the concept of "survival of the fittest" from natural to social analysis.

Whereas Common Sense psychology posited individuals within society, albeit a society whose rules were ultimately sanctified by its metaphysics, the evolutionary viewpoint displaced the individual-community dynamic with an individual-cosmos relationship. Both individual and society stood in an equivalent relationship to nature; the actions of each were determined by the same principles of evolutionary law. This process of analogy is central to Spencer's general theory of evolution. All the sciences are supposed to work by these same principles, and methods of analysis were in important respects interchangeable. This is, no doubt, why Spencer, trained as an engineer, felt himself qualified to pronounce on a variety of social issues. His *Principles of Psychology* (1855), for example, contains numerous digressions on various physical and chemical phenomena and very few clinical or behavioral observations. These digressions would seem rather pointless were it not Spencer's aim to ground psychological theory in the physical sciences. This integration of psychology into a holistic vision that spanned the sciences and the social sciences responded to the disciplinary needs of late-nineteenth-century psychologists in a way that Common Sense psychology could not. Not only could recent physiological discoveries now be integrated into the discipline, but historical changes also could be accounted for. Yet, particularly to adherents of orthodox Christian visions of human nature, Spencer's assertion that the higher mental faculties, such as reason, were merely complex instinctual or reflex responses proved threatening.[22] No qualitative difference was posited between presumably unique human characteristics and those of simpler organisms. Despite (from the moralistic position) this apparent shortcoming, evolutionary theory could not simply be ignored. The task of adjusting Spencer's ideas to an essentially Christian framework was undertaken by Howells's friend, John Fiske.

In *Outlines of Cosmic Philosophy*, first published in 1874, Fiske made his most comprehensive attempt to preserve universal moral principles within an evolutionary framework. His analysis of social behavior owed much to Spencer's analogy between the social and the biological realms. But according to Fiske, the progress of human nature could be charted not by simple adaptation to external circumstance but by specifically ethical criteria: "The fundamental characteristic of social progress is *the continuous weakening of selfishness and the continuous strengthening of sympathy.* Or—to use a more convenient and somewhat more accurate expression suggested by Comte—it is a gradual supplanting of *egoism* by *altruism.*"[23] Fiske appropriated Comte's term, *altruism,* to place it in a dialectical opposition with *egoism.*[24] This dialectical pattern accounts for historical and social progress. Fiske thereby reconciled an evolutionary view of human nature with Christian metaphysics and a progressive interpretation of American history. Moreover the opposition has a clear analogue in Howells's name for utopia, Altruria, and the Altrurian name for the United States, Egoria.

Fiske, like his Common Sense predecessors, located the basis for all social feelings in the infant-parent bond. Fiske suggested that the prolonged period of human infancy, characterized by reliance on parents, forms the source of all altruistic feeling. And, when this feeling is encoded by a set of ethical precepts, such as Christianity, the result is progress. The more advanced altruistic cultures—to Fiske, the western European nations along with the United States—are the result of "a slow process of breeding, of adaptation, of acclimatization—mental and moral, as well as physical" (*Outlines*, 202). This breeding process presumably is verifiable by historical observation; Fiske charted the course of history from beginnings in clans, to Greek patriotism, on to Christianity: "The spirit of Christianity, first rendered possible by Roman cosmopolitanism, has made, and is ever making, wider and deeper conquests as civilization advances" (*Outlines*, 207). According to Fiske, the influence of the Christian religion has been in large part responsible for what he considered the more advanced states of humanity.

Fiske identified cultures as primitive or modern according to their adherence to egoistic or altruistic principles. To classify, Fiske compared "the ideal types of perfect manhood at the two extremes of civilization within our ken. The primitive man is the man of intense personality, with an enormous sense of his own importance, easily roused to paroxysms of anger, brooking no contradiction, disregardful of the feelings of others, domineering over all within his reach. The modern type is the man of mild personality, shunning the appearance of self-assertion, slow to anger, patient of contradiction, mindful of the feelings of those around him" (*Outlines*, 207-8).

In short, Fiske's modern man resembles Howells's Aristides Homos. Fiske used his categorizations of primitive and modern not only to note Western cultural changes but also to contrast Western with other world cultures:

> Over a large part of the earth's surface the slow progress painfully achieved during thousands of prehistoric ages has stopped short with the savage state, as exemplified by those African, Polynesian, and American tribes which can neither work out a civilization for themselves, nor appropriate the civilization of higher races with whom they are brought into contact. Half the human race, having surmounted savagery, have been arrested in an immobile type of civilization, as in China, in ancient Egypt, and in the East generally. It is only in the Aryan and some of the Semitic races, together with the Hungarians and other Finnic tribes subjected to Aryan influences, that we can find evidences of a persistent tendency to progress. [*Outlines*, 255]

Although Fiske denied an inherent racial tendency toward progress, attributing it to "a concurrence of favorable circumstances" (*Outlines*, 256), his racial hierarchy corresponded to the conventional Western view of itself as the disseminator of advanced culture.

Fiske's vision of social evolution also affirmed an ideal character type, an important consideration to both the earlier Common Sense psychology and Spencerian psychology as well. Fiske preserved Common Sense ethical idealism by aligning it with Spencer's notion of successful adaptation: the altruistic personality represents the highest degree of cultural success. In Fiske's model, the individual, empowered by the advanced culture, had the option to choose moral, altruistic behavior. This would enable the individual to freely operate and consequently escape Spencer's tragic determinism. Such an optimistic interpretation of evolutionary theory provided the basis for the comic slant of the Altrurian Romances in place of the tragic or tough-minded outlook more commonly associated with a Spencerian stance.

As editor for the *Atlantic Monthly* and *Harper's Monthly* from the 1860s through the 1880s, Howells naturally was familiar with evolutionary theories. Despite his substantial acceptance of evolution, reflected particularly in his ideas about realist criticism,[25] Howells expressed qualms about the ethical effects of Spencerian determinism and its disparagement of human intellectual processes. In an 1874 review of Dickens for the *Atlantic,* Howells reveals these misgivings when contrasting the comforts of religious belief against faith in an unsentimental evolution theory: "We suppose that nowadays Evolution is to console and support us—not with the hope of heavenly peace somewhere, but with the elevating consciousness of primordial jelly."[26] Years later, in his 1901 obituary for John Fiske, Howells was to maintain this same tone of concern: "John Fiske was first an apostle to the scientific heathen, and preached Darwin and Spencer and Huxley to the multitude. . . . When he had dissatisfied himself with the psychological outcome [of evolutionary science] he began to speak as one having authority, and to say those things, new and glad, of God and of the Soul which are possibly more important than anything said of either in our darkened day."[27]

Howells found encouragement in Fiske's version of evolution theory, particularly in its preservation of religious belief. Fiske's hierarchical classification of cultures according to altruistic criteria, which he had adapted from Spencer, also appealed to Howells, but the most significant aspect of Fiske's modification of Spencerian theory from Howells's perspective, a corollary of the preservation of conventional religious belief, was its insistence on the importance of free will. The individual's ability to transcend external circumstance and exercise free will recurs thematically in Howells's later fiction. The plots of such novels as *The Rise of Silas Lapham* (1885) and *The Minister's Charge* (1887) directly deal with the struggles of characters to overcome deleterious environmental influences. And even as early as 1872, in a review of a Lincoln biography, Howells cites

Lincoln's success despite the limitations of his frontier environment as evidence against strict determinism.[28] Howells plainly wanted to believe that humans could freely choose between good and evil in their actions—like John Fiske, Howells was willing to concede a strong environmental influence on individual behavior, but he was unwilling to subscribe to utter determinism.[29]

The polemics and the narrative structure of the Altrurian Romances denote Howells's commitment to a vision of individual free will that negotiates tensions between communal demands and personal freedom. The progression of consciousness in the three narrative viewpoints suggests a groundwork for individual freedom. Twelvemough, to whom perceptions about the social effects of American economics arise as momentary intrusions, manifests only a minimal capacity for thought counter to his identification with the leisure class. Homos, in marked contrast to Twelvemough, has a far more flexible and sympathetic view of people. But Homos's perspective, though more advanced, is similar to Twelvemough's in that each is a true product of his environment. A qualitative leap occurs when Eveleth assumes the narrative role. Despite her wealthy American background, she begins with a compassionate attitude toward people and, unlike Homos, she shows an ability to change as she becomes more Altrurian. This narrative movement toward an ideal of free will and personal freedom suggests that these ideals exist as great utopian goals, but Altrurian personal freedom is unlike the American variety. Although everyone is obligated to spend three hours daily in communal work, the remaining time may be used for other pursuits. Thus, for example, in his American lecture, Homos claims that Altrurians "regard all artists, who are in a sort creators, as the human type which is likest the divine" (160). But the Altrurian artist, though allowed to claim exclusion from the universal work rule, rarely does so. This expression of free will by conformity to social rules characterizes Altrurian society. Hence, punishment for crimes is unnecessary. An encounter with a murderer who is "'pursued by remorse that gives him no peace'" (391) convinces Eveleth, after some debate, that the Altrurian penitential method is best. Altrurians so thoroughly internalize their social code that external pressures are obviated. Individual free will and social good simply do not conflict.

The reason individual and collective identities merge so seamlessly is the institution of the family, a crucial feature of the ideal (for some) of the utopian village as refuge from a complex of changes occurring in late-nineteenth-century American cities. As Homos repeatedly notes in *A Traveler*, the family is the basis for Altrurian society: "The home is the very heart of the Altrurian system" (162). Moreover, Altrurian society is regarded as a kind of extension of the family, as indicated by the title of their national anthem, "Brothers All." Altruria dramatizes Fiske's notion that the family is the source of all benevolent impulses. And Altruria, by recognizing the family's importance, represents the highest level of social development within Fiske's comparative model. The action in *Through the Eye of the Needle* centers on the idea of family: several weddings are either planned or take place, and in the end the mutinous sailors return to their new Altrurian home. In place of social divisiveness, the image of family prevails, and individual differences are inevitably sublimated in deference to the higher unity.[30]

The ideal of the family, however, displays two contradictory aspects. Like the comic work of "social signification" that establishes behavioral and attitudinal boundaries that define a community,[31] the image of the family involves either inclusion within the Altrurian community or exclusion from it. In the Altrurian Romances, the community may be established either within the text, as when certain characters share values or understand a joke, or outside the text, as when, for example, reader and author agree to find Twelvemough's conformity ludicrous, or, alternatively, when the reader agrees that "'America and Altruria are really one at heart'" (23). But not all may join the Altrurian family. The question of who is to be included and who excluded from Howells's utopian realm hangs on a point of great significance to Fiske and Spencer—the hierarchy of cultures.

Altruria, the realm of human freedom, uneasily rests on the pinnacle of human development. By definition the main threat to Altruria arises not from within but from the less highly developed outside world. This threat is not one of direct attack; Altruria has remained unknown to other countries. But Aristides Homos, while apparently encouraging his American listeners' utopian impulses, insinuates the Altrurian anxiety about the precariousness of their well-being: "Ah, you mustn't go to Altruria! You must let Altruria come to *you*" (177). Like late-nineteenth-century nativists in the United States, Altrurians understand their primary threat to be the arrival of immigrants.

Throughout Howells's career, immigration was an important issue, particularly as it became more obvious to Americans toward the turn of the century. In fact, the percentage of foreign-born Americans was barely greater in 1910 than it had been in 1860—14.5 percent, as opposed to 13.2 percent, of the population.[32] But the growing number of immigrants from southern and eastern Europe in the late 1800s introduced a population with different languages, social customs, and political traditions. These differences stimulated resistance from more than one segment of the population. One example of an upper-class anti-immigrant response was the Immigration Restriction League, founded in Boston early in 1894. This organization advocated adoption of literacy tests to limit the influx of "'Slav, Latin, and Asiatic races, historically down-trodden, atavistic, and stagnant.'"[33] Although President Cleveland eventually vetoed it, the popularity of the ideas of the Immigration Restriction League was apparent in Congress's passage of a bill that would have excluded illiterate immigrants. Concern about immigration was not restricted, however, to upper-class Americans. For reasons other than common cultural or ethnic motives, such as anti-Catholic sentiment, working-class Americans also feared immigration. Ethnic differences were routinely used by employers to obstruct unionization and to drive down wages. For example, Chinese laborers were imported into Massachusetts during the 1870s by shoe manufacturers for this purpose; and Slavic workers were effectively used by the coal industry to destroy the miners' union in 1875. Such competition helped stimulate anti-immigrant sentiment among supporters of trade union activity.[34] Immigrants also frequently introduced broad critiques of capitalism as well as ideas about labor organization that were at odds with American trade unions, which tended to avoid political involvement and economic analyses in favor of a narrower focus on wages and working conditions.[35]

Howells's own responses to immigration reflect considerable ambivalence. On the one hand, he must be recalled as the one who promoted the English-language publications of the American Jewish journalist and novelist Abraham Cahan.[36] And his courageous defense of the Haymarket anarchists in 1887 similarly bespeaks a commitment to cultural diversity. Yet, on the other hand, contradictory impulses may be discerned in his journalistic writings. For example, in one early *Atlantic* column he sarcastically expresses fear over the prospect of "the American race accomplish[ing] its destiny of dying out before the populatory foreigner."[37] In another, Howells looks ahead to a future dominated by "the oblique-eyed, swarthy American of that time."[38] Similarly, in comments occasioned by some wanderings through a local neighborhood, he observes with displeasure the effects of Irish immigration ("It is pretty certain that the general character of the population has not gained by the change"), he notes that "the encroachment of the Celtic army" and "the well-known ambition of Dubliners to rule the land—[will] one day make an end of us poor Yankees as a dominant plurality," and he concludes with the following query: "We wait with an anxious curiosity the encounter of the Irish and the Chinese, now rapidly approaching each other from opposite shores of the continent. Shall we be crushed in the collision of these superior races?"[39]

The kinds of anxieties about immigration and its effects that Howells, a Welsh immigrant's grandson, displays in these writings appear in the Altrurian Romances, but the utopian work transmutes them, first by handling with comic irony questions of immigration and foreign influence in the United States. In *A Traveler from Altruria*, Homos, a foreigner, is treated condescendingly by the self-deluded Twelvemough, to whom there is no doubt that immigrants are inferior beings. At one point, Twelvemough describes domestics as "ignorant foreigners, fit for nothing else" (17); and later, condemning some farmers from England who complain about their poverty, an upper-class companion smugly opines, "these foreigners have no self-respect" (86). More humorously, Twelvemough expresses his fear of being "attainted" by the "enmity" and "explicit vulgarity" of the distinctly more peaceful and sensitive Homos (72). But despite Howells's ridicule of the xenophobic Twelvemough's narrow-mindedness, Howells's exemplar Homos *also* expresses negative opinions about immigrants. His comments about Italians, quoted earlier, are characteristic of Homos's observations on lower-class, immigrant New Yorkers in the "Letters." Whether the source is a mysterious ethnic essence or a result of American economics, immigrants somehow undergo a "malign change" in the United States that causes them to acquire only the most noxious American characteristics.

The Altrurian anxieties over immigration appear in Homos's comments about immigrants and his desire to encourage native utopianists in the United States to build their own ideal society rather than emigrate to Altruria. In *A Traveler*, Homos declares that "America and Altruria are really one at heart" (23). This intrinsic unity leads Homos, in his concluding sermon, to maintain that, if American political ideals were applied to the economic sphere, the "Evolution" that peacefully transformed Altrurian society could do the same for the United States. Yet Homos's encouraging affirmations of the altrurianism implicit in Americans only obscure the significance of Altruria's social composition. Homos hints at this when he notes in his sermon that he is the first Altrurian to travel abroad *as* an Altrurian. Altruria has remained secret because it is a closed society: although shipwrecked sailors are made welcome, immigration clearly is not desired. When one of the farmers expresses his eagerness to leave the inequities of the United States behind and emigrate, Homos responds by insisting, "You must let Altruria come to *you*." Similarly, when Twelvemough introduces Eveleth's and Homos's narratives in *Through the Eye of the Needle*, he observes that "a people living in conditions which some of our dreamers would consider ideal, are forced to discourage foreign emigration, against their rule of universal hospitality, and in at least one notable instance are obliged to protect themselves against what they believe an evil example by using compulsion with the wrong-doers" (273). Twelvemough's comment highlights his incongruous consonance with the Altrurians on the issue of foreign contamination.

The specific incident to which Twelvemough alludes, in which the shipwrecked Thrall family and their servants are coerced into communal labor, reveals the underlying fear of cultural corruption. Eveleth, reflecting her adoptive Altrurian viewpoint, comments on the wealthy Thralls: "It could not be said that they were molestive in the same sense as the sailors [who had killed animals for food, to the distress of the vegetarian Altrurians], but they were even more demoralizing in the spectacle they offered the neighborhood of people dependent on hired service" (415). The fear of demoralization by contact with people from capitalist society is usually not so overtly stated in *Through the Eye*. More typically, when the crew of the ship that had brought Aristides and Eveleth mutinies and asks to stay in Altruria, Aristides explains to Eveleth that "the Altrurians are not anxious to have the men stay, not merely because they are coarse, rude, or vicious, but because they think they ought to go home . . . to found an Altrurian Commonwealth of their own" (371-72). The sailors, when allowed to present their plea to stay, describe their situation in revealing terms.

Eveleth relates the first mate's account of their miserable working conditions and the tonic effect of his arrival in Altruria: "When he got ashore here in Altruria, and saw how *white* [Howells's emphasis] people lived, people that *used* each other white, he made up his mind that he would never go back to any ship alive" (376). In response, the captain apologizes for the sailors' working conditions and remarks that he also finds it difficult to return to the United States after his time in Altruria: "Don't you suppose *I* would like to spend the rest of my days, too, among *white* people?" (377). The captain adds that he was afraid to let his wife come ashore "'to let her see what a white man's country really was, because I felt so weak about it myself'" (378). The figural significance of *whiteness* recalls Homos's earlier comments on the White City at the 1893 Columbian Exposition.[40]

Homos, utterly taken with the classical architecture of what he terms "the Fair City," discovers there "the illusion of Altruria" because of its classical design and cleanliness. Against this citadel of purity, he contrasts the Midway Plaisance outside:

> In the Fair City, everything is free; in the Plaisance everything must be paid for. . . . The Orient, which has mainly peopled the Plaisance, with its theaters and restaurants and shops, takes the tint of the ordinary American enterprise, and puts on somewhat the manners of the ordinary American hustler. It is not really so bad as that, but it is worse than American in some of the appeals it makes to the American public, which is decent if it is dull, and respectable if it is rapacious. The lascivious dances of the East are here, in the Persian and Turkish and Egyptian theaters; . . . One must be aware that the citizens of the Plai-

sance are not there for their health, as the Americans quaintly say, but
for the money there is in it. [205]

Homos's stark contrast between the White City and the surrounding Plaisance, disingenuous insofar as it ignores the military display in the White
City sponsored by the German munitions maker Krupp, simultaneously
evokes the image of utopian Altruria surrounded by the materialist world
and that of an America besieged by immigrants.[41]
     The idea that the most advanced nation would have problematic rela-
tions with its neighbors is hardly unique to Howells. John Fiske's popular
lecture, "Manifest Destiny," published in *Harper's Monthly* while Howells was editor, presents a relevant treatment of this issue. Fiske, in keeping
with the Spencerian cultural hierarchy echoed in *Cosmic Philosophy*,
states that "the development of industry is largely dependent upon the ces-
sation or restriction of warfare."[42] This peaceable quality, the triumph of
the altruistic over the egoistic in culture, has, however, a somewhat paradoxical military mission: "In order that the pacific community may be able
to go on doing its work it must be strong enough and warlike enough to
overcome its barbaric neighbors, who have no notion of keeping peace."[43]
Fiske justifies his racial hierarchy through an appeal to the virtues of "local
self-government combined with central representation," which he credits
to the Teutonic influence, and he concludes with a frankly imperialist pre-
diction:

> The work which the English race began when it colonized North
> America is destined to go on until every land on the earth's surface
> that is not already the seat of an old civilization shall become English
> in its language, in its religion, in its political habits and traditions, and
> to a predominant extent in the blood of its people. The day is at hand
> when four-fifths of the human race will trace its pedigree to English
> forefathers, as four-fifths of the white people in the United States trace
> their pedigree to-day.[44]

Fiske's statement, which complements Howells's earlier fear of a future of
"oblique-eyed, swarthy" Americans, relies on an aggressive interpretation
of cultural authority.
     By contrast, Howells's vision in the Altrurian Romances appears
more peaceful. Because it has remained mysteriously hidden in the Aegean
Sea, Altruria has no need for a military force, and its few shipwrecked immigrants pose only a limited threat to the prevalent culture. Expressing
Howells's idealization of small rural towns, Mrs. Gray, Eveleth's mother,
comments that life in Altruria, which at first she had feared, "took her
back to the America she used to know" (383). The nostalgic approval of

Altruria given by Mrs. Gray, an early doubter of Homos, suggests Howells's attempt to find a utopian future in an idealized, almost childlike, past, in which everyone was a member of an extended family.

Altruria's organization into villages rather than industrial cities and its glorification of farming rather than industry imply a desire to retreat to a supposedly simpler rural life. Homos remarks in his lecture that farming is the most honored pursuit in Altruria (161). And in the Altrurian Romances the only working people with whom Homos has any sustained interactions are farmers. Despite Homos's sympathy with New York's poor in the "Letters," urban and industrial workers are described generically and are notably absent as characters.[45] Howells's avoidance of this issue reflects the difficulties he had in earlier novelistic treatments of economic problems. In *Annie Kilburn*, for example, Howells criticizes philanthropic schemes to ameliorate the living conditions of workers. And in his most programmatic attempt to present the social disarray of industrial society, *A Hazard of New Fortunes*, it is the ultimately ineffectual Christian faith of young Conrad Dryfoos that is compared favorably to the more radical politics of the immigrant Lindau. Howells does present Lindau with a certain sympathy; yet, as his deeply accented speech signifies, Lindau's political solutions were imported and not truly germane to America and its needs.

In place of potentially explosive working-class political solutions, Howells uses Homos's direct address to his readers in the "Letters" to affirm a faith in the American middle class: "It is from those who have not been forced to toil so exhaustively that they cannot think clearly; it is from the comfortable middle class . . . that the good time is to come" (192). Instead of "a wild revolt of the poor against the rich, of laborer against capitalist, with all the sanguinary circumstance of such an outbreak" (191), the middle class offers a relatively disinterested, almost Altrurian outlook. Howells infuses the middle class with a nostalgic Midwestern agrarian vision: "Of course the vast majority of Americans are of the middle class, and with them you can still find the old American life, the old American ideals, the old American principles; and if the old America is ever to prevail, it must be in their love and honor of it" (190). Howells, identifying the middle class with his symbol of a preindustrial America free from the threat of cultural diversity, advances his vision of a place where Christian idealism would go unchallenged and all threats would be external.

Howells's critique of social Darwinist individualism and his appeal to the "old America," his nostalgic vision of a rural society, are strategic responses to evolutionary determinism and a call for political change. When determinism is used to justify as natural current social conditions, Howells bristles. Thus he objects to such social Darwinist apologetics for economic inequities as those voiced by Twelvemough in familiar terms: "'The divisions among us are rather a process of natural selection'" (14). And he also objects to the vision of human nature as a static entity, while he argues instead that change for the better is possible. In place of the newer evolutionary determinism, Howells's ideal of an "old America" recalls the earlier Common Sense outlook in which the individual will is bounded by community morality instead of natural laws.

A desire for an effective community morality is also reflected on a structural level by the comic tone and action of the Altrurian Romances. The "vigilant sense of a collective supervision," noted by Meredith as an attribute of comedy, along with a comic "utilitarian aim of general improvement," cited by Bergson, guides Howells's utopian work. Rather than engage in bitter, potentially alienating polemics, Howells argues that turn-of-the-century American conditions are foolish and of benefit to no one, not even members of the upper class. The new Altrurian community, ideally to be composed of those readers willing to take up Homos's challenge to build their own Altruria, presents itself as open to all who would embrace Altrurian ideals. This inclusive and optimistic tone is matched by both the plot of *Through the Eye of the Needle,* in which the newest members of the Altrurian family return home, and the progression of narrative points of view in the Altrurian Romances, which shows evolutionary development in the three successive states of mind of the narrators.

Howells's comic vision of the individual in society, an attempt at incorporating moral precepts within an evolutionary framework, represents a distinct and telling alteration of the prevalent nineteenth-century accounts of the evolution of human behavior. In Spencer's model, the individual and the culture are both products of the natural environment. Fiske preserves the cause-effect relationship between culture and environment, but he posits culture as a mediating force between the individual and nature. On the level of relations between cultures, Fiske maintains a Spencerian outlook. The operation of Spencer's evolutionary law demands conflict between competing cultures.

In contrast to Spencer's and Fiske's emphases on war between cultures, Howells addresses the question of the assimilation of immigrants into American society. Howells accepts Fiske's idea of the culture as a mediating force, which he then problematizes by introducing the issue of immigration and the idea that an individual be loyal to more than one culture. In Howells's utopia, the national symbol of Altruria contains an implicit call to give up ties to the old in favor of the newer, more highly evolved society. But even the enthusiastic Eveleth, despite her desire to become Altrurian, finds the process of assimilation slow and disorienting. Her situation would appear to dramatize the difficulties faced by immigrants during Howells's time: with their dual allegiances to the new

American society and to their ethnic cultures, the transformation to American identity was difficult. Yet, despite his recognition of this problem from Eveleth's immigrant standpoint, Howells insists in the name of cultural unity that immigrants have an undivided allegiance to their adoptive homeland. The underside of the comic "collective supervision" emerges in a strategy of exclusion toward those who do not accept membership solely in the dominant community. Earlier, in his *Atlantic* essays, Howells had perceived with marked anxiety the presence of other ethnic groups; similarly, in the Altrurian Romances any ethnic identity is a threat to his utopian vision.

Howells defends his vision in the name of evolutionary progress: Altruria is the most highly developed society, and, therefore, other cultures will inevitably become like it. And, of course, the United States stands next in line in the cultural hierarchy. Howells evokes a symbol he calls "old America," but American identity has not necessarily resided in a common cultural history or set of traditions. Symbols of national unity in America often have derived from an orientation toward the future, a desire to create a country that would live up to utopian dreams. While politically conservative visions of the future have tended to emphasize organic and traditional social structures, more progressive political outlooks customarily have stressed democratic principles.[46] In the end, Howells, by stressing the desire to reconstruct society according to ethical ideals, aligns himself with politically progressive forces. But in his appeal to an "old America," which connotes an exclusion of other cultures and runs counter to his political idealism, Howells reveals an ambivalence toward immigration and a general discomfort with an urban industrial society.

By emphasizing communal consensus and morality, Howells tries to eliminate the threat of cultural pluralism while he attempts to reproduce the older Common Sense emphasis on legitimation of the individual. Like Hawthorne, who used the image of the individual's return home to dramatize the reliance of the individual on the community, Howells ends the Altrurian Romances with the return of the ship to its new Altrurian home. But, unlike the Puritans in Hawthorne's romance, these sailors have come to a New World that is already perfect. If they—and Howells's Altruria— are to survive, they must shed completely their old identities, thereby eliminating the threat of competing cultures. Perhaps it was this anxiety that prompted Howells, referring to himself in the third person, to mention in his introductory comments that he had to "admit the possibility of imperfection even in the ideal commonwealth of Altruria; or in other terms, he suffered his dream of it to experience slight touches of nightmare" (4).

5

The Ironic Construction of Selfhood

William James's *Principles of Psychology*

In their fiction, Hawthorne and Howells dramatized problems of the relationship between the self and the community within nineteenth-century American thought. For Hawthorne, contemporary social issues and the advent of association psychology complicated but did not overturn his Common Sense understanding of the individual's reliance on the community. The Common Sense analysis of the individual psyche, which constituted a part of every educated person's instruction in moral philosophy, remained powerful even after the Civil War. In large part the Common Sense analysis held its ground because it articulated on a theoretical level the tension between the individual and society, which has been an important part of America's cultural heritage since Puritan times. This tension, derived from the need to locate truth within the individual while the individual paradoxically remained subordinate to community ethical and behavioral standards, was depicted by Hawthorne in his short stories, his children's histories, and, most prominently, *The Scarlet Letter*. For Hawthorne's fictional characters, claims to knowledge of truth that contradict social conventions precede self-imposed isolation and even madness. Hawthorne's strongest character, Hester Prynne, evades this fate only through membership in a reconfigured community and reconciliation with the Puritans.

The Common Sense description of mental activity, with its emphasis on introspection, worked well to describe an educated population that shared common assumptions and cultural mores. But with growth and the changes in nineteenth-century immigration patterns, it became increasingly difficult to rely on the common associations advocated as an aesthetic goal by Archibald Alison and others. While the diversification of the American population challenged the notion of cultural unity, evolutionary theory threatened the religious and ethical bases of American life. Despite its threatening aspects, however, evolutionary theory, with its postulated hierarchy of cultures, situated the United States and England at the pinnacle of human development, thus containing the menace of non-anglophone immigrant cultures and reiterating the universalist tone, if not the content, of traditional psychologies. But while evolutionist theory cer-

103

tified the doctrine of anglophone superiority, it did so at the expense of the individual free will. By arguing that anglophone cultures were objectively superior because they had developed in response to natural conditions, writers like Herbert Spencer abandoned the idea of individual volition in favor of a thoroughgoing materialism. For William Dean Howells, among others, the issue was unavoidably ethical: without a firm basis in the possibility of free choice, individual morality was an impossibility. Despite his general adherence to an evolutionist outlook, Howells was unwilling to discard the possibility of free individual will. A tension between free will and evolutionary determinism, though masked by a comic structure, pervades the Altrurian Romances and displays a cultural malaise. Howells ineffectually attempts to resolve the issue by asserting a version of Kant's categorical imperative: the truly enlightened individual would recognize that the highest possible moral action is that which benefits all.[1]

The ultimate inadequacy of Howells's attempt to resolve this important late-nineteenth-century problem through a return to traditional philosophy was underscored by the appearance in 1890 of William James's *The Principles of Psychology*. This work's initial prominence was in part attributable to its deft, comprehensive survey of the state of psychology, a discipline then undergoing revolutionary change. But despite its now outdated physiological descriptions and the philosophical psychology, obsolete even then, that it refutes, *The Principles* is still read. In large part the appeal of *The Principles* is rooted in the problem it addresses: we still wrestle with the conflict between explanations of human behavior based in material circumstance and those based in a philosophy of individual will. But *The Principles* also engages our interest because of its colloquial style and narrative structure, an apparently personal account of an intellectual struggle. We seem to witness, even accompany, James as he sorts through empirical evidence and inherited beliefs to suggest how we are best to diagnose the human condition. An examination of the narrative structure of *The Principles*, an unusual structure in what ostensibly is a college psychology textbook, can provide insights into James's attempt to rearrange the discipline of psychology. In addition, attention to the prevalent figures of speech will indicate the effect of rhetorical structures on James's ideas about the individual's relationship to the environment, social and material.[2]

Although it reflects James's extensive knowledge of philosophy, *The Principles* is not simply a philosophical work. Remaining true to his background in medicine and physiology, and while maintaining an equanimous tone, James weighs the claims of physiologists against those of moral philosophers. James displays characteristic balance in the opening sentence of *The Principles:* "Psychology is the Science of Mental Life, both of its phenomena and of their conditions."[3] This definition encompasses the division that pervades the structure of his study. On the one hand, James declares the importance of the "phenomena" of mental life: "The phenomena are such things as we call feelings, desires, cognitions, reasonings, decisions, and the like" (15). As James notes, these assorted mental events comprise the Common Sense fusion of faculty and association psychologies. Against this old philosophical psychology, however, James introduces "the conditions" of mental life, physiology. With his call for an exploration of the material conditions associated with thought, James treats the new psychology of the late 1800s on equal terms with the old. In the very first statement of *The Principles,* James thus fuses two opposed approaches to human psychology.

To appreciate the implications of this opening gesture, it is helpful to recall the state of American psychology during the 1890s, a time when academic disciplines were becoming increasingly professionalized. Physiological psychology, a recent import from German universities, was growing in popularity, largely because it meshed well with prevalent evolutionary theories. With its emphasis on the body and the environment, this new psychology threatened the older philosophical Common Sense psychology, which, since its American inception with the works of Benjamin Rush, had been highly oriented toward Christian morality.[4] Because it challenged the centrality of the moral free will, environmental determinism in any form was abhorrent to Common Sense theorists. Accordingly, in what was to be the final volley from the retreating ranks of Common Sense psychologists, James McCosh of Princeton opened his two-volume *Psychology* with the definition, "Psychology is the science of the soul."[5] This retrogressive assertion coincided with the declaration of a contemporary that knowledge of psychology "is not possible by way of physiology"; physiological study would alter nothing to defenders of the old psychology because "in any case the mental facts remain what they always were."[6] And, at Harvard, the regnant psychology was Francis Bowen's amalgam of Common Sense realism and Unitarian metaphysics.

More than constituting a simple theoretical problem for one with contrary beliefs, the domination of psychology at Harvard by Francis Bowen, who had taught there since the early 1830s, obstructed James's professional goals. As Howard Feinstein notes, "at the small institution that Harvard was in the 1870s, a new teacher who aspired to teach a new discipline had to move a previously well-established professor out of the way."[7] Although James had achieved some professional security with his promotion in 1876 to an assistant professorship in biology, he was anxious to leave behind his scientific background and abandon physiology for philosophy. *The Principles of Psychology,* conceived as a textbook for the psychology course James wished to teach, was part of an overall effort to displace Bowen and the old psychology. Like many no-longer-young professors, James further hoped his first full-length publication would strengthen his bid for professional advancement, and in 1878 he contracted with Henry Holt to write a psychology text. What was to have been a two-year project extended to twelve and, ironically, James's successful attempt to move psychology out of the realm of philosophy was responsible for his own professional movement out of physiology and into Harvard's philosophy department.

In *The Principles,* James legitimizes his professional designs by circumscribing the old philosophical view of the discipline. His technique is to question established presuppositions. For example, though in his opening sentence James cites the importance of mental "phenomena," he rapidly surveys the established philosophical positions with respect to mental faculties and finds them inadequate: *"the faculty does not exist absolutely, but works under conditions;* and *the quest of the conditions* becomes the psychologist's most interesting task"* (17);[8] therefore, "a certain amount of brain-physiology must be presupposed or included in Psychology" (18). James begins *The Principles* by defining his discipline, only to undermine promptly his own definition—material conditions limit, if not determine, the operation of mental faculties. Yet James also asserts the presence of a quality that historically had been ascribed to the will: *"The pursuance of future ends and the choice of means for their attainment are thus the mark and criteria of mentality* in phenomena" (21). In his opening chapter, then, James does not merely present his reader with a fundamental approach and organizational scheme for the study of psychology. Instead, his alternation between mentalist and materialist viewpoints reveals his radical questions about the proper disciplinary focus for his declared area of study.

With no clearly defined object of study, *The Principles of Psychology* occupies the strange role of a textbook in search of its discipline.[9] In *The Principles,* James guides the reader in a review of contemporary psychological theories. The two primary viewpoints are the mentalist, esteemed for its long philosophical history and its affirmation of the human will, and the materialist, justified by the findings of physiological experimentation and the status of evolutionary science. Each had an established theory of knowledge and a distinct methodology; neither was willing to accept the definitions and the findings of the other. The psychology of moral philosophers was clearly inadequate in the face of physiological psychology. No location for the human soul could be found by anatomists, and the philosophical categories or faculties did not correspond to the findings of laboratory researchers. But physiological psychology was a problematic venture as well. Because it tended to view humans as nothing more than their physical bodies, it suffered from the same problem as did evolutionary psychology: change could be accounted for only by chance or by an altered environment. Most significantly, it eliminated the possibility of free will.

The conflicted vision initially apparent in his introduction intensifies as James articulates his criticism of both mentalist and materialist schools. In chapter 5, "The Automaton-Theory," for example, he accuses those who subscribe to a purely physiologic approach of their own kind of "philosophic faith, bred like most faiths from an aesthetic demand" (138). James goes on to debunk the supposed objectivity of scientists: "The desire on the part of men educated in laboratories not to have their physical reasonings mixed up with such incommensurable factors as feelings is certainly very strong." Playing on the cliché of scientists who seek the purity of the laboratory, James suggests that their positivistic conclusions arise more from an unrecognized desire to order the universe than to observe often inconsistent natural phenomena.

Because physiological research expanded the realm of psychological research, James suggests it had a salutary effect. But because it excluded from consideration many of the complexities of human existence, he indicates it did not go far enough. To remedy this situation, James reintroduces a methodological principle of philosophical psychology: "*Introspective Observation is what we have to rely on first and foremost and always*" (185). Despite his defense of the introspective method, James acknowledges its limits. Introspective evidence, although necessary, may be distorted by what we now call psychological defenses and unconscious motivations. Therefore, James warns, "*we must never take a person's testimony, however sincere, that he has felt nothing, as proof positive that no feeling has been there*" (208).

The relationship of physiology to mentation further complicates the issue. James values the study of physiology because "*no mental modification ever occurs which is not accompanied or followed by a bodily change*" (18). James expands on this when he discusses the James-Lange theory (first introduced in 1884). Briefly, this theory argues that "*the bodily changes follow directly the perception of the exciting fact, and that our own feeling of the same changes as they occur IS the emotion*" (1065). The priority, both temporal and logical, of physiology over introspective analyses reaches its peak with this theory. Indeed, James disparages earlier psychological descriptions of emotional states: "I should as lief read verbal descriptions of the shapes of the rocks on a New Hampshire farm as toil through them again" (1064). Yet in the chapters on "The Automaton-Theory" and "The Mind-Stuff Theory," James, hoping to "perhaps force some of these materialistic minds to feel the more strongly the logical respectability of the spiritualistic position" (181), finds fault with those who would admit only physiological evidence into psychology.

This oscillation between the polarities of materialist and mentalist disciplinary visions constitutes the structure of *The Principles*. Within such individual chapters as "Habit," "Discrimination and Comparison," "Association," and "Instinct," for example, James shifts back and forth between philosophy and physiology. This same pattern holds true for *The Principles* as a whole. The movement from the early chapters on physiology to a more traditional, moralistic treatment of habit characterizes the narrative flow. Chapters 2 and 3 ("The Function of the Brain" and "On Some General Conditions of Brain-Activity") provide the physiological basis that is subsequently applied to behavior in chapter 4, "Habit." James then devotes chapters to criticism of materialist psychology ("The Automaton-Theory" and "The Mind-Stuff Theory") and advocacy of the introspective method ("The Methods and Snares of Psychology"). With this call for a return to introspection, James proceeds, in such chapters as "Attention," "Association," "The Perception of Time," "Memory," and "Sensation," to discuss topics hitherto defined as intellectual states. James follows these with chapters on "The Emotions" and "The Will."[10]

Given the uncertainty of the proper subject matter of psychology, the format of *The Principles* may seem arbitrary. But if we compare the organization of *The Principles* to earlier writings, a pattern emerges. In their works, Common Sense psychologists such as Thomas Reid and Dugald Stewart progress from treatments of the intellect to the emotions to the will. Thomas Upham, in his popular psychology textbook, the *Abridgement of Mental Philosophy*, adheres to this tripartite faculty psychology. James ironically simulates this same mentalist structure to call into question the old psychology. Given his interest in the physiological bases of emotional response, it is no surprise that he devotes only one chapter each to the emotions and the will.[11]

In the concluding chapter, James summarizes his beliefs about such problems as the relationship of experience to thought, the possibility of innate mental structures, and the origin of instincts. His closing remarks, in which he again disparages association and Spencerian psychologies, are revealing. Although he states that the evolutionary, "so-called Experience-philosophy has failed to prove its point," he makes only conservative claims for his own beliefs:

> The causes of our mental structures are doubtless natural, and connected, like all our other peculiarities, with those of our nervous structure. Our interests, our tendencies of attention, our motor impulses, the aesthetic, moral, and theoretic combinations we delight

in . . . have all grown up in ways of which at present we can give no account. Even in the clearest parts of Psychology our insight is insignificant enough. And the more sincerely one seeks to trace the actual course of *psychogenesis,* the steps by which as a race we may have come by the peculiar mental attributes which we possess, the more clearly one perceives "the slowly gathering twilight close in utter night." [1280]

This apparent skepticism over "our insight" into psychology is noteworthy in light of the chapter-by-chapter organization of *The Principles.* James uses a faculty psychology structure to attack mentalist psychology as well as materialist psychology. This ironic use of a faculty-psychology format accords with the concluding tone of *The Principles.*

In addition, the search for an object of disciplinary inquiry itself has an ironic structure. The kind of ironic structure I refer to here is that described in Kenneth Burke's dramatistic "The Four Master Tropes."[12] According to Burke, when dramatic roles are replaced by ideas, dramatic conflict becomes dialectic. This dialectical conflict may ultimately be resolved by recourse to a Hegelian higher synthesis; or, like Adorno's negative dialectic, the conflict may remain irresolvable. In an ironic conflict, no subsuming higher viewpoint is available, and we are presented instead with a double vision. Each side fends off the attacks of the other, but neither side is sufficiently powerful to prevail.

This lack of resolution characterizes *The Principles.* James uses two opposed psychological viewpoints to create a mutual critique. He objects to the idealism of the old psychology: too much scientific evidence exists to allow one to discount physiology and environmental influences. Yet, in materialist psychology, James finds a correspondingly questionable inherent idealism. Because neither overcomes the other and because the two prevalent viewpoints could not be unified, *The Principles* ironically fails in its search for the proper basis of psychology. Neither the philosophical conception of the individual nor the materialist stress on the body adequately defines the disciplinary subject matter.

Notwithstanding his criticisms of the two major psychological approaches, James finds value in each. With its emphasis on the physical conditions of mental actions, the new psychology proposed a scientific basis for psychological research. One scientific concept, the reflex arc, would be significant in the chapter on habit and, more remotely, to the idea of the stream of thought. With its emphasis on environment and physiological conditions, materialist psychology also challenged the notion of subjectivity central to the old psychology. The old, soul-centered psychology, derived from Christian beliefs, nevertheless incorporated elements

James would find useful to his inquiry. The traditional philosophical method of psychological investigation, introspection, proves essential to James. In "Habit," for example, James initially bases his idea on the physiological notion of the reflex arc, the neural pathway formed in response to a stimulus.[13] But before long, James begins to support his idea of habit with devices typical of philosophical psychology, introspection and anecdote: "The writer well remembers how, on revisiting Paris after ten years' absence, and, finding himself in the street in which for one winter he had attended school, he lost himself in a brown study, from which he was awakened by finding himself upon the stairs which led to the apartment in a house many streets away in which he had lived during that earlier time, and to which his steps from the school had then habitually led" (119). Attempting to persuade the reader by an appeal to common experience, James continues in this vein: "We all of us have a definite routine. . . ." Shared routine experience entices the reader to participate in the learned, reasonable, balanced discourse of *The Principles*.

The introspective method founds its claim to truth on experience. Unlike other experiences, however, the results of introspection cannot be directly verified. This introspective method, retained by James, and later by phenomenologists, from earlier moral-philosophy discourse, is best understood in *The Principles* as a means of persuasion, an attempt to draw the reader into the narrative.[14] Throughout *The Principles*, James assumes a populist, egalitarian pose from which he derides the motivations of philosophers and scientists. Nevertheless, he also uses philosophical and scientific methods, intimating to the reader that they are readily comprehensible. His tone is evident in the footnote that concludes the introduction: "Nothing is easier than to familiarize one's self with the mammalian brain. Get a sheep's head, a small saw, chisel, scalpel and forceps (all three can best be had from a surgical-instrument maker), and unravel its parts . . ." (24). Matter-of-fact instructions suggest easy participation by the reader in a symbolic unraveling of the brain.

James also relies on one other essential of the old psychology, the will. Despite the substantial critique of the self implicit in materialist psychology, James retains this primary expression of selfhood. Numerous critics, beginning notably with Ralph Barton Perry, have discovered in James's recurrent episodes of depression and varied physical ailments during his twenties the origin of his assertion of the will. His self-cure during that difficult time provides the source. Because the physiologic approach to psychiatric problems implied that melancholia, along with all other emotional ills, had its basis in one's physical constitution, the outlook for James was bleak. But during an emotional crisis in 1870, he invoked a philosophical approach to amend the physical etiological assessment of depression.

I think that yesterday was a crisis in my life. I finished the first part of Renouvier's second *Essais* and see no reason why his definition of Free Will—"the sustaining of a thought *because I choose to* when I might have other thoughts"—need be the definition of an illusion. At any rate, I will assume for the present—until next year—that it is no illusion. My first act of free will shall be to believe in free will. For the remainder of the year, I will abstain from the mere speculation and contemplative *Grublei* in which my nature takes most delight, and voluntarily cultivate the feeling of moral freedom.[15]

However one wishes to assess the incident, his refusal to allow physical determinism to overwhelm the will thematically recurs in James's writings.

The debate during the nineteenth century over free will frames what otherwise might seem a purely personal problem. By the late nineteenth century, earlier defenses of free will appeared irrelevant. Despite notable academic holdouts, such as proponents of Common Sense psychology, evolutionist thought in the physical and the social sciences was the norm. On the social level, the evolutionary doctrine of Manifest Destiny effectively justified cultural hierarchies and the obliteration of Native American cultures. Social Darwinism similarly rationalized the inequities of social classes. Yet the power of the old individualism remained. One reason *The Principles of Psychology* proved an acceptable alternative to the old psychology was that, unlike materialist psychology, it stressed the individual will. No doubt his defense of the will has resulted in the critical characterization of James as an individualist. But the solutions he suggests in *The Principles* to the conflict between materialist and mentalist psychologies indicate that James was no simple defender of the free individual will. In his chapters on "Habit," "The Consciousness of Self," and "The Stream of Thought," James offers an alternative to traditional conceptions of the individual, and he implicitly justifies his textbook, so ironic in a Burkean sense.

James's chapter on habit contains some of his most renowned statements on mental health and education: "The great thing, then, in all education, is to *make our nervous system our ally instead of our enemy*. It is to fund and capitalize our acquisitions, and live at ease upon the interest of the fund" (126). In what might appear positivistic and old-fashioned bromides, James insists on the value of proper thought and, of yet greater value, action: "With mere good intentions, hell is proverbially paved" (129). These suggestions for the inculcation of a proper predisposition to correct action merely conclude James's assertion of the centrality of habit in human life; when excerpted from the chapter as a whole, they do not convey his questions about human will.[16] Accordingly, I will first turn to the opening statement of this chapter, in which James, following the lead of evolutionist psychologists, suggests a close relationship between the behaviors of humans and those of other organisms: "When we look at living creatures from an outward point of view, one of the first things that strike us is that they are bundles of habits. In wild animals, the usual round of daily behavior seems a necessity implanted at birth; in animals domesticated, and especially in man, it seems, to a great extent, to be the result of education" (109). By associating the higher activity of reason with animal instinct—both instinct and habit serve the function of guiding ordinary activity—James claims a theoretical kinship with evolutionary psychologists. More significantly he establishes a basis from which to examine human thought as behavior that exists in response to the world.

This responsiveness is essential to a living organism. Evolutionary science decreed that organisms unable to adapt to changes in surroundings would be unable to survive. James calls this ability to adapt *plasticity:* "*Plasticity,* then, in the wide sense of the word, means the possession of a structure weak enough to yield to an influence, but strong enough not to yield all at once" (110). Whereas a simple organism may have an extremely limited set of potential responses to a given situation, the almost limitless possibilities of response offered by a complex organism must be restricted for the very practical reason that one would spend all of one's time confronting the world anew were it not for habitual response. As James puts it, "*the phenomena of habit in living beings are due to the plasticity of the organic materials of which their bodies are composed*" (110). The complexity of the human body mandates habit. Without habit, the principle of plasticity would reign, and mental chaos would result.

On both the literal and the figural levels, this assessment is rooted in nervous-system sensitivity. In sensory organs, this function exhibits itself when an external stimulus triggers a neuronal response, which initiates transmission to the brain. Impulse transmission from the brain then leads to an appropriate muscle response. A classic example of this process is the rapid and unconscious muscle response that follows contact with fire. James describes nervous system performance as "nothing but a system of paths between a sensory *terminus a quo* and a muscular, glandular, or other *terminus ad quem*" (113). He observes that habit relies on the physiology of neuronal response: "A path once traversed by a nerve-current might be expected to follow the law of most of the paths we know, and to be scooped out and made more permeable than before . . . until at last it might become a natural drainage channel" (113). By grounding habit formation in the process of transmission and the science of physiology, James strengthens his later suggestions about mental health and ethics.

Concurrently, with the phrase "natural drainage channel," he invokes a prevalent metaphor: fluid dynamics.[17] James consciously makes use of this metaphor; earlier he states that "the philosophy of habit is thus, in the first instance, a chapter in physics rather than in physiology or psychology" (110). He quotes from an essay on habit, his source for this metaphor: "'Water, in flowing, hollows out for itself a channel, which grows broader and deeper; and, after having ceased to flow, it resumes, when it flows again, the path traced by itself before'" (111). James borrows a metaphor from an essay on the philosophy of habit, applies it to neurophysiology, and then, its physical basis established, returns to it in his later thoughts on habit. This use of a fluid metaphor to describe psychological action is by no means unique—Freud uses hydraulics as the underlying physical metaphor for his theory of drives.[18] But for James the metaphor of fluidity primarily reveals the tendency toward equilibrium.

The metaphor of fluidity and the tendency toward equilibrium is apparent in three important aspects of *The Principles*. In addition to the routine, habitual flow of nerve impulses noted above, James relies on the nature of fluidity and equilibrium to create his analytic framework. In the attempt to produce a balanced vision, the ironic dialectic of *The Principles*, with its recurrent shifts of perspective, enacts on a structural level the metaphor of fluidity. The final, and ultimately most significant, effect of the fluid metaphor relates to James's conception of the relationship between the individual and the environment. Unlike Freud, whose drive theory draws on the notion of a closed system that builds pressure until a release must be found, James envisions an ongoing interaction between the individual and the environment, in which habit facilitates the homeostatic process by which levels of tension are equalized. Nerve impulses, like water, flow according to the path of least resistance to equalize tension.

To James, the individual and the world interact dynamically. A useful discussion of response to external stimulus, clearly influenced by *The Principles*, is John Dewey's essay of 1896, "The Reflex Arc Concept in Psychology." Dewey criticizes contemporary thought about the reflex arc because it did not account for change. In its simplest form, the reflex arc describes the way a sensory stimulus evokes a neurological response, such as the movement to pull the hand away from a flame. But Dewey argues that this classic stimulus-response model represents only a portion of the entire process and that to use it to signify the whole of human behavior is terribly misleading. According to Dewey, nothing can on its own act as a stimulus—it takes an act of the mind to edit and choose from among the variety of available sensory input. The completed response itself is then incorporated back into the stimulus, and perception is thereby changed. By definition perception is oriented toward future behavior. Instead of the image of an active world working on a relatively passive human physiological system, Dewey offers a classic pragmatist statement in which both response *and* stimulus reflect an orientation toward the world. And the response is itself integrated into the action that attends to stimulation.

By exchanging the image of the arc for that of a completed circuit, Dewey asserts the future orientation characteristic of a pragmatist psychology. The analogous philosophical formulation had been furnished in 1877 by Charles S. Peirce's "The Fixation of Belief." Peirce, defining belief as that on which we are willing to act, rejects Cartesian doubt as the origin of philosophy. Instead Peirce asserts that doubt and belief necessarily involve action in the world: "Belief does not make us act at once, but puts us into such a condition that we shall behave in a certain way, when the occasion arises. Doubt has not the least effect of this sort, but stimulates us to action until it is destroyed."[19] Peirce rejects deductive reasoning and authority as foundations for belief: the proper test of belief resides in interaction with the world. Doubt ceases when action proves the validity of belief, and belief is sustained so long as it provides a reliable predisposition to future action.

Like Dewey's reflex arc and Peirce's belief, habit has a proleptic orientation. But James's idea of habit limits the operation of choice and free will. This is evident in the fact that habit can persist beyond its value as a useful behavior. Because habits are so difficult to change, James asserts, habit provides the basis for behavioral continuity:

> Habit is thus the enormous fly-wheel of society, its most precious conservative agent. It alone is what keeps us all within the bounds of ordinance, and saves the children of fortune from the envious uprisings of the poor. It alone prevents the hardest and most repulsive walks of life from being deserted by those brought up to tread therein. . . . It dooms us all to fight out the battle of life upon the lines of our nurture or our early choice, and to make the best of a pursuit that disagrees, because there is no other for which we are fitted, and it is too late to begin again. [125]

The reason habit maintains its behaviorally conservative function is that we do not alter our habitual behavior, even when problematic, because we cannot perceive alternatives. Only when we can believe—in Peirce's sense—that an alternative exists can we act on it.

In habit James locates a basis for the comprehension and classification of human behavior. With his claim that "the laws of Nature are nothing but the immutable habits which the different elementary sorts of matter follow in their actions and reactions upon each other" (109), James universalizes habit. The physical and physiological analogies ground James's later, more

philosophically and moralistically inclined statements. This strategy, following the general tendency of the environmental determinism associated with
evolutionary thought, seemingly denigrates the function and place of free
will in human activity. James even eliminates the will as a possible origin for
most habitual activities when he claims that "though many, perhaps most,
human habits were once voluntary actions, no action, as we shall see in a
later chapter, can be *primarily* such. While an habitual action may once have
been voluntary, the voluntary action must before that, at least once, have
been impulsive or reflex" (113). When James's early tribute to the exercise
of will in the development of habit is considered in light of the chapter as a
whole, the compensatory nature of his emphasis on the will becomes apparent: the importance of the will is inverse to its relative influence.

By restricting the operation of the will in accord with habit, James
diminishes the philosophical foundation for the self. To Common Sense
philosophers, the will was a vital human attribute because of its moral
function. While not acceding to the Spencerian view, according to which
human thought is epiphenomenal, James nevertheless renders this traditional basis of human selfhood and individuality problematic with his
formulation of habit. And if, as Peirce suggests, doubt is the only possible
basis for a reevaluation of belief, and doubt arises only when belief, habitual behavior, is shown to be deficient in its ability to provide suitable results, then the conservative nature of habit is confirmed. Without doubt no
alternative behavior is conceivable. The will, severely constrained by the in-
ertia of habitual action, is further restricted by the lack of awareness of the
very possibility of change.

This conservatism engendered by habit works at both the personal
and social levels. As Freud and later psychoanalytic thinkers have shown,
personal history profoundly shapes one's perceptions of reality. By recre-
ating behavioral matrices, the conflicted individual relives unresolved problems with family members long after these individuals are absent. The
social effects of habitual behavior are, perhaps, even more striking. James
declared that habit is the basis of social stability. People inevitably respond
to symbolic constructs that may have very little, if anything at all, to do
with their current living situations. An example is the recreation of au-
thoritarian relationships in society. Naturalized by the patriarchal family
structure, hierarchical social divisions appear more than simply the norm;
they seem comfortable in their stability and seductive in the implied promise of care associated with parent-child relations. James shows his keen
awareness of this function when he asserts that habit is the "most precious
conservative agent."

The conservatism of habit and the interplay between the individual
and the social environment shape James's discussion of the self. In a

lengthy chapter that confronts the orthodox foundation of moral philosophy, the self, James explores the conventional theoretical bases of selfhood
while he attempts to articulate an object for disciplinary inquiry. The first
half of "The Consciousness of Self" is worthy of sustained attention, not
merely because of its conclusions about selfhood but because the analytic
and discursive method is characteristic of *The Principles of Psychology* as
a whole.[20]

The chapter opens with a deceptively clear statement of intent and
design: "Let us begin with the Self in its widest acceptation, and follow it
up to its most delicate and subtle form, advancing from the study of the
empirical, as the Germans call it, to that of the pure, Ego" (279). James
outlines the investigation as three aspects of the self, its "constituents,"
"feelings and emotions," and "the actions to which they prompt" (280).
This tripartite division recapitulates the orderly division of Common Sense
psychology into sensory and intellectual functions, emotions, and the will.
James promptly subdivides the first category into different aspects of the
"constituents" of the self: the material, the social, the spiritual, and the
pure ego. By recalling the philosophical approach to the self, with its scho-
lastic categorizations, he ostensibly advocates an essentialist model of
selfhood. James, however, uses this traditional format to show the shortcomings of the old philosophical approach. Instead of a self derived from a
recondite essence, the self in James's hands becomes manifest through a
process of differentiation from externals.

James's discussion of the spiritual self exemplifies the method by
which he reveals the inconsistencies that lurk in traditional notions. He defines the spiritual self as "a man's inner or subjective being, his psychic
faculties or dispositions, taken concretely" (283). To consider this entity,
more abstract than the material and social selves, James introspects. But
introspection opens the door to numerous potential problems, for if
thought is to ground the spiritual self, only a portion of it may provide the
basis for selfhood. Although we have an abundance of thoughts, James
notes that we identify only a few as peculiarly characteristic of ourselves.
These thoughts are "felt by all men as a sort of innermost centre within the
circle, of sanctuary within the citadel, constituted by the subjective life as a
whole. Compared with this element of the stream [of thought], the other
parts, even of the subjective life, seem transient external possessions, of
which each in turn can be disowned, whilst that which disowns them remains. Now, *what is this self of all the other selves?*" (285). Having posed
this question about the essence of identity, couched in terms of possession,
James moves further into the introspective realm and begins to cite his own
experience. This self-exploration yields the disquieting confession that "*it
is difficult for me to detect in the* [introspective] *activity any purely spirit-*

ual element at all. . . . all [I] *can ever feel distinctly is some bodily process, for the most part taking place within the head"* (287). After assuming the role of an explorer in the most highly refined mental regions, James returns to report that in this purportedly spiritual realm he finds only assorted physical sensations. He concludes his introspection with the comment that "our entire feeling of spiritual activity, or what commonly passes by that name, is really a feeling of bodily activities whose exact nature is by most men overlooked" (288). In his identification of the spiritual essence as subtle physical activity, James refutes the notion of a metaphysical origin for the so-called spiritual self.

By recalling the structures and categories of moral philosophers only to refute them, James duplicates in "The Consciousness of Self" the larger organizational strategy of *The Principles*. In a particularly ironic move, James uses an introspective method to dispute the usefulness of traditional categories. But introspection, with its implied invitation to the reader to affirm the results of his scientific study, also serves a powerful rhetorical role. In a gesture reminiscent of his early invitation to the reader to dissect a sheep's head, James invites the reader to participate in his learned disputation with the authorities. His refutation of Common Sense relies on the strategy and method of Common Sense philosophy. Consequently, his initial structure, derived from mentalist psychology categories, breaks down, and James, without comment, abandons his neatly organized discussion.

In his treatment of the ego, James begins to define his alternative conception of selfhood. He establishes the terms of his investigation by asking whether "this consciousness of personal sameness may be treated either as a subjective phenomenon or as an objective deliverance, as a feeling, or as a truth" (314). In keeping with the empirical nature of his study and his skepticism toward received wisdom, James focuses on the feeling of continuity with earlier states of consciousness. He argues that the transcendental ego derives from our feelings of "warmth and intimacy" with recollected earlier states of consciousness (316). From this physical origin James concludes, much as David Hume did a century earlier, that the sense of continuous personal identity "must not be taken to mean more than these grounds warrant, or treated as a sort of metaphysical or absolute Unity" (318).[21] The core of identity is twofold: an identification with ideals of thought, attitude, or behavior; and a concomitant pleasure, based on familiarity, at the recollection of these mental states. The repetition of these thoughts and associated feelings, with its source in the function of habit, forms the essence of the self. And the transcendental ego, the necessary premise of philosophical psychology, is revealed to be an error of logic, a placement of final things first.

Although habit describes the operation of self-identity, James never-theless has questions about the object of self-love: "What is this abstract numerical principle of identity, this 'Number One' within me, for which, according to proverbial philosophy, I am supposed to keep so constant a 'lookout'?" (303). James answers his own question with his description of an ideal self, a self that is "the true, the intimate, the ultimate, the perma-nent Me" (301). Instead of originating in some hidden recess of the self, this "true" self is comprised of those socially derived beliefs and attitudes that one identifies as ideal and toward which one aspires. These beliefs and attitudes, which comprise the best part of one's self, become the object of one's self-love. Self-love is not "love for one's mere principle of conscious identity"; rather, it is love for ideals that originate outside the self, thoughts that are relatively "superficial, transient, liable to be taken up or dropped at will" (307). James thereby deduces the paradox of self-love when the core of selfhood consists of identification with externals.

The self, constituted by the physiology of habit and identification with ideals, is generated in the structure of consciousness James describes in "The Stream of Thought." Despite Thomas Reid's earlier use of the phrase "stream of thought" specifically to describe the association of ideas, James appropriates the term and successfully displaces the earlier definition.[22] To discuss the stream of thought, James invokes the introspective method of the moral philosophers, stating, "We now begin our study of the mind from within" (219). In his application of introspection, James demands empirical honesty, and he criticizes earlier introspective psychologies for their adher-ence to philosophical dogma and their lack of attention to the experience of thought: "Most books start with sensations, as the simplest mental facts, and proceed synthetically, constructing each higher stage from those below it. But this is abandoning the empirical method of investigation. No one ever had a simple sensation by itself. Consciousness, from our natal day, is of a teeming multiplicity of objects and relations, and what we call simple sen-sations are results of discriminative attention" (219). In much the same manner as Dewey would later insist, James contends that thought be under-stood as a unified process rather than as a compilation of simple com-ponents or associated ideas. His basic assertion that "*the first fact for us, then, as psychologists, is that thinking of some sort goes on*" (219) rejects evolutionist psychology because it implies that thought is epiphenome-nal. More significantly, James subordinates physiology in favor of an intro-spective methodology. After going to great lengths in earlier chapters to diminish its importance, James preserves a philosophical approach to psy-chology. At the same time, he rejects conventional notions of subjectivity; hence, he asserts that "*thought goes on*" (220), a statement explicitly void of a human grammatical subject.

James outlines five characteristics of thought: thought is personal, it is always changing, it appears continuous, it seems to deal with things external to itself, and it involves some choice in perception. In abandoning the old additive categorization of intellectual processes, James substitutes the principle of movement from the internal to the increasingly external. The traditional model, with its structural metaphor of a spatial hierarchy, discarded, James substitutes the metaphor of fluidity, earlier introduced in the chapter on habit. The fluid metaphor shapes the chapter title, "The Stream of Thought," and the conception of the thought process. No longer a logical point of origin, the individual becomes a channel of thought. The individual's permeable boundaries are suggested by the movement from the internal to the external in the categorization of thought components. The fluid nature of thought reflects the physiological recognition that sensation constantly modifies brain physiology: "Experience is remoulding us every moment, and our mental reaction on every given thing is really a resultant of our experience of the whole world up to that date" (228). James revises the Heraclitan formula to read that each time it is a different "I" who steps into the river.

The effect of the fluid metaphor appears in James's observation that, despite (or perhaps because of) the constant alterations in thought, thought appears to us as a continuous phenomenon. "Consciousness, then, does not appear to itself chopped up in bits. Such words as 'chain' or 'train' do not describe it fitly as it presents itself in the first instance. It is nothing jointed; it flows. A 'river' or a 'stream' are the metaphors by which it is most naturally described" (233). This continuous flow accounts for the sense of a coherent, continuous identity. The unity of thought only appears to be broken by observations of different objects. This distinction, between the process of thought and the objects of thought, is vital to James's psychology because it grounds his basic argument against association psychology, which he accuses of confusing the two.[23] The apparent continuity of thought is the result of signification. As Peirce explains in his response to the question of the existence of an intuitive self-consciousness, "Questions Concerning Certain Faculties Claimed for Man" (1868), each thought functions as a sign. Although cognition of external objects points toward the existence of an originary consciousness, this consciousness cannot be located in any pure form. The process of signification explains the final attribute of the stream of thought: selection.

The importance of selection as a function of consciousness appears in the observation that some things appear more interesting and worthy of attention than do others. But this process by which things become salient derives from a vision of the world as a place we construct based on our choices: "Out of all present sensations, we notice mainly such as are significant of absent ones; and out of all the absent associates which these suggest, we again pick out a very few to stand for the objective reality" (275). Consciousness synecdochically works to create a vision of the world; sensory input is edited, and signs are interpreted to habitually reconstruct the world in a familiar manner. In the case of conscious selection, in the realms of aesthetics and ethics, the power to evade an utterly deterministic philosophy rests on the capacity not simply to choose but to perceive the very possibility of choice. In these realms the tension between habit and will reaches its highest pitch.

The individual usually defines himself or herself on the basis of these choices, apparently derived from a unified consciousness. But, as James has shown, consciousness is not so much unified as it is a process of reference. Despite this referentiality, and the question of the ultimate source of consciousness, we must return to James's preliminary observation with respect to the stream of thought: "Every thought tends to be part of a personal consciousness" (220). Thought is inherently based in our corporeal structure, and no proximity or similarity with another can span the division between human minds. Whatever philosophical problems might be implied by an insistence on the integrity of the subject, from James's psychological viewpoint, the existence of a self has a biological basis.

In *The Principles of Psychology,* James recasts the contemporary conflict of mentalist and materialist psychologies and offers an alternative vision of the individual's relationship to the community. Without relying on the discredited mentalist model of selfhood, James retains the function of the self. He manages this by positing a performative model of selfhood: from one moment to the next the self is reconstituted by the apparently continuous phenomena of experience. In what amounts to a semiotic model of selfhood, James, after deconstructing the essentialist self in "The Self," calls the stream of thought the basis of selfhood.[24] The trope of fluidity informs James's descriptions of both neuronal physiology and the consciously experienced stream of thought. The self, always in flux, interacts with the world, and in these interactions it strives for an equalization of pressures, a resolution of tensions. This fluidity likewise shapes the dialectical, ironic structure of James's narrative. In *The Principles,* the oscillation from one position to another denotes the balance characteristic of fluid behavior. As each position becomes untenable, however, it is abandoned. The narrator does not lose his identity when he adopts contradictory positions; instead, the narrative flow back and forth indicates a normal mental function. And the reader, invited by the narrator to join in the search, participates in this enactment of selfhood.

But James's attempt to invite the reader through an appeal to introspection and experience introduces a potential difficulty. Historically, the introspective method of philosophers operated as a form of proof—the experience of the individual writer was validated through an appeal to consensus. And readers were similarly advised which aspects of their experiences were to be accorded philosophical legitimacy. The problem with this method was that it legitimized only one type of experience, that of the dominant social group. With its reliance on introspection, *The Principles* seems to revert to an essentialist vision of selfhood, and James's attempt to involve the reader apparently conflicts with the fluid, dialectical structure of his textbook. But if we regard James's use of introspection more as a technique of communication and less as a attempt to prove the truth, his psychology breaks from the dominant mentalist-materialist polarization of late-nineteenth-century psychology. With this break, James sets forth a socially oriented model of the self primarily derived from individual experience. This theoretical maneuver proves valuable because it does not seek to validate experience through the consensual evaluation of the dominant class or social group. Instead, without ordering them into the kind of social hierarchy associated with Spencerian psychology, it legitimates the variety of lived experiences, because membership in no one community is automatically accorded greater intrinsic worth. And the possibility of willed individual action, albeit limited by habit formation and conditioned by the social environment, remains intact.

6

Selfhood, Pragmatism, and Literary Studies

Who Do We Think We Are?
And What Do We Think We're Doing?

Poststructuralist and revisionist theorists of literature and culture have effectively challenged the concept of the self as a unified locus of intention. If the self may no longer be considered the center of intentionality in an older, more positivistic sense, then we are left to inquire whether it still has value in discussions of literary theory. Is it possible—and useful—to talk about the self as something other than artifact and artifice, as other than an antiquarian dream to be disrupted while the discipline progresses toward new knowledge? The first issue at hand, if such a possibility exists, would appear to be the need for some terms that do not immediately involve us in a pendulum swing between the grandiosity of imperial selfhood and the implied powerlessness of historical overdetermination. Such a terminology that avoids these polarities and accommodates the specificity of experience may be found in the work of pragmatists and symbolic interaction theorists.

A useful starting place for a discussion of selfhood in literary discourse is provided by William James's chapter on the self in his redaction of the much longer *Principles of Psychology*, the one-volume *Psychology: The Briefer Course*. James distinguishes between "the self as known, or the *me*," and "the self as knower, or the *I*."[1] The self as the object of inquiry—as opposed to the yet more elusive self that functions as a knowing subject (which James treats in his chapter on "The Stream of Thought")—that self which we investigate is of particular interest because of how it is constituted. Its constitution is especially complex because, as James comments, "a man has as many social selves as there are individuals who recognize him."[2] James thus implies that individual self-image involves a process by which one internalizes the perceived attitudes of others. This distinctly social account of selfhood serves as the starting point for George Herbert Mead, who further explores the communicative and interactive aspects of selfhood.

To Mead, like James, the self as an object of reflection begins with internalized attitudes. According to Mead, "The individual experiences himself as such, not directly, but only indirectly, from the particular standpoints of other individual members of the same social group, or from the

generalized standpoint of the social group as a whole to which he be-
longs."[3] Mead here proposes the image of a self that is, in effect, the site of
an ongoing discussion. He distinguishes his semiotic conception of selfhood from those that identify the self as a simple composite of corporeal
existence, stating, "It is obvious when one comes to consider it that the self
is not necessarily involved in the life of the organism, nor involved in what
we term our sensuous experience."[4] Instead, as the words "not necessarily" imply, the self has resources beyond bodily experience, social
resources that arise from the communicative structure of the self. Because
Mead's theory suggests that the self is the site of flux involving the internalized attitudes of others, it avoids the image of a self that revolves
around some static core or essence. Instead, the self continually undergoes
change in response to a variety of symbolic structures, and, moreover,
these symbolic structures themselves are continually reproduced, and peri-
odically transformed, through internalized dialogues. Mead's description
of mental operations as dialogue stresses the importance of language, but
his is not a language that awaits mastery by the exemplary individual. Language as a cultural medium also reflects specific situations in ways that
may be of greater consequence to the critic who examines the instabilities
and differences in language over time and between communities. The fact
that language is itself mutable and therefore demands interpretations by its
users forms the basis of symbolic interaction theory.

Symbolic interactionism, a theory derived from the work of Mead
and developed by Herbert Blumer, takes into account social forces without
insisting that these forces operate on individuals in a deterministic manner.
Blumer, arguing against behavioristic reductions, states that "human beings
interpret or 'define' each other's actions instead of merely reacting to each
other's actions. Their 'response' is not made directly to the actions of one
another but instead is based on the meaning which they attach to such actions. Thus, human interaction is mediated by the use of symbols, by
interpretation, or by ascertaining the meaning of one another's actions."[5]
According to Blumer, interaction is based on the interpretation of symbols,
and as a result any situation can generate multiple interpretations. These
interpretations—and misinterpretations—become part of how the self perceives the social and material environment.[6]

The contingent nature of selfhood, the tenacity of symbolic identifications, and the importance of interpretive processes are evident throughout nineteenth-century literature. Particularly dramatic examples of how
these things play out in response to one another may be found in *Uncle
Tom's Cabin*. The title character of Stowe's novel finds that defining himself in terms of a religious identity is vital to his sense of self, which then
furnishes the grounds for his choices of action. When it comes to resolving

the conflicting demands of membership in human and spiritual communities, Tom has to balance his very human wish for freedom from slavery against his spiritual commitment to being a Christian, an identity that at times conflicts with his desire for freedom. As Stowe repeatedly points out, Tom is consistently willing to sacrifice the possibility of freedom, and even his life, for his evangelical Christian ideals, and, accordingly, Tom finds himself in situations that display his idealism in increasingly dramatic fashion. The purest example of his evangelical motivation occurs after Augustine St. Clare promises Tom his freedom. Tom is naturally overjoyed at the prospect of freedom and a return to his family, but, to St. Clare's (and the twentieth-century reader's) astonishment, Tom chooses to stay in order to bring about his master's conversion. Tom's decision to remain St. Clare's slave most forcefully dramatizes his willingness to make sacrifices so as to be a member of the evangelical community.

From a symbolic interactionist perspective, such an imagined process of community membership can be complex and subtle. Because membership in social groups is symbolic, identification with a community is not necessarily based on shared or commensurate experiences. Individuals also may identify with either higher motives or abstracted communities of people not immediately present. William James calls this process of identification the "potential social me," a phrase that succinctly conveys the process of compensation for perceived inadequacies by identification with an ideal.[7] In *Uncle Tom's Cabin,* a desire for identification with the ideal shapes the climactic scene, in which Tom is beaten to death by two slaves who readily follow Legree's command. These slaves, exposed only to the power of the slave master, respect no force other than that which could enslave and brutalize, and under these circumstances, they cheerfully perform Legree's brutal work. But Legree's inability to coerce Tom into renouncing Christianity overwhelms the two slaves, who then inquire as to the source of Tom's strength. Exposed for the first time to Christian theology, the two immediately embrace the Christianity espoused by the dying Tom. Their sudden conversion experiences reflect a belief that conversion comes unexpectedly through the grace of God.

Their conversions also mark, from a symbolic interactionist perspective, the way attention can suddenly shift. Legree's failure to break Tom exposes a shortcoming in the slave master's power, and the two slaves, seeking to resolve the unprecedented cognitive crisis created by this failure, find that Tom's Christian beliefs achieve greater salience. The processes affecting cognitive shifts form the bases of John Dewey's "The Reflex Arc Concept in Psychology" as well as William James's chapters on "Attention" in both of his psychology texts, but C.S. Peirce offered what may well stand as the most influential philosophical consideration of the matter, in two essays, "The Fixation of Belief" and "How to Make Our Ideas Clear." In these essays, Peirce explores the questions that accompany a recognition of the fact that perceptions of the environment change when the individual recognizes shortcomings in cognition and interpretation. Peirce concludes that belief is that (and only that) on which we base action: "The essence of belief is the establishment of habit, and different beliefs are distinguished by the different modes of action to which they give rise."[8] Thus, Peirce dismisses speculative or metaphysical doubt as merely illogical thought about belief; only the recognition of ineffective behavior, as in the case of Tom's torturers, who see that their acts do not lead to the desired result, authentically predicates a crisis in belief. In *Uncle Tom's Cabin,* the answer to such cognitive and interpretive problems routinely is provided by Stowe's version of Christianity. The two formerly brutal slaves offer Tom their apologies and some physical comforts as their imaginations are captivated by the symbolic identification that sustains Tom. The novel remains fascinating in part because it dramatizes how it is possible to ally oneself with ideal categories, whether in religious or other terms. Sudden instances of conversion, of redefinitions of selfhood in accord with new allegiances, make for exciting (or implausible) action within stories. More to the point for a symbolic analyst, they serve to highlight the subtle ways that ideologies compel people to live their lives according to sets of beliefs that may do little to improve their physical well-being and may even promote self-destructive behaviors.

Uncle Tom's Cabin thus accentuates a couple of important features of selfhood. The first is that identity does not remain static. For example, it may change with the apparent abruptness of Sambo's and Quimbo's sudden conversions, or it may show a steady process of refinement toward an ideal state, as it does with Tom. In both cases, though, their senses of self repeatedly alter in response to the situations in which they find themselves. Another way of saying this is that selves may be understood as agglomerations of multiple social roles in addition to other, more distinctly symbolic identifications. The second significant feature of this model of selfhood is that there are moments when irreconcilable conflicts between social roles and other symbolic identifications become too apparent to be accommodated without some kind of transformation.

Interpretations of the ways in which identifications with social groups and belief systems shape conflicts in nineteenth-century literature require some understanding of social and intellectual history. Thus, to Stowe and those of her readers steeped in an evangelical Christianity, Tom's acts of self-sacrifice would serve as a model of ethical behavior. And, as I have argued earlier, from the perspective of antebellum Common Sense psychology, Hawthorne's solipsistic characters, such as young Goodman

Brown, Arthur Dimmesdale, and Roger Chillingworth, display unethical and potentially insane behaviors. In both sets of situations, selfhood and ethical issues are closely linked. The link between conceptions of selfhood and ethics is worth pursuing, particularly as it emerges in response to the question of the potential impact on literary and cultural studies of non-essentialist models of selfhood. To begin an exploration of this link, we first must turn our attention to questions about the work done by students of literature and culture.

Despite revisionist disturbances of so much received disciplinary wisdom, the definitions of the terms *theory* and *practice* have remained relatively inert. *Theory* and *practice*, in their common uses, have designated the work of the critic in specific and presumably complementary ways. As a rule, *theory* has come to denote the reading and writing of metacritical along with philosophically oriented, discourses. *Practice*, by contrast, has routinely signified the reading of texts usually understood to reflect a more traditionally literary character. Because *practice* normally refers to critical engagements with poetry and narrative, as well as other prose deemed to possess sufficiently literary merit to qualify it as literature, *theory* ends up referring to discourse about almost anything else that ultimately pertains to literary studies. What the terms *theory* and *practice* share in common is a description of the primary activities associated with each—reading, interpretation, and, at times, writing. *Theory* and *practice* then can be distinguished from each other not by an account of how the critic engaged in either activity actually passes time; rather, their objects of inquiry differ.

This distinction between the respective objects of inquiry associated with *theory* and *practice* is itself derived from disciplinary and generic categories. Thus, the difference between *theory* and *practice* rests on a foundation of genre definitions. Poststructuralist critiques of language and writing have rendered problematic any definitions, such as those of *theory* and *practice*, that ultimately rely on discriminations between the genres of literary and nonliterary languages and texts. In perhaps the classic poststructuralist disruption of such traditional discriminations, "White Mythology: Metaphor in the Text of Philosophy," Derrida states, "From philosophy, rhetoric," thus succinctly reversing the historical progression of pre-Socratic rhetoric to Greek philosophy.[9] From a Derridean perspective, the philosophical attempt to use language to transcend itself appears as an effective story, nothing more (nor less) authoritative. We may be in a better position to locate that which has been designated as *theory* if we transform Derrida's title and look for *philosophy* in the text of *literature*. The word *philosophy* here designates one necessary function of literary discourse: guidance toward certain types of interpretations of language structures.

This does not refer to the kind of specific methodological procedures used in textual explication. Rather, this kind of guide is that which usually creates academic interest in a text. To best illustrate this, we may return to *Uncle Tom's Cabin* and Jane Tompkins's well known essay about it.

In "Sentimental Power: *Uncle Tom's Cabin* and the Politics of Literary History," the point that ultimately had the greatest impact was Tompkins's contention that sentimental fiction fails as great literature only when it is interpreted by the apparently "universal standards of aesthetic judgment" associated with patriarchal academic criticism. Sensitivity to the way popular sentimental novels represents "a monumental effort to reorganize culture from a woman's point of view" is the mark of a good reader, one who grasps the importance of being attuned to the ways the most interesting literature makes particular interpretive demands of its readers.[10] The particular demand of *Uncle Tom's Cabin*—the philosophy in the text of this literature—is its insistence that readers interpret the words of the novel in a certain way and, most crucially, its insistence that readers interpret the world differently. What helped make Tompkins's argument so persuasive was that it asserted a theory of reading inhered *within* Stowe's novel. Generally speaking, the argument that a particular text elicits a particular type of interpretation has created the kind of interest among critics that may lead to the text's inclusion in the conversation of critics and, consequently, the literary canon.

If theory may be adduced from literary texts, and metaphor is the ground of philosophy, then the basis for a distinction between theory and practice must be found elsewhere. One way to reestablish such a distinction is to look at ends rather than origins. The practice of academics may be found not in some particular type of reading but rather in the work that fills so much of our days: teaching. The designations *reading* and *teaching* more effectively describe the critic's work than do troublesome and tortuous distinctions between different types of reading.

Although there has been a recent increase in attentiveness to pedagogy in English departments, it is important to note that an interest in pedagogy is hardly a new thing. Academics engaged in rhetoric and composition, unlike those who are predominantly occupied with literary studies, historically have been attuned to the importance of pedagogy. Pedagogy also has assumed importance in reader-response theories, many of which have provided insights that both derive from and readily translate into classroom practices. The link between composition and reader-response ideas goes beyond a simple attention to pedagogy. Theorists in both areas have responded to a common question: How may teachers come to terms with the experiences, attitudes, and needs of individual students? The disciplinary problems these theorists have encountered in their attempts to respond to individual experiences and needs substantially derive from certain entrenched notions of selfhood, in particular the unspoken formalist commitment to the ideal reader. One of the many reasons that formalist ideas about idealized, coherent selfhood have persisted is that formalist theory proposed an interpretive methodology that was readily and successfully translatable into classroom activity. As Gerald Graff explains it, close attention to the text appeared to obviate similar attentiveness to cultural tensions and histories: "The explicative method made it possible for literature to be taught efficiently to students who took for granted little history by professors who took for granted a little more history."[11] The display of textual explication through the classroom lecture has endured in large part because it effectively shows how formalist explication can translate emotional responses into an apparently standardized format. The vocabulary of aesthetics furnishes a guide, not especially dissimilar from that of nineteenth-century faculty psychology, as to which of the individual's affective responses are legitimate and which ones are not. Formalist explication also has endured because the alternative to the disciplinary guidelines it suggests appears to be the chaos of undisciplined, personal responses.

The foremost pragmatist theorist of the twentieth century, John Dewey, offered an alternative to formalist pedagogy that remains relevant and provocative. Dewey's postulate that education must be responsive to experience is counterpoised by the idea that the teacher's role is to create situations in which a "directed, cumulative, ordered reconstruction of experience" may take place.[12] An especially suitable subject matter for the "reconstruction of experience" among traditional, college-aged students is that of selfhood. This need not necessarily involve depictions of role models. Rather, the question of education, in its broader sense, and its relationship to constructions of selfhood may be explored in works that create conceptual difficulties at the same time as they reinforce certain late-twentieth-century ideals. Once again, the works of Harriet Beecher Stowe, a writer who was very attentive to the implications of education, are germane.

Stowe's attitudes toward education appear to have shifted somewhat between the publication of *Uncle Tom's Cabin* (1851) and that of the lesser-known *Pink and White Tyranny* (1871), and her ideas about education raise questions about selfhood. A significant constancy unites these two works, a tenacity of moral purpose that leads Joan Hedrick to label Stowe's writing a "ministry" comparable to those of her father and brothers.[13] Although Stowe routinely exhibited a concern about societal characteristics and policies, from her Protestant perspective individuals and their individual souls would have been the appropriate objects for religious and moral education—it is within each particular individual that the processes of conversion or regeneration would presumably occur. Stowe's particular bent as a moral educator has been described as distinctly middle-class.[14] But consistent as Stowe's commitments to middle-class values and the theological goal of education may have been, there was room for certain significant changes in emphasis, changes that display an altered understanding of selfhood.

In *Uncle Tom's Cabin,* the most important process an individual can undergo is that of conversion, and the conversion process itself is one that arises in an unexpected and mysterious manner. The conversions of Sambo and Quimbo during Tom's dying moments are typical of the novel: conversion suddenly erupts, here largely in response to the charismatic Tom. The idea that conversion comes abruptly also is borne out by the differing results enjoyed by Miss Ophelia and Eva during their attempts to evangelize Topsy. Miss Ophelia's rigid and judgmental character is described by Stowe as typical of New England, and her theology reflects "a severe and somewhat gloomy cast."[15] Her inability to respond successfully to Augustine St. Clare's challenge to inculcate Protestant dogma into the character of Topsy contrasts unfavorably with Eva's immediate success. Eva's success, according to the story, derives from her love for Topsy, and, somewhat analogously, Augustine St. Clare's own conversion at the moment of his death comes with the presence of Tom and the memory of his mother. The suddenness of conversion reveals Stowe's well-known Calvinistic tendencies, and it is also consistent with what Henry May identifies as "the tearful revivalistic vein which had . . . become increasingly dominant in American Christianity."[16] Stowe's ideal of religious education would maintain this emotional component, but only with respect to the need for the educator's love. The emotionalism of the sudden conversion in *Uncle Tom's Cabin* would later be displaced by an emphasis on gradualism and rational processes.

In *Pink and White Tyranny,* the source of religious change is the education process despised in *Uncle Tom's Cabin.* Education in the later novel unfolds in two arenas, the personal and the social. The story of personal education largely revolves around Lillie Ellis. The novel begins with her courtship and marriage to the virtuous and wealthy John Seymour, and the bulk of the action that ensues shows John's attempts to indulge this shallow young woman, whose depredations include reading French novels, lying about her age, and attempting to get her husband to serve wine with dinner. In contrast to Lillie, John's sister, Grace, "was one of those women formed under the kindly severe discipline of Puritan New England," a discipline that here leads to more fortunate results than it did with Miss Ophelia.[17] Consistent with her adherence to "high principle," Grace, after almost three hundred pages of forbearance, finally tells her distressed brother that he must treat Lillie as "a moral invalid," advice he quickly follows (315). Lillie's moral invalidism presages her rapid physical decline, and on her death-bed she gives evidence of John's effectiveness by voicing her moral awakening.

Education as a means of promoting individual conversion experiences also fortuitously meshes with Stowe's ideas about class and ethnicity. In *Pink and White Tyranny*, it is the function of the upper class to spiritually elevate the lower, thus assuring their salvation, their integration into Protestant America, and their acceptance of an American class hierarchy. One of Lillie's first shocks comes on learning that her new husband manages and teaches his workers at a Sunday school, an institution that became widespread after the Civil War. Lillie argues that John is exposing himself to disease, and, besides, his students are repulsive: "That working-class smell is a thing that can't be disguised" (79). John, however, insists that "they are the laborers from whose toils our wealth comes; and we owe them something" (79). John's attitude of noblesse oblige obviously reflects Stowe's interest in education, but Lillie's disgust with immigrant laborers and their culture also finds expression within the novel. For example, when pointing out John's consternation at discovering Lillie's lie about her age, Stowe expresses a typically nineteenth-century attitude about race and ethnicity: "The Anglo-Saxon race have, so to speak, a worship of truth; and they hate and abhor lying with an energy which leaves no power of tolerance." By contrast, "The Celtic races have a certain sympathy with deception. They have a certain appreciation of the value of lying as a fine art" (96). The Seymours' Irish domestics also lack a developed work ethic; without Grace's oversight, Bridget and the others "declined in virtue" (131). Virtue comes to the working people and is maintained through paternalistic oversight, Sunday school education, and the good examples of the thrifty Grace and the abstemious John.

The shift from *Uncle Tom's Cabin* to *Pink and White Tyranny* is clear: whereas in the earlier novel salvation comes not from the privileged but from the lowly—a slave and a female child—in the later work it is the function of the privileged to benevolently manage the lower class. In addition, the gradual effects of moral education are depicted as reliable in *Pink and White Tyranny*, departing from the precipitous emotional conversion experiences of *Uncle Tom's Cabin* associated with the presence of charismatic characters. The first of these two changes reinforces the idea that Stowe displayed a commitment to the nineteenth-century American class system; Stowe may have been a committed abolitionist, but there were limits to her fictional elevation of the lowly. The second suggests that, as Henry May has remarked about *Oldtown Folks*, Stowe's writings reveal the way she wrestled with her Calvinist heritage. In the case of *Pink and White Tyranny,* her religious thinking reflects a greater sense of the importance of environment, the typical post–Civil War reaction to Darwinist thinking that Howells's writings also displayed. If immigrants and the working class can be educated, Stowe appears to be arguing in *Pink and White Tyranny,* they will not disrupt the preindustrial New England society she had earlier celebrated in her nostalgic *Oldtown Folks.*

These changes in Stowe's depictions of fictional characters and their responses to education and religious experiences represent only one facet of selfhood in fiction. The persons of both author and reader may here arise in a discussion of the dynamics of selfhood in literature. In the case of Stowe, we may note how her work, particularly *Uncle Tom's Cabin,* is a profound critique of antebellum American society. At the same time, though, we can note how her work, especially the later novels, reflects typically nineteenth-century social thinking: a fear of lost social cohesion, a desire for class stability, and an implicit vision of an ethnic hierarchy. How we as readers react to the dissonance between Stowe's antipatriarchal ideal of abolitionism and her more conventional social ideals depends, at least in part, on our desire for writers who advocate social change and who are themselves suitable subjects for advocacy. The greater the desire to advocate the works of a neglected writer on moral grounds, the more problematic are the kinds of attitudes present in Stowe's later novel, attitudes that symptomatize cultural power rather than criticize it. The complexity of the situation may, however, encourage a flexible view of authorial selfhood, and it can promote a recognition of the unpredictable effects of writing on the reader, an awareness of the ways identity may be fissured and conflicted according to one's allegiances. The fact that these allegiances arise in response to the reader's historical situation encourages a critical return to the topic of selfhood and individualism in American culture.

John Dewey's return to the question of individualism is worth recalling, for it features a nuanced understanding of how individualism has been used in American culture while it maintains the position that a progressive individualism may prove an effective resource for social critics. In a collection of essays written during the late 1920s and early 1930s, *Individualism, Old and New,* Dewey notes the discrepancy between American rhetoric of individual opportunity and the facts of economic oppression for so many. Dewey observes that, in practice, individualism "has become the source and justification of inequalities and oppressions."[18] The possibility of social reform nevertheless exists: "A stable recovery of individualism waits upon the elimination of the older economic and political individualism, an elimination which will liberate imagination and endeavor for the task of making corporate society contribute to the free culture of its members. Only by economic revision can the sound element in the older individualism—equality of opportunity—be made a reality."[19] Dewey's observations on American uses of individualism are instructive because, even though he is well aware of the way individualism has been used to justify corporate practices, he feels that it provides a resource useful to democratic practices. And the place for the development of this resource is the school.

From Dewey's perspective, the school can serve as a proving ground to test theories and to create the conditions for social progress and democracy. Dewey is quite straightforward about this second point. A typical comment from an 1897 essay, "My Pedagogic Creed," presents the view that his writings in successive decades would apply and amplify: "Education is the fundamental method of social progress and reform."[20] Dewey's writings on the subjects of democracy, social progress, and education consistently present the idea that schools can help socialize students to participate in a democratic society. Richard J. Bernstein observes that as far as Dewey is concerned democracy and education are essentially linked: "Democracy is a reflective faith in the capacity of all human beings for intelligent judgment, deliberation, and action *if the proper conditions are furnished*" (my emphasis).[21] These *proper conditions* will be approached as entrenched economic and social disparities are diminished.

Bernstein's cautionary remark about the limits of education is noteworthy because Dewey was well aware that education by itself could not transform society. As he stated in *Individualism, Old and New*, "Only by economic revision can the sound element in the older individualism—equality of opportunity—be made a reality." This comment is especially germane during a time when scholars increasingly are exploring the politically and socially transformative capacities of their work. Discussions of politics in the profession may be a welcome change from times of comparative quiescence. Yet intellectuals and social critics would do well to recall that, as Nancy Fraser observes, we occupy "specifiable locations in social space" and thus are not "free-floating individuals who are beyond ideology."[22] Fraser's contention is instructive as a reminder that teaching and related activities have social implications. At the same time, though, this suggests that, although teachers may engage in educational practices that comport with democratic ideas, we should be cautious when assessing the effects of our occasional sessions with our students.

Notes

1   Translating the Self

1. Charles Horton Cooley, *Human Nature and the Social Order* (1902; reprint, New York: Schocken Books, Inc., 1964), 188. His general outlook is well summed up in his phrase, "Self and society are twin-born" (idem, *Social Organization* [1909; reprint, New York: Schocken, 1962], 5).

2. The lengthy history of criticism that relates representations of selfhood to questions of freedom will be treated later in this chapter, yet it is worth noting that numerous critics have found in American individualism a cultural problem. Most notoriously, the typical American protagonist was described as immature and on the run from social responsibilities in Leslie Fiedler, *Love and Death in the American Novel* (New York: Criterion, 1960). Quentin Anderson's *The Imperial Self: An Essay in American Literary and Cultural History* (New York: Knopf, 1971) treats the "extrasocial commitment" of Emerson, Whitman, and Henry James as an evasion of pressing social issues. Sacvan Bercovitch, in *The Puritan Origins of the American Self* (New Haven: Yale Univ. Press, 1975), is critical of the effects of individualism and interprets it as a secularized form of socialization based in Puritan theology. D.H. Lawrence furnished the most acerbic observation on the rhetoric of freedom: "The most unfree souls go west, and shout of freedom" (D.H. Lawrence, *Studies in Classic American Literature* [New York: Thomas Seltzer, 1923], xx).

3. William James, *The Principles of Psychology* (1890; reprint, Cambridge: Harvard Univ. Press, 1983), 277.

4. Ibid., 233.

5. Ralph Waldo Emerson, *Essays and Lectures,* ed. Joel Porte (New York: Library of America, 1983), 10; hereafter cited in text.

6. The question of the extent of Stowe's radicalism is treated in Myra Jehlen, "The Family Militant: Domesticity versus Slavery in *Uncle Tom's Cabin,*" *Criticism: A Quarterly for Literature and the Arts* 31 (Fall 1989). Along related lines, Mark Seltzer has raised questions about the New Historicist tendency "to replace an identification of women with the natural with an identification of women with the social" (Mark Seltzer, "The Still Life," *American Literary History* 3 [1991]: 462). For a more general discussion of nineteenth-century domestic fiction and the tension between its oppositional stances as contrasted with its textual inscriptions of social authority, see Richard Brodhead, *Cultures of Letters: Scenes of Reading and Writing in Nineteenth-Century America* (Chicago: Univ. of Chicago Press, 1993), chapter 1. A fuller consideration of how this tension manifests itself in Stowe's fiction will be offered in chapter 6 of this study.

7. J. Hector St. John de Crèvecoeur, *Letters from an American Farmer and Sketches of Eighteenth-Century America,* ed. Albert E. Stone (New York: Penguin, 1986), 201.

8. Ibid., 201.

9. Native Americans figure ambivalently in *Letters.* Crèvecoeur excepts them from this profligate tendency—he observes that they "are respectable, compared with this European medley" of settlers in the wilderness, but his acceptance seems qualified (ibid., 77).

10. Alexander Hamilton, James Madison, and John Jay, *The Federalist Papers* (New York: Mentor, 1961), no. 10, 77.

11. Martha Banta, "Introduction," in *The House of Mirth,* by Edith Wharton (New York: Oxford Univ. Press, 1994), vii.

12. W.E.B. Du Bois, *The Souls of Black Folk* (New York: Bantam, 1989), 3.

13. Bruce D. Dickson Jr. notes the relationship between the most well known idea of this chapter, first published as an essay in 1897, and Emerson's "The Transcendentalist"; see Bruce D. Dickson, Jr., "W.E.B. Du Bois and the Idea of Double Consciousness," *American Literature* 64 (1992): 299-309.

14. Henry Adams, *The Education of Henry Adams* (Boston: Houghton Mifflin, 1973), 457.

15. Ibid., 498.

16. Ibid., 9.

17. Ralph Waldo Emerson, *Society and Solitude,* new and rev. ed., vol. 7 of *Complete Works* (Boston: Houghton Mifflin, 1887), 20.

18. The twentieth-century reception of Scottish Common Sense philosophy and its effects on literary criticism will be discussed in chapter 2. Association psychology, which reiterated rather than resolved the tensions inherent in Common Sense psychology, will be treated in chapter 3. For general accounts of American psychology before 1900, see William R. Woodward and Mitchell G. Ash, eds., *The Problematic Science: Psychology in Nineteenth-Century American Thought* (New York: Praeger, 1982); Gardner Murphy, *Historical Introduction to Modern Psychology,* rev. ed. (New York: Harcourt, Brace, 1949); and Jay Wharton Fay, *American Psychology before William James* (New Brunswick, N.J.: Rutgers Univ. Press, 1939).

19. William J. Scheick observes that "Emerson's antinomian stress on feeling always was balanced, in his artistry as well as his thought, by a unitarian emphasis on order"; see William J. Scheick, *The Slender Human Word: Emerson's Artistry in Prose* (Knoxville: Univ. of Tennessee Press, 1978), 23. On the dialogical structure of Emerson's "polarized self," see Evan Carton, *The Rhetoric of American Romance: Dialectic and Identity in Emerson, Dickinson, Poe, and Hawthorne* (Baltimore: Johns Hopkins Univ. Press, 1985), 25-46.

Distinguishing between Emerson's conception of the hero and that of British Romantics, Sacvan Bercovitch observes that American selfhood is "a mode of personal identity intended to embrace both the individual and society, without allowing either for Romantic-antinomian hero-worship or for the claims of social pluralism"; see Sacvan Bercovitch, "Emerson the Prophet: Romanticism, Puritanism, and Auto-American-Biography," in *Emerson: Prophecy, Metamorphosis, and Influence,* ed. David Levin (New York: Columbia Univ. Press, 1975), 20-21. Bercovitch emphasizes the continuity between Emersonian thought and American Puritanism, describing Transcendentalism as the secular development of certain Puritan presentations of the self. The Puritan tension between the individual (who must interpret sacred writings) and the community (which validates interpretation) interestingly corresponds to the Common Sense psychology of Emerson's time, in which individual perceptions were to be validated consensually. More recently, David M. Robinson describes the trajectory of Emerson's career in terms of "a growing valorization of the social aspects of experience," a trajectory that suggests Emerson is "best regarded as a moral or ethical philosopher"; see David M. Robinson, *Emerson and the Conduct of Life: Pragmatism and Ethical Purpose in the Later Work* (New York: Cambridge Univ. Press, 1993), 6. Maurice Gonnaud's *An Uneasy Solitude: Individual and Society in the Work of Ralph Waldo Emerson* (trans. Lawrence Rosenwald [Princeton, N.J.: Princeton Univ. Press, 1987]) uses Emerson's journal entries to dispute the characterization by Stephen Whicher and others that Emerson's late work was utterly derivative of his earlier writings and thus unworthy of sustained critical interest; see especially chapter 13, "A Surrogate Optimism."

20. Although historians debate about precisely when the shift from a communally oriented society to an individualistic one characteristic of a market economy took place, the rhetoric of benevolence was not substantially displaced in the political realm by that of individualism until after the 1820s. William Appleman Williams argues that the transition to a decisively individualistic laissez-faire economics began in the 1820s primarily as a result of increasing conflict between the established upper class and upwardly mobile entrepreneurs; see William Appleman Williams, *The Contours of American History,* (Cleveland: World, 1961), 225-35. Lawrence Frederick Kohl similarly asserts that "the central concern of the Jacksonian generation was the transition from a society based on tradition to a society based on an ethic of individualism" (Lawrence Frederick Kohl, *The Politics of Individualism: Parties and the American Character in the Jacksonian Era* [New York: Oxford Univ. Press, 1989], 6).

21. Abraham Lincoln, "The Perpetuation of Our Political Institutions: Address before the Young Men's Lyceum of Springfield, Illinois," in *Abraham Lincoln: His Speeches and Writings*, ed. Roy P. Basler (Cleveland: World, 1946), 77.

22. R.W.B. Lewis, *The American Adam: Innocence, Tragedy, and Tradition in the Nineteenth Century* (Chicago: Univ. of Chicago Press, 1955), 91.

23. For critical treatments of these interests, see Lora Romero, "Vanishing Americans: Gender, Empire, and New Historicism," *American Literature* 63 (1991): 385-404; Nina Baym "How Men and Women Write Indian Stories," in *Recent Essays on* The Last of the Mohicans, ed. H. Daniel Peck (New York: Cambridge Univ. Press, 1992); and Jane Tompkins, *Sensational Designs: The Cultural Work of American Fiction, 1790-1860* (New York: Oxford Univ. Press, 1985), 94-121.

24. James Fenimore Cooper, *The Last of the Mohicans: A Narrative of 1757,* in *The Leatherstocking Tales*, vol. 1 (New York: Library of America, 1985), 469; hereafter cited in text.

25. "About half [of critics evaluating Cooper] have decided that despite superficial allegiances to republican democracy, Cooper was at heart an American aristocrat; half, that his inconsistencies can be described by regarding him as an orthodox Jacksonian democrat" (Stephen Railton, *Fenimore Cooper: A Study of His Life and Imagination* [Princeton: Princeton Univ. Press, 1978], 10).

26. Paul Boyer, *Urban Masses and Moral Order in America, 1820-1920* (Cambridge: Harvard Univ. Press, 1990), 7.

27. Ralph Waldo Emerson, *Journals and Miscellaneous Notebooks*, vol. 4, ed. William H. Gilman et al (Cambridge: Harvard Univ. Press, 1962), 335.

28. Louise K. Barnett illuminates the question of language use in her discussion of the last Leatherstocking tale, *The Deerslayer*, a work that features much talk. The continuity of Cooper's attitudes and concerns is apparent, for speech serves in the later novel as "an index of the speaker's morality" (Louise K. Barnett, *Authority and Speech: Language, Society, and Self in the American Novel* [Athens: Univ. of Georgia Press, 1993], 36). Cooper also asserts here that the operation of political rhetoric transcends cultural boundaries: "Next to arms, eloquence offers the great avenue to popular favor, whether it be in civilized or savage life" (James Fenimore Cooper, *The Deerslayer; or, The First War-Path* [Albany: State Univ. of New York Press, 1987], 489).

29. Self-restraint also differentiates Magua from his peers. While the others were "gorging" themselves, "Magua alone sat apart . . . apparently buried in the deepest thought" (584). The self-control that makes it possible for him to manipulate others has its limits. When describing the source of his animus toward Munro, he blames the whipping he received at Munro's orders, a whipping that was not only disgraceful to the warrior but also offended his sense of fairness: "Is it justice to make evil [i.e., distribute liquor], and then punish for it! Magua was not himself; it was the fire-water that spoke and acted for him!" (588). Cooper here presents Magua as failing to master his passions, a failure reinforced by his obsession with Cora.

30. Fiedler, *Love and Death*, 187. The question of sociality leads Charles Hansford Adams to observe that Cooper's "sense of full identity as the integration of the individual with his social and historical role in the world . . . demands throughout his career efforts to consolidate public and private identity" (Charles Hansford Adams, *"The Guardian of the Law": Authority and Identity in James Fenimore Cooper* [University Park: Pennsylvania State Univ. Press, 1990]), 80.

31. Henry Nash Smith, *Virgin Land: The American West as Symbol and Myth* (Cambridge: Harvard Univ. Press, 1950), 60.

32. See I.A. Richards, *Poetries and Sciences* (New York: Norton, 1970), chapter 6, "Poetry and Beliefs," 57-66; E.D. Hirsch, Jr., *Cultural Literacy: What Every American Needs To Know* (Boston: Houghton Mifflin, 1987).

33. The hiring statistics for the 1991-92 school year, consistent with those of earlier years, reflected this tendency: the distribution of advertised positions for specialists in British and American literature were 17.8 and 10.1 percent, respectively. (Subsequent MLA studies have not distinguished between areas of specialization in this manner.) See "Number of Positions Advertised in MLA's *Job Information List* Continues to Decline," *MLA Newsletter* 24.2 (Summer 1992): 12-17.

34. For discussions of this history, see William E. Cain, *The Crisis in Criticism: Theory, Literature, and Reform in English Studies* (Baltimore: Johns Hopkins Univ. Press, 1984), chapter 5; also see Richard Ruland, *The Rediscovery of American Literature: Premises of Critical Taste, 1900-1940* (Cambridge: Harvard Univ. Press, 1967), chapter 1.

35. Van Wyck Brooks, "On Creating a Usable Past," *Dial* 64 (11 April 1918): 337.

36. Vernon Louis Parrington, *Main Currents in American Thought: An Interpretation of American Literature from the Beginnings to 1920* (New York: Harcourt, Brace, 1930), 1: vi.

37. Ibid., 1: 307, 180. While claiming individualism for his political perspective, Parrington noted its complex and difficult nature. For example, he acknowledged the contradiction between the British "self-seeking" and French "humanitarian" individualisms that informed American thought (ibid., 1: 272-73). For contextual background and responses to *Main Currents,* see Kermit Vanderbilt, *American Literature and the Academy: The Roots, Growth, and Maturity of a Profession* (Philadelphia: Univ. of Pennsylvania Press, 1986), 301-32; a more theoretical assessment of Parrington is available in Wesley Morris, *Toward a New Historicism* (Princeton: Princeton Univ. Press, 1972), 35-51.

38. Lionel Trilling, *The Liberal Imagination* (New York: Doubleday, 1950), 3.

39. Georg Lukács, *The Theory of the Novel,* trans. Anna Bostock (Cambridge: MIT Press, 1971), 66.

40. Ibid., 32.

41. On these and other characteristics of modernist thought, see Michael H. Levenson, *A Genealogy of Modernism: A Study of English Literary Doctrine, 1908-1922* (New York: Cambridge Univ. Press, 1984); and Sanford Schwartz, *The Matrix of Modernism: Pound, Eliot, and Early Twentieth-Century Thought* (Princeton: Princeton Univ. Press, 1985).

42. Kenneth Burke, *Counter-Statement,* 2d ed. (1953; reprint, Berkeley: Univ. of California Press, 1968), 68.

43. Ibid., 111.

44. Parrington, *Main Currents,* 2: 445.

45. F.O. Matthiessen, *American Renaissance: Art and Expression in the Age of Emerson and Whitman* (New York: Oxford Univ. Press, 1941), xv; hereafter cited in text.

46. Myra Jehlen, "Introduction," in *Ideology and Classic American Literature,* ed. Sacvan Bercovitch and Myra Jehlen (New York: Cambridge Univ. Press, 1986), 2. Other significant theoretical reassessments of Matthiessen's *American Renaissance* include William Cain, *F.O. Matthiessen and the Politics of Criticism* (Madison: Univ. of Wisconsin Press, 1988), 179-201; Jonathan Arac, "F.O. Matthiessen: Authorizing an American Renaissance," in *The American Renaissance Reconsidered,* ed. Walter Benn Michaels and Donald E. Pease (Baltimore: Johns Hopkins Univ. Press, 1984), 90-112; Donald Pease, *Visionary Compacts: American Renaissance Writers in Cultural Context* (Madison: Univ. of Wisconsin Press, 1987), 246-48; and Gary Lee Stonum, "Undoing American Literary History," *Diacritics* 11 (1981): 2-12. Matthiessen's project, as later critics agree, involved an attempt to reconcile the conflict between historicist scholars and New Critics; on this conflict, see Gerald Graff, *Professing Literature: An Institutional History* (Chicago: Univ. of Chicago Press, 1987), 136-44.

47. Pease, *Visionary Compacts,* 24. Richard Pells argues that insincerity was characteristic of American intellectuals after the Second World War, and he thereby accounts for their limited dissent, commenting, "Intellectuals were starting to enjoy the rewards of affluence and the perquisites of power" (Richard H. Pells, *The Liberal Mind in a Conservative Age: American Intellectuals in the 1940s and 1950s* [New York: Harper and Row, 1985], 120). Donald Pease, in the opening and closing chapters of *Visionary Compacts,* similarly argues that American critics during the Cold War were guilty of political cowardice or dishonesty. Although advanced more obliquely, a similar position is adopted in Russell Reising, *The Unusable Past: Theory and the Study of American Literature* (New York: Methuen, 1986), 37-47. While the argument that careerism was among the motivations of

post-World War II literary intellectuals is plausible, there is little evidence to suggest that their motivations and commitments to social change were radically different from those of most present-day scholars.

48. Eric J. Sundquist, *To Wake the Nations: Race in the Making of American Literature* (Cambridge: Harvard Univ. Press, 1994), 18.

49. Ibid., 18.

50. Ibid., 4.

51. Ibid., 538.

52. Ibid., 538.

53. Du Bois, *The Souls of Black Folk,* 189.

54. Ibid., 189.

55. Wai-Chee Dimock, "Feminism, New Historicism, and the Reader," *American Literature* 63 (1991): 601.

56. Ibid., 602.

57. Ibid., 612.

58. See, for example, Frank Lentricchia, *Ariel and the Police: Michel Foucault, William James, Wallace Stevens* (Madison: Univ. of Wisconsin Press, 1988), 70-75. Along these lines, Brook Thomas remarks, "Historicists who do attempt to replace unmasked ideologies with ideological positions of their own find themselves contradicting their own historicist premises, sometimes going as far as to reemploy teleological narratives, even if told from different points of view" (Brook Thomas, *The New Historicism and Other Old-Fashioned Topics* [Princeton: Princeton Univ. Press, 1991], xii.)

59. Gayatri Chakravorty Spivak, "Acting Bits/Identity Talk," *Critical Inquiry* 18.4 (Summer 1992): 774.

60. Ibid., 788.

61. Sacvan Bercovitch, *The Office of* The Scarlet Letter (Baltimore: Johns Hopkins Univ. Press, 1991), 22.

62. Ibid., xiii.

63. Cornel West, *The American Evasion of Philosopyy: A Genealogy of Pragmatism* (Madison: Univ. of Wisconsin Press, 1989), 7.

64. Emily Miller Budick, "Sacvan Bercovitch, Stanley Cavell, and the Romance Theory of American Fiction," *PMLA* 107 (Jan. 1992): 89. Also see idem, *Engendering Romance: Women Writers and the Hawthorne Tradition* (New Haven: Yale Univ. Press, 1994), 1-9.

65. Steven Mailloux, *Rhetorical Power* (Cornell Univ. Press, 1989), 133. Mailloux illustrates this movement, along with a consideration of its theoretical consequences throughout his discussion of "rhetorical hermeneutics" in *Rhetorical Power.* Two noteworthy instances of similar interpretive strategies may be found in Janet Gabler-Hover, *Truth in American Fiction: The Legacy of Rhetorical Idealism* (Athens: Univ. of Georgia Press, 1990) and Louise Barnett's *Authority and Speech.* By remaining receptive to the ideas of referentiality implicit in nineteenth-century rhetoric, Gabler-Hover opens her inquiry to the way major fictional works "invite rather than merely tolerate readings that offer closure and a distinctive moral/ethical program" (*Truth,* 3). By acknowledging this, in light of the poststructuralist critique of referentiality, her work pursues questions about the construction of the reading self, and it engages with questions of ethics. Similarly, Barnett looks to fictional speech as a site charged with the struggle between personal intentionality and ideological constraint, yet her investigation is one that does not insist on the inevitable priority of the one or the other. Barnett finds within this interplay, as does

Gabler-Hover, the potential for questions about the processes and cultural significations of reading.

2   Hawthorne's Drama of the Self

1. Henry James, "Hawthorne," in *Literary Criticism: Essays on Literature, American Writers, English Writers,* ed. Leon Edel and Mark Wilson (New York: Library of America, 1984), 426; hereafter cited in text.

2. Henry James, *The American Scene* (Bloomington: Indiana Univ. Press, 1968), 196.

3. The question of James's meaning in *The American Scene,* though not treated here, is a significant one. Leon Edel defends James against the possible charge of racism that initially had been raised by F.O. Matthiessen, noting that, despite the general tenor of his observations about Jewish and Italian immigrants, James was capable of explicitly recognizing their humanity. Of perhaps greater interest is James's lack of commentary in *The American Scene,* on Irish immigrants; see Leon Edel, "Introduction," in James, *Scene.* James limits himself to a very few remarks about the Irish, such as his observations about the threat to Boston of "the Irish yoke" and his associating himself, albeit ironically, with the departed "Boston of history, the Boston of Emerson, Thoreau, Hawthorne" (*Scene,* 245).

4. As Habermas notes when discussing the mutual reliance of the private and public realms, "next to political science, psychology arose as a specifically bourgeois science during the eighteenth century" (Jürgen Habermas, *The Structural Transformation of the Public Sphere: An Inquiry into a Category of Bourgeois Society,* trans. Thomas Burger and Frederick Lawrence [Cambridge: MIT Press, 1989], 29).

5. As social historian Mary Blewett observes, "between 1810 and 1840 the economy of southern New England shifted rapidly from subsistence farming and the commercial maritime activities of seacoast towns to the development of a series of factory centers and mill villages" (Mary H. Blewett, *Men, Women, and Work: Class, Gender, and Protest in the New England Shoe Industry, 1780-1910* [Urbana: Univ. of Illinois Press, 1990], 21). For discussions of the new industrial morality and the ideological complexities and struggles associated with antebellum industrial development, see Alan Dawley and Paul Faler, "Workingclass Culture and Politics in the Industrial Revolution: Sources of Loyalism and Rebellion," in *American Workingclass Culture: Explorations in American Labor and Social History,* ed. Milton Cantor (Westport, Conn.: Greenwood, 1979), 61-75; also see Jonathan A. Glickstein, *Concepts of Free Labor in Antebellum America* (New Haven: Yale Univ. Press, 1991).

6. Charles Sellers, *The Market Revolution: Jacksonian America, 1815-1846* (New York: Oxford Univ. Press, 1991), 387.

7. Gary B. Kulik makes the point that the history of labor objections to capitalist development, "lost for so long, undercuts the Tocquevillian assumption, underlying most of American historiography, that industrial capitalism sank its roots into American soil quickly and without opposition" (Gary B. Kulik, "Patterns of Resistance to Industrial Capitalism, Pawtucket Village and the Strike of 1824," in *American Workingclass Culture,* ed. Cantor, 232).

8. Nathaniel Hawthorne, *The Snow-Image and Uncollected Tales,* vol. 11 of *The Centenary Edition of the Works of Nathaniel Hawthorne,* ed. William Char-

vat, Roy Harvey Pearce, and Claude M. Simpson (Columbus: Ohio State Univ. Press, 1974), 299; hereafter cited in text as *Snow-Image*. Cf. similar sentiments about Irish immigration in Nathaniel Hawthorne, *The American Notebooks,* vol. 8 of *Centenary Edition* (1972), 39-41, 63.

9. For his discussion of James's effect on the history of Hawthorne criticism, see Michael Colacurcio, "Introduction: The Spirit and the Sign," in *New Essays on The Scarlet Letter,* ed. Michael J. Colacurcio (New York: Cambridge Univ. Press, 1985), 1-28. This essay continues the attack on those who attend exclusively to the aesthetic elements of Hawthorne's writings, an argument developed in Michael Colacurcio, *The Province of Piety: Moral History in Hawthorne's Early Tales* (Cambridge: Harvard Univ. Press, 1984).

10. Fred G. See, using modern psychological terms, suggests the complexities of this process: "Hawthorne developed a thematics of desire which neither accepted nor repudiated the metaphysical dimension central to the writers of domestic sentiment, like Mrs. Stowe, whose works he famously condemned" (Fred G. See, *Desire and the Sign: Nineteenth-Century American Fiction* [Baton Rouge: Louisiana State Univ. Press, 1987], 7).

11. Arlin Turner, *Nathaniel Hawthorne: A Biography* (New York: Oxford Univ. Press, 1980), 36. Thomas C. Upham is not to be confused with Charles Wentworth Upham, well known to Hawthorne scholars for his involvement in Hawthorne's removal from the Salem customhouse in 1849. In addition to his familiarity with Upham, Hawthorne read works by Common Sense philosophers, such as Dugald Stewart, Thomas Brown, Francis Hutcheson, and Lord Kames; see Randall Stewart, *Nathaniel Hawthorne: A Biography* (New Haven: Yale Univ. Press, 1948), 17; also see Marion L. Kesserling, *Hawthorne's Reading, 1828-1850: A Transcription and Identification of Titles Recorded in the Charge-Books of the Salem Athenaeum* (New York: New York Public Library, 1949), 45-54.

12. Bercovitch, *Office*; Emily Miller Budick, "Hester's Skepticism, Hawthorne's Faith: or, What Does a Woman Doubt? Instituting the American Romance Tradition," *New Literary History* 22 (1991): 199-211.

13. Nathaniel Hawthorne, *The Letters, 1813-1843,* vol. 15 of *Centenary Edition* (1978), 494.

14. Edwin Haviland Miller, *Salem Is My Dwelling Place: A Life of Nathaniel Hawthorne* (Iowa City: Univ. of Iowa Press, 1991), 16. For alternative characterizations, see James R. Mellow, *Nathaniel Hawthorne in His Times* (Boston: Houghton Mifflin, 1980); and Gloria Erlich, *Family Themes and Hawthorne's Fiction: The Tenacious Web* (New Brunswick, N.J.: Rutgers Univ. Press, 1984).

15. Lauren Berlant, *The Anatomy of National Fantasy: Hawthorne, Utopia, and Everyday Life* (Chicago: Univ. of Chicago Press, 1991); T. Walter Herbert, *Dearest Beloved: The Hawthornes and the Making of the Middle-Class Family* (Berkeley: Univ. of California Press, 1993).

16. The most influential treatment of Common Sense realism and its effects on American literature, Terence Martin's *The Instructed Vision: Scottish Common Sense Philosophy and the Origins of American Fiction* (Bloomington: Indiana Univ. Press, 1961), established this assessment of Hawthorne's relationship to Common Sense thought. According to Martin, the philosophy of Common Sense offered an "extremely effective means of controlling the imagination," and as such it created problems for American writers by making "fiction more difficult to imagine as an independent, autonomous kind of expression" (vi-vii). His thesis posits an antagonistic relationship between writer and society, and it privileges a

Romantic individualism as the means by which American writers could best escape conformity and conservatism. In particular, Martin focuses on Hawthorne as one who sought an alternative to the conventional notion of "the imagination as a place of terror"; instead Martin proposes that the imaginative realm has the capacity to "desocialize experience" so as to allow one to approach reality "exempt from social prescription" (107-8; 143). See n. 35, below, on this characterization by twentieth-century critics of Hawthorne's purported iconoclasm.

17. Fay, *American Psychology*, 52. These texts were fixed by the "Report of the Yale Faculty in 1827"; after 1827, they were supplemented by American texts that tended to follow the Scottish models.

The conservatism of Scottish Common Sense realist philosophy and psychology has led most twentieth-century commentators to condemn its influence, particularly its Christian moralizing. The classic twentieth-century attitude is expressed by Herbert Schneider, *A History of American Philosophy* (New York: Columbia Univ. Press, 1946), 232-57. More balanced, revisionary assessments are offered by Elizabeth Flower and Murray G. Murphy, *A History of Philosophy in America* (New York: Capricorn, 1977), 1: 203-73; also see Daniel Walker Howe, *The Unitarian Conscience: Harvard Moral Philosophy, 1805-1861* (1970; reprint, Middletown, Conn.: Wesleyan Univ. Press, 1988), 27-40. On the pedagogical influences of Common Sense thinkers, see Lawrence Cremin, *American Education: The National Experience, 1783-1876* (New York: Harper and Row, 1980), 19-28; also see James Berlin, *Writing Instruction in Nineteenth-Century American Colleges* (Carbondale: Southern Illinois Univ. Press, 1984), 19-41.

18. The feminist reassessment of sentimental literature has begun to lead to a rethinking of the relationship between early sentimental novels, such as *The Coquette* and *Charlotte Temple*, and the prevalent Common Sense thought of the time, which was at its most enthusiastic, skeptical of the moral effects of popular fiction. This trajectory can be noted in Cathy Davidson's change from her earlier suggestion that *The Coquette* represents an attempt by its author Hannah Foster, to subvert patriarchal social forms (see Cathy Davidson, "Mothers and Daughters in the Fiction of the New Republic," in *The Lost Tradition: Mothers and Daughters in Literature,* ed. Cathy N. Davidson and E.M. Broner, [New York: Ungar, 1980], 115-27) to her later self-revision in which she states, "*The Coquette,* however, does not openly challenge the basic structure of patriarchal culture but, instead, exposes its fundamental injustices through the details and disasters of the plot" (Cathy Davidson, *Revolution and the Word: The Rise of the Novel in America* [New York: Oxford Univ. Press, 1986], 144).

19. G. Stanley Hall's well-known polemics against his precursors are best understood as responses to the philosophy of Princeton's James McCosh. Hall advocated basing philosophy on psychology—and psychology on physiology—like his German contemporaries. In its time, Hall's fervor was not inappropriate, given the fact that most texts were dominated by orthodox Christian beliefs. See G. Stanley Hall, "Philosophy in the United States," *Mind* (1880): 89-105.

20. Martin cites Reid's attack on the theory of association of ideas as problematic to writers of fiction since without the power of association imaginative work is secondary to reality. This was not the point Reid tried to make when, in his *Essays on the Intellectual Powers of Man,* he refuted Hume's skepticism of the possibility of knowledge based on the reasoning process; the fallibility of reasoning powers could not be avoided or corrected, according to Hume, since the only way to evaluate them was through a second chain of reason, itself subject to the same risk of

error. Reid saw the flaw in Hume's argument as a logical consequence of the Lockean idea that the mind does not know things by direct means and that consequently all the mind can know are ideas. Hume followed this idea to the logical conclusion that the reasoning process was a closed system that had no demonstrable link with material reality. Reid's retort was to argue for a system in which information about the world was available through the external senses. This argument is, of course, crucial to theoretical coherence—or its absence—in Common Sense thought. Reid's critique of association was, however, basically irrelevant to questions of imagination. And, later, Dugald Stewart and other Common Sense thinkers recognized this and had no problem with incorporating association of ideas into their philosophical and psychological scheme.

21. The distinctions between the disciplines of philosophy and psychology did not have the same force in the nineteenth century as they do today. Psychology as we know it developed in the latter half of the nineteenth century, a fusion of elements derived from moral philosophy, biology, and physics. In this discussion, *psychology* will generally be used to designate that field of philosophy which dealt specifically with descriptions of mental functions (i.e., exclusive of logic).

22. See Fay, *American Psychology*, 90-128. Upham's textbooks were still in print and for sale in 1886; his *Disordered Mental Action* "gained wide distribution as a cheap reprint in Harper's Family Library" (Marvin Laser, "'Head,' 'Heart,' and 'Will'" in Hawthorne's Psychology," *Nineteenth-Century Fiction* [1955]: 133). Wayland's book sold 130,000 copies by 1860. And Hickok's "was the textbook for many of the older generation of present-day [1930s] American psychologists" (Fay, *American Psychology*, 120).

23. Horatio Bridge, *Personal Recollections of Nathaniel Hawthorne* (New York: Harper Bros., 1893), 53; Nehemiah Cleaveland, *History of Bowdoin College* (Boston: J.R. Osgood, 1882), 132.

24. Upham practiced what he preached—in 1819, his *American Sketches*, a collection of poems based on American themes and locales, appeared. With respect to his more well known writings, Herbert Schneider remarks that Upham was "the first great American textbook writer in mental philosophy" (Schneider, *History*, 240). Unfortunately, Upham has been afforded relatively little consideration by Hawthorne scholars. Frederick Crews established the critical climate of the 1960s with his attack on those who argued the importance of Upham's psychology (Frederick Crews, *The Sins of the Fathers: Hawthorne's Psychological Themes* [New York: Oxford Univ. Press, 1966], 259-60). Martin dismisses Upham, saying his work essentially restates that of Reid and Stewart (Martin, *Vision*, 25). Discussions of Hawthorne's philosophical milieu elicit only passing mention of Upham in John E. Holsberry, "Hawthorne's 'The Haunted Mind': The Psychology of Dreams, Coleridge and Keats," *Texas Studies in Literature and Language* 21 (1979): 307-31; and John Franzosa, "Locke's Kinsman, William Molyneux: The Philosophical Context of Hawthorne's Early Tales," *ESQ* 29 (1983): 1-15. Attention to Upham's advocacy of free will and the possibility of moral improvement as an influence to dispute the claim that Hawthorne was a fatalist is offered by Claudia D. Johnson, *The Productive Tension of Hawthorne's Art* (University: Univ. of Alabama Press, 1981), and Joseph Schwartz, "A Note on Hawthorne's Fatalism," *Modern Language Notes* 70 (1955): 33-36. Rita K. Gollin (*Nathaniel Hawthorne and the Truth of Dreams* [Baton Rouge: Louisiana State Univ. Press, 1979], 19-30) offers the most balanced discussion of Hawthorne's relationship to Common Sense psychology, although she addresses the work of Dugald Stewart rather than Upham's

and is primarily concerned with questions of imagination; accordingly, she finds that Stewart's ideas about dreams influenced Hawthorne.

25. See Fay, *American Psychology*, 96; also see Schneider, *History*, 241. Earlier works on abnormal psychology that stressed proper treatment of psychiatric patients had been produced by Isaac Ray (*A Treatise on the Medical Jurisprudence of Insanity* [1834; rpt. Cambridge: Harvard Univ. Press, 1962]) and, more notably, by Benjamin Rush (*Medical Inquiries and Observations upon the Diseases of the Mind* [Philadelphia: Kimber and Richardson, 1812]). Although Rush was more original, in that he believed physiological problems to be the bases of mental disorders, Upham was the first to discuss psychiatric problems within the context of an overall psychological theory.

26. Upham's discussion of the will, not introduced as a separate category until 1834, was, for its time, an innovative feature.

27. Thomas C. Upham, *Abridgement of Mental Philosophy, including the Three Departments of the Intellect, Sensibilities, and Will: Designed as a Textbook for Academies and High Schools* (New York: Harper, 1886), 19; hereafter cited in text.

28. Dugald Stewart, *Elements of the Philosophy of the Human Mind*, vol. 2 of *The Collected Works*, ed. William Hamilton (Boston, 1884), 8.

29. The emphasis on classification might seem an archaism to those more familiar with literary expressions of psychological theory. This impression would quickly be dispelled upon examination of *The Diagnostic and Statistical Manual of Mental Disorders* (DSM-IV), the manual of the American Psychiatric Association, which gives all the names of officially recognized psychopathologies and assigns each a code number.

30. Thomas C. Upham, *Outlines of Imperfect and Disordered Mental Action* (New York: Arno, 1973), 257.

31. Ibid., 259.

32. Nathaniel Hawthorne, *The Scarlet Letter*, vol. 1 of *Centenary Edition* (1962), 36; hereafter cited in text.

33. One example of this occurs in Hawthorne's preface to *The Marble Faun*, in which the author seems to despair over the possibility of communicating with a sympathetic audience.

34. Parrington, *Main Currents*, 2: 447.

35. Hawthorne's artistic expression of psychological states has led critics to classify him as a Romantic. Some assessments of Hawthorne as a Romantic artist, such as those of Frederick Crews, Terence Martin, and Richard Harter Fogle ("Art's Illusion: Coleridgean Assumptions in Hawthorne's *Tales and Sketches*, in *Ruined Eden of the Present*, ed. G.R. Thompson [West Lafayette, Indiana: Purdue Univ. Press, 1981], 109-28), were understandable responses, developed during the 1950s and 1960s, to earlier depictions of Hawthorne as a latter-day Puritan. It is important to recall that Crews's argument—like Martin's—was a protest against the normalization of Hawthorne during the "Christian revival of the 1950s" (Crews, *Sins*, 5). Leslie Fiedler stated this revisionist position most explicitly when he objected to the then recent scholarship (including Randall Stewart's biography) that rejected the image of Hawthorne as reclusive, "putting in its place an active, practical, hard-working Hawthorne: a *bon bourgeois*, good husband and father, with a taste for athletics and backroom politics" (Fiedler, *Love and Death*, 486). The assessment to which Fiedler objected was itself in large part a response to Parrington's earlier charges against Hawthorne on the grounds of his purported

aestheticism and social isolation. Interestingly, even more historically oriented inquiries during this era reflected this revisionism; see Henry Nash Smith, *Democracy and the Novel* (New York: Oxford Univ. Press, 1978); and Leo Marx, *The
Machine in the Garden: Technology and the Pastoral Ideal in America* (New York:
Oxford Univ. Press, 1964).

A qualified assessment of Hawthorne as a Romantic nevertheless remained
prevalent through the 1970s and the early 1980s. For example, Nina Baym argued
for a vision of Hawthorne as Romantic artist who simultaneously embodied the
unromantic image of professional writer (Nina Baym, *The Shape of Hawthorne's
Career* [Ithaca, N.Y.: Cornell Univ. Press, 1976]); Claudia Johnson asserted that
Hawthorne "shared the dark vision of his Puritan ancestors" (Johnson, *Productive
Tension,* 4) while he simultaneously made use of Romantic aesthetics; and David
Pancost similarly argued that "Hawthorne's metaphysics, like his concept of artistic creation, is a mixture of a conservative philosophical tradition and a more
radical Romanticism" (David W. Pancost, "Hawthorne's Epistemology and On-
tology," *ESQ* 19 [1973]: 12). The radical Romanticism referred to by Pancost
may well be understood as an expression by Hawthorne of certain elements of
the Common Sense philosophy—such as interest in the imagination and introspection.

36. Nathaniel Hawthorne, *Twice-Told Tales,* vol. 9 of *Centenary Edition*
(1974), 121; hereafter cited in text as *Tales.*

37. James Mellow notes that in Hawthorne's fiction one repeatedly does
"encounter that mysterious father" in questions of uncertain paternity (Mellow,
Hawthorne in His Times, 14). But Hawthorne not only presents this problem in
his fiction; at times he resolves it with images of family reconciliation, such as the
final scaffold scene between Pearl and Dimmesdale in *The Scarlet Letter,* which
precedes little Pearl's vast inheritance from Chillingworth, her other, legal, father;
see discussion of *The Scarlet Letter* in chapter 3.

38. The "Haunted Mind" has inspired intermittent critical interest. Martin
regards it as representative of Hawthorne's rejection of Common Sense philosophy's supposed hostility to fiction (Martin, *Instructed Vision,* 145-48). A Jung-
ian approach to "The Haunted Mind" is employed in an attempt to universalize
the experience in Barton Levi St. Armand, "Hawthorne's 'The Haunted Mind': A
Subterranean Drama of the Self," *Criticism* 13 (1971): 1-25. Hyatt Waggoner's account, less dogmatic than the two mentioned above, treats the story as a model for
Hawthorne's idea of mental activity; see Hyatt H. Waggoner, *The Presence of
Hawthorne* (Baton Rouge: Louisiana State Univ. Press, 1979), 17. Norman Hostetler follows Martin's characterization of "The Haunted Mind" as an affirmation of
Romantic psychology (Norman H. Hostetler, "Imagination and Point of View in
'The Haunted Mind,'" *American Transcendental Quarterly* 39 [1978]: 266). For
a most thorough discussion of philosophical background, particularly Lockean influence and the importance of association psychology, see John E. Holsberry,
"Hawthorne's 'The Haunted Mind.'" It is worth recalling here that American academics had no special difficulty aligning their Common Sense allegiances with an
acceptance of Lockean empiricism; see Howe, *The Unitarian Conscience,* 36-40.

39. In essence, his argument was that the arbitrariness of association could
easily lead to solipsism. Instead, he posited a theory of natural signs by which there
would be continuous interaction between the individual mind and the world.

40. Nathaniel Hawthorne, *Mosses from an Old Manse,* vol. 10 of the *Centenary Edition* [1974], 268; hereafter cited in text as *Mosses.*

41. A flurry of interest was initiated by the mention of some of these as possible influences on Hawthorne in Daniel J. Barnes, "'Physical Fact' and Folklore: Hawthorne's 'Egotism; or the Bosom-Serpent,'" *American Literature* 43 (1971): 117-21. Sargent Bush, Jr., disagreed with earlier critics who focused on single definitive sources for "Egotism," arguing instead that there was a considerable body of bosom serpent lore; see Sargent Bush, Jr., "Bosom Serpents before Hawthorne: The Origins of a Symbol," *American Literature* 43 (1971): 181-99. Thomas Werge added poetic precursors, and Jackson Campbell Boswell insisted his list of classical precursors completed the discussion; see Jackson Campbell Boswell, "Bosom Serpents before Hawthorne: Origin of a Symbol," *English Language Notes* 12 (1975): 279-87, and Thomas Werge, "Thomas Shepard and Crèvecoeur: Two Uses of the Image of the Bosom Serpent before Hawthorne," *Nathaniel Hawthorne Journal* 4 (1974): 236-39.

A more psychologically oriented analysis is provided in Sharon Cameron, *The Corporeal Self: Allegories of the Body in Melville and Hawthorne* (Baltimore: Johns Hopkins Univ. Press, 1981), 102-3, which argues that the physical disorder does not represent a social condition but indicates a psychic fracture customarily repressed. Edgar Dryden (*Nathaniel Hawthorne: The Poetics of Enchantment* [Ithaca: Cornell Univ. Press, 1977], 25) acknowledges the social power of sympathy while also arguing that the basic problem is internal rather than interpersonal.

42. Hawthorne, *American Notebooks*, 22, 228.

43. Hawthorne, *Letters, 1813-1843*, 495.

44. Imagery of chains or linkage resonates throughout the body of Hawthorne's writings. For example, in *The Marble Faun*, Hawthorne describes how the crazed Donatello had thrown the model over the edge of the precipice and Miriam's subsequent expression of guilt: "We two slew yonder wretch. The deed knots us together for time and eternity, like the coil of a serpent" (Hawthorne, *The Marble Faun: Or, the Romance of Monte Beni*, vol. 4 of *Centenary Edition* [1968], 174). The narrator then expands on the consequences: "It was closer than a marriage-bond. So intimate, in those first moments, was the union, that it seemed as if their new sympathy annihilated all other ties, and that they were released from the chain of humanity." And, as a result of this release, "moral seclusion . . . had suddenly extended itself around them" (175). Similarly, in *The House of the Seven Gables*, the image Hawthorne uses to stand in for the principle that connects people in society, the "whole sympathetic chain of human nature," reflects an underlying ambivalence (Hawthorne, *The House of the Seven Gables*, vol. 2 of *Centenary Edition* [1974], 141). This image of linkage recalls a similar concept expressed in the sentimental novel *The Coquette*: "'Are we not all links in the great chain of society, some more, some less important; but each upheld by others, throughout the confederated whole?'" (Hannah Foster, *The Coquette* [New York: Oxford Univ. Press, 1986], 40). The image of the chain and linkage will be discussed further in the next chapter.

45. The critical discussion of "Wakefield" generally seems to focus on the psychology of the character. For example, Arnold Weinstein stresses an existential, psychologistic reading of the story when he claims that the absence of motive and interiority reflects Hawthorne's obsession "with the notion of his own insubstantiality, his ghostliness, his secret identity as Nobody" (Arnold Weinstein, *Nobody's Home: Speech, Self, and Place in American Fiction from Hawthorne to DeLillo* [New York: Oxford Univ. Press, 1993], 19).

46. Barnett, *Authority and Speech*, 1.

47. Ely Moore, "Labor Unions," in *Social Theories of Jacksonian Democracy: Representative Writings of the Period, 1825-1850,* ed. Joseph L. Blau (Indianapolis: Bobbs-Merrill, 1954), 290.

48. Ibid., 292.

49. Kesserling, *Hawthorne's Reading,* 53-61.

50. Norman S. Fiering, "Irresistible Compassion: An Aspect of Eighteenth-Century Sympathy and Humanitarianism," *Journal of the History of Ideas* 37 (April-June 1976): 195.

51. Adam Smith, *The Theory of Moral Sentiments,* ed. D.D. Raphael and A.L. Macfie (New York: Oxford Univ. Press, 1976), 38-40.

52. Francis Hutcheson, *An Inquiry into the Original of Our Ideas of Beauty and Virtue (1725)* (Hildesheim: Georg Olms, 1971), 250; 159. Hutcheson followed Shaftesbury in condemning self-love as inimical to benevolence. Others, such as David Hartley, argued that self-love and benevolence need not conflict. For a presentation of the range of views of this debate, see D.H. Monro, *A Guide to the British Moralists* (London: Fontana, 1972), 31-144.

53. Thomas Brown, *Lectures on the Philosophy of the Human Mind* (Andover: M. Newman, 1822), 3: 340.

54. The family in Hawthorne's work has been treated at length by Gloria Erlich and T. Walter Herbert. Their studies seem to have been motivated in part by the perception that psychological approaches to Hawthorne, no matter how potentially interesting, are necessarily incomplete and even ineffective when not historically grounded. Both Erlich and Herbert rely on family documents and attend primarily to Hawthorne's personal history; and they agree on the idea that Hawthorne needed to cultivate personal and artistic independence to become successful, though Herbert is more inclined to describe Hawthorne's writing as an exploration of "the entanglement of misery and beatitude that was native to the domestic ideal" (Herbert, *Dearest Beloved,* xvi).

55. This is the basic position in Michael Davitt Bell (*Hawthorne and the Historical Romance of New England* [Princeton: Princeton Univ. Press, 1971]) and Michael Colacurcio (*Province,* 283-313). Crucial background on Hawthorne's awareness of spectre evidence may be found in David Levin, "Shadows of Doubt: Spectre Evidence in 'Young Goodman Brown,'" *American Literature* 34 (1962): 346. A historical study that takes a different tack in its emphasis on the significance of revival meetings as "demonic aspects of Protestant zeal" during Hawthorne's time is Frank Shuffleton, "Nathaniel Hawthorne and the Revival Movement," *American Transcendental Quarterly* 44 (1979): 315.

56. To some extent, discussions that assert the integrity of Brown's dream against community values are attenuated versions of Crews's argument; Crews's Freudian understanding was that "Young Goodman Brown" served as "a psychological paradigm for other struggles" (Crews, *Sins,* 99), one more enactment of the Oedipal conflict. An exception to this critical tendency is Norman Hostetler's analysis of Brown's perceptual problems as a reflection of Lockean psychology, which notes that the ability of Hawthorne's characters to align sense perceptions with mental processes "frequently governs their ability to develop a sound moral relationship with other people" (Norman H. Hostetler, "Narrative Structure and Theme in 'Young Goodman Brown,'" *Journal of Narrative Technique* 12 [1982]: 221).

57. Colacurcio, *Province,* 285.

58. See, *Desire and the Sign,* 39-40.
59. Budick, "Sacvan Bercovitch, Stanley Cavell," 89.

3   "But the Past Was Not Dead"

1. Baym, *Shape,* chapter 1.
2. J. Hillis Miller, *Hawthorne and History: Defacing It* (Cambridge: Basil Blackwell, 1991), 82.
3. Recent historicist inquiries have moved beyond pure questions of source and ideology to treat more fully their relationships to Hawthorne's stylistic innovations. Sacvan Bercovitch treats stylistic uncertainty as a correlate of liberal dissent: "Ambiguity brings [the tendency toward fragmentation] under control, gives it purpose and direction, by ordering the facts into general polarities" (Bercovitch, *Office,* 26). Also, in her study of nineteenth-century rhetoric, Janet Gabler-Hover makes the case for a general acceptance of universal moral truths (consistent with Hawthorne's schooling in conventional rhetorical theory) as a counterbalance against Hawthorne's more famous ambiguities: "This faith in and reverence for the truth was an omnipresent theme throughout the nineteenth century, and, strangely enough, despite the increasing scientific skepticism as the century wore on about the epistemological status of such concepts as truth, the rhetorical conception of truth was sufficiently entrenched within the culture to ensure that truthful language retained its integrity for many Americans" (Gabler-Hover, *Truth,* 36).
In addition, Michael Colacurcio argues that Hawthorne's tales dealt with moral problems from an assumed Puritan point of view to be judged from a Romantic outlook in order to provide a mutual critique and an alternative to a positivistic epistemology; see Colacurcio, "Introduction: The Spirit and the Sign," 1-28. Other historicist studies that emphasize the historical bases of Hawthorne's fictions similarly controvert simple characterizations of Hawthorne as a proto-modernist or a Romantic; see Kenneth Dauber, *The Idea of Authorship in America: Democratic Poetics from Franklin to Melville* (Madison: Univ. of Wisconsin Press, 1990); Rita Gollin, "Hawthorne and the Anxiety of Aesthetic Response," *Centennial Review* 28 (1984): 94-104; and Gordon Hutner, *Secrets and Sympathy: Forms of Disclosure in Hawthorne's Novels* (Athens: Univ. of Georgia Press, 1988).
4. See, for example, John Carlos Rowe, *Through the Custom-House: Nineteenth-Century American Fiction and Modern Theory* (Baltimore: Johns Hopkins Univ. Press, 1982); and Michael Davitt Bell, "Arts of Deception: Hawthorne, 'Romance,' and *The Scarlet Letter,*" in *New Essays,* 29-56.
5. Larzer Ziff, *Literary Democracy: The Declaration of Cultural Independence in America* (New York: Viking, 1981), 118; Laura Laffrado, *Hawthorne's Literature for Children,* (Athens: Univ. of Georgia Press, 1992), 8.
6. Samuel Johnson, *Johnson on Shakespeare,* vol. 7 of *The Yale Edition of the Works of Samuel Johnson,* ed. Arthur Sherbo (New Haven: Yale Univ. Press, 1968), 84.
7. Ibid., 87, 80.
8. Ibid., 59-60.
9. William Charvat, *The Origins of American Critical Thought: 1810-1835* (Philadelphia: Univ. of Pennsylvania Press, 1936), 1. Charvat based his research on American and popular foreign literary magazines. M.F. Heiser observed that neoclassical aesthetics, much like Common Sense philosophy, "contained in its ad-

mission of 'rational individualism' the seeds of its own dissolution" (M.F. Heiser, "The Decline of Neoclassicism, 1801-1848," in *Transitions in American Literary History,* ed. Harry Hayden Clark [Durham, N.C.: Duke Univ. Press, 1953], 154). Accordingly, Charvat noted that the influence of Wordsworth and British Romanticism was gradual and acceptable to Americans because Wordsworth's philosophy relied so heavily on Scottish and English thought (Charvat, *Origins,* 70-76). Wordsworth's religious orientation, didacticism, and intelligibility made his idealism and belief in the edifying power of nature more palatable to American critics of the 1820s.

10. Charvat, *Origins,* 4.

11. Ibid., 7-23. Rush Welter observes a corresponding "conservative commitment to public schooling [that] was often essentially illiberal, a means of coming to terms with modern evils that was intended primarily to curb popular discussion" (Rush Welter, *The Mind of America, 1820-1860* [New York: Columbia Univ. Press, 1975], 284). The comparable argument that education served the purposes of "elite control" is made in Joel Spring, *The American School, 1642-1990,* 2d ed. (New York: Longman, 1990), 108. For a less polemical version of this argument that nevertheless makes the similar observation that education was understood to be especially important in the promulgation of republican values, see Cremin, *American Education,* chapters 4-7 *passim.*

12. Review of *Twice-Told Tales* in the *Salem Gazette* (14 March 1837), in *Hawthorne: The Critical Heritage,* ed. J. Donald Crowley (London: Routledge and Kegan Paul, 1970), 53.

13. Andrew Preston Peabody, review of *Twice-Told Tales* in the *Christian Examiner* (Nov. 1838), in *Hawthorne: The Critical Heritage,* ed. Crowley, 64.

14. The treatment given Coleridge's *Aids to Reflection* is instructive. First published in England in 1825, it was presented in this country in 1829 with an influential preface by James Marsh. Marsh asserted that Coleridge's work was primarily a means to associate "the study of words with the study of morals and religion" (James Marsh, "Introduction" in *Aids to Reflection,* by Samuel Taylor Coleridge [Burlington, Vt.: C. Goodrich, 1840], 10). Once again, as the writings of Thomas Upham attest, the imagination, though not proscribed, was circumscribed by the social realm.

15. William Cullen Bryant, *Representative Selections,* ed. Tremaine McDowell (New York: American Book, 1935), 190.

16. Ibid., 197.

17. William Charvat, *The Profession of Authorship in America, 1800-1870,* ed. Matthew J. Bruccoli (1968; rpt. New York: Columbia Univ. Press, 1992), 64; William Ellery Channing, *The Works of William E. Channing* (Boston, 1890), 126.

18. First published in 1790, Alison's book received little attention before a laudatory review appeared in 1810. The first reference to it in American magazines came in 1818 (Charvat, *Origins,* 48-51). Washington Irving helped popularize Alison in the United States, and Bryant's "Lectures" reflected his knowledge of Alison as well; see Harry H. Clark, "Changing Attitudes in Early American Literary Criticism: 1800-1840," in *The Development of American Literary Criticism,* ed. Floyd Stovall (Chapel Hill: Univ. of North Carolina Press, 1955), 26; 29. Hawthorne's library record indicates an awareness of Alison's theories and familiarity with the contemporary magazines that advanced the critical positions identified by Charvat; see Kesserling, *Hawthorne's Reading,* 43-64.

19. Archibald Alison, *Essays on the Nature and Principles of Taste* (Edinburgh, 1817), 1: xvi; hereafter cited in text as *Essays*.

20. A similarly normalized association appears in the opening chapter of Henry Home, Lord Kames, *Elements of Criticism* (New York, 1859), 29-37.

21. Hawthorne's first children's story, "Little Annie's Ramble," was published in 1835. Aside from other short pieces directed toward a juvenile audience, Hawthorne wrote a "Universal History" for the Peter Parley series in 1836. After the *Grandfather's Chair* series, Hawthorne wrote his moralized versions of classical myths, *A Wonder Book for Girls and Boys* (1851) and *Tanglewood Tales* (1853).

22. Nathaniel Hawthorne, *True Stories from History and Biography*, vol. 6 of *The Centenary Edition* (1972), 214. This volume also contains *The Whole History of Grandfather's Chair*; hereafter cited in text as *True Stories*).

23. Carol Billman, "Nathaniel Hawthorne: 'Revolutionizer' of Children's Literature?" *Studies in American Fiction* 10 (1982): 111. Billman specifically refers to Hawthorne's bowdlerizations of classical tales in *A Wonder Book* and *Tanglewood Tales*. Children's literature in the United States did not take the imaginative turn it did in Europe during the early nineteenth century, and she notes that Hawthorne's writings were no exception to this tendency: "He domesticates characters and situations and draws moral lessons from sometimes inconclusive stories" (Billman, "'Revolutionizer,'" 112). Hawthorne's statement about revolutionizing children's literature was made in a well-known overture to Longfellow suggesting they collaborate (21 March 1838): "Possibly we may make a great hit, and entirely revolutionize children's literature" (Hawthorne, *Letters*, 266).

24. Between 1820 to 1850, "somewhere between 25 and 30 American romances were based, wholly or in part, on the history of seventeenth-century New England" (Bell, *Hawthorne*, ix).

25. "The frame, in which Grandfather and the children identify themselves with history, has the same purpose as 'The Custom-House': it forges an imaginative link between the present and the past that serves not only to reanimate the past with the life of the present, but to implicate the present in the life of the past" (John W. Crowley, "Hawthorne's New England Epochs," *ESQ* 25 [1979]: 64). Elsewhere Hawthorne uses physical devices such as the town pump, the scarlet letter, the house of the seven gables, and the Province-House to link the present with the past.

26. A similar situation is repeated in *The Scarlet Letter*. Although most of the women outside the prison door counsel death for Hester Prynne, one advises mercy. Apparently unable to withstand the rigors of the New World, the dissenter later dies. See Frederick Newberry, "Tradition and Disinheritance in *The Scarlet Letter*," *ESQ* 23 (1977): 1-9; Bell, *Hawthorne*, 117-20.

27. Lawrence Buell, *New England Literary Culture: From Revolution through Renaissance* (New York: Cambridge Univ. Press, 1986), 214. John McWilliams situates *Grandfather's Chair* in the "commemorative tradition" of histories and argues that only occasionally do Grandfather's responses reflect ambivalence; see John P. McWilliams, Jr., *Hawthorne, Melville, and the American Character: A Looking-Glass Business* (New York: Cambridge Univ. Press, 1984), 38-39. Nina Baym, who has treated Hawthorne's children's writings extensively and has championed their worth for scholars, similarly asserts that only with the writing of *The Scarlet Letter* did Hawthorne reflect ambivalence; see Baym, *Shape*, chapter 3.

Those who conversely locate in *Grandfather's Chair* a historical vision that would inform *The House of the Seven Gables* and *The Scarlet Letter* include

Crowley ("Hawthorne's New England," 60), and Ziff (*Literary Democracy*, 118). More recently, both Laura Laffrado and Lauren Berlant assert the subversive potential of *Grandfather's Chair*. Berlant sees in the children's history a counterbalance to official history, one authorized not by an allegiance to official sources "but because of his unique voice, as one among many sources of knowledge," a testimony to alternative, popular sources (Berlant, *Anatomy of National Fantasy*, 197). Laffrado similarly argues for the subversive impact of the body of Hawthorne's children's literature, and she suggests that *Grandfather's Chair* displays the power of the narrator to transform reality in the service of a deeper truth: "In his diligent and sincere attempt to write such narratives, Hawthorne managed to slip the bonds of the present and enter the full reality of all times and places" (Laffrado, *Hawthorne's Literature*, 40).

28. Buell, *Literary Culture*, 217.

29. Quoted in Welter, *Mind*, 27.

30. George Dekker regards it as the tension informing *The Scarlet Letter* (George Dekker, *The American Historical Romance* [New York: Cambridge Univ. Press, 1987], 171), and Sacvan Bercovitch identifies its expression as "the ritual of a culture on an errand—which is to say, a culture based on a faith in process" (Sacvan Bercovitch, *The American Jeremiad* [Madison: Univ. of Wisconsin Press, 1978], 23).

31. Grandfather's debt to George Bancroft may have been theoretical, but Hawthorne's was more material: Bancroft had a hand in Hawthorne's political appointments during two Democratic administrations.

32. Hawthorne, *Twice-Told Tales*, 68-69.

33. Ibid., 95, 88.

34. The most prominent of recent critical works on ideology in *The Scarlet Letter*, Bercovitch's *The Office of* The Scarlet Letter, notes that "Hawthorne makes it the office of the narrator to abandon and, after her return, to enclose her still resisting self in history and community" (150). Hester's rebellion is thus ritualized, and American dissent effectively contained.

35. Budick, "Hester's Skepticism," 207.

36. Hawthorne, *The Scarlet Letter*, 31; hereafter cited in text.

37. James Mellow notes, "Throughout the pitched battle that centered on his dismissal, Hawthorne maintained an attitude of aggrieved innocence, the bewilderment of a man who has been thoroughly wronged"—the same tone Hawthorne assumes in the preface to the second edition. But, Mellow continues, "As a shrewd politician, he had been anticipating his probable removal for several months." Mellow, *Hawthorne in His Times*, 292.

38. Given the vitriolic response of the Salem Whigs to Hawthorne's fictional attack, the return of the past also functions to mute the threat of the present. For example, the Salem *Register* (21 March 1850) was scandalized by Hawthorne: "The most venomous, malignant, and unaccountable assault is made upon a venerable gentleman, whose chief crime seems to be that he loves a good dinner. . . . This chapter has obliterated whatever sympathy was felt for Mr. Hawthorne's removal from office" (quoted in Stewart, *Nathaniel Hawthorne*, 98).

39. Emerson, *Essays*, 7.

40. Carton, *Rhetoric of American Romance*, 154.

41. A.N. Kaul remarks that Hawthorne uses the historical setting so as to comment on a nineteenth-century cultural problem: "The loss of a sense of

community, obsession with self, exploitative individualism—Hawthorne's major themes—are thus the dangers latent in democratic society" (A.N. Kaul, *The American Vision: Actual and Ideal Society in Nineteenth-Century Fiction* [New Haven: Yale Univ. Press, 1963], 153). More recently, Charles Swann has observed along similar lines that "For Hawthorne, social being is at the core of all identity and of all virtue" (Charles Swann, *Nathaniel Hawthorne: Tradition and Revolution* [New York: Cambridge Univ. Press, 1991], 84).

42. Emerson, *Essays,* 7.

43. As John McWilliams comments, "by connecting past to present directly, [Hawthorne] could remind contemporaries that they need not worship patriarchal demigods and could not create themselves anew" (McWilliams, *Hawthorne, Melville,* 107).

44. E.A. Duyckinck, review in *Literary World* (30 March 1850, in *Hawthorne: The Critical Heritage,* ed. Crowley, 155; George Bailey Loring, review in the *Massachusetts Quarterly Review* (Sept. 1850), in *Hawthorne: The Critical Heritage,* ed. Crowley, 168; Orestes Brownson, review in *Brownson's Quarterly Review* (Oct. 1850), in *Hawthorne: The Critical Heritage,* ed. Crowley, 179. Also see examples of the stereotypical "narrow Puritan" in Bell, *Hawthorne,* 85-104 passim.

45. The word *sympathy* had specific technical meaning to Common Sense philosophers and sentimental novelists alike. It recurs with great frequency in *The Scarlet Letter,* e.g., "The feeling that it so evidently manifested, rather than the direct purport of the words, caused it to vibrate within all hearts, and brought the listeners into one accord of sympathy" (67). Although scholars have observed the importance of sympathy, they have at times displaced the concept onto a specifically Romantic setting; see Pancost, "Hawthorne's Epistemology," 8; also see Roy R. Male, "Hawthorne and the Concept of Sympathy," *PMLA* 68 (1953): 138. More recently, Lester Hunt notes Hawthorne's reliance on Adam Smith's definition in most aspects of the term (Lester Hunt, "*The Scarlet Letter:* Hawthorne's Theory of Moral Sentiments," *Philosophy and Literature* 8 (1984): 75-88). And Stephen Railton, suggesting a correlation between Hawthorne's rhetorical stance and the idea of sympathy, observes that Hawthorne analogizes the author/reader relationship with that of the alienated character and members of his/her community (Stephen Railton, *Authorship and Audience: Literary Performance in the American Renaissance* [Princeton: Princeton Univ. Press, 1991], 107-31).

46. Hawthorne, *Snow-Image,* 99. The importance of the "chain" to both sympathy and proper perception is suggested by the following passage from *The House of the Seven Gables:* "So long as you should feel [her hand's] grasp, soft as it was, you might be certain that your place was good in the whole sympathetic chain of human nature. The world was no longer a delusion" (141). See chapter 2, n. 44, above.

47. Hawthorne further challenges the interpretation of phenomena: "Oftener, however, its credibility rested on the faith of some lonely eyewitness, who beheld the wonder through the colored, magnifying, and distorting medium of his imagination, and shaped it distinctly in his after-thought" (155).

48. This phrase is echoed later after Dimmesdale's return to rewrite his election sermon: "That self was gone! Another man had returned out of the forest" (223). Yet, as the conclusion shows, Dimmesdale never relinquishes his social role.

49. Gabler-Hover, *Truth,* 98-9.

50. Ibid., 99.

51. Hester Prynne's rebelliousness and Hawthorne's presentation of it perseveres as a difficult area for critical interpretation. Some critical works continue to explore the heroic dimensions of Hester Prynne; these include Leland S. Person, Jr., *Aesthetic Headaches: Women and a Masculine Poetics in Poe, Melville, and Hawthorne* (Athens: Univ. of Georgia Press, 1988), and Joyce Warren, *The American Narcissus: Individualism and Women in Nineteenth-Century American Fiction* (New Brunswick, N.J.: Rutgers Univ. Press, 1984). Others, however, are more inclined to find equivocation in Hawthorne's most notable character; for example, Sacvan Bercovitch perceives in her an embodiment of the dissent with which Hawthorne struggles: "We might say that the problem of dissent in *The Scarlet Letter* lies in the paradox of Hester's sainted individualism" (Bercovitch, *Office,* 121). Along similarly complex lines, Lauren Berlant observes, "Hawthorne's women emerge as uncanny, paradoxical, politically unintelligible: as fantasy projections of patriarchal fear about the imminent end of male hegemony within the political public sphere, as occasions for serious critique of that same patriarchal culture, and as eroticized subjects who speculate that other forms of collective life might be imaginable, even within America" (Berlant, *Anatomy,* 9).

52. Richard Brodhead finds in *The Blithedale Romance* a narratively problematic and culturally symptomatic conjunction between the private and the family. To Brodhead, Hawthorne's fusion of what might be termed public or relational aspects of the self with a radically disjunct spectatorial function is the mark of a particular moment in antebellum literary culture; see Brodhead, *Cultures of Letters,* 48-68. This fusion—and the corresponding failure of domestic relationships—in *Blithedale* highlights by its absence the function of sympathy.

53. Buell, *Literary Culture,* 264.

4   The Altrurian Romances

1. Hawthorne, *The Scarlet Letter,* 263.

2. Bellamy's *Looking Backward* is most similar in its call for an "ethical revelation that makes social upheaval unnecessary" (John L. Thomas, *Alternative America: Henry George, Edward Bellamy, Henry Demarest Lloyd and the Adversary Tradition* [Cambridge: Harvard Univ. Press, 1983], 243). Kenneth Roemer has noted the appearance of "153 utopian, partially utopian, and anti-utopian works" (274) between the years 1888 and 1900; see Kenneth M. Roemer, "'Utopia Made Practical': Compulsive Realism," *American Literary Realism* 7 (1974): 273-76.

3. Dominick LaCapra, *Rethinking Intellectual History: Texts, Contexts, Language* (Ithaca: Cornell Univ. Press, 1983), 44. LaCapra's remark is particularly relevant because it raises two issues central to a study of Howells: a split perspective and social criticism. The argument that Howells's social criticism was superficial had its most forceful and influential exponent in H.L. Mencken. Mencken, in his essay "The Dean" (1917), characterizes Howells as "a placid conformist" and "a contriver of pretty things" who perceives "through a pink fog" and "has nothing to say, for all the charm he gets into saying it"; Mencken further claims that "His psychology is superficial, amateurish, often nonsensical" (H.L. Mencken, *Prejudices, First Series* [New York: Knopf, 1919], 52-58). During the 1950s, several significant critical studies appeared to refute the critical frame of reference that Mencken had established. Disputing Mencken's characterization of

Howells, Everett Carter cast Howells in the role of the tough-minded realist who, along with the pragmatists, embraced "the flux and change of experience" (Everett Carter, *Howells and the Age of Realism* [Philadelphia: J.B. Lippincott, 1954], 154). Edwin H. Cady's two biographical studies of Howells (*The Road to Realism: The Early Years of William Dean Howells, 1837-1885* [Syracuse: Syracuse Univ. Press, 1956] and *The Realist at War: The Mature Years of William Dean Howells, 1885-1920* [Syracuse: Syracuse Univ. Press, 1958]) were particularly important because they attended to Howells's emotional problems and treated his writings as complex responses to both social and personal issues.

Much of the scholarship on Howells in the past two decades has followed along the lines established by Cady. Kenneth Lynn's biography succinctly states the contemporary defense of Howells's psychological complexity: "Despite what his critics have said about him, Howells was a man of modern sensibility, whose awareness of life was rooted in radical doubt and anxiety" (Kenneth Lynn, *William Dean Howells: An American Life* [New York: Harcourt Brace Jovanovich, 1971], 12). Other significant explorations of the psychological complexities of Howells's vision include Kermit Vanderbilt, *The Achievement of William Dean Howells: A Reinterpretation* (Princeton: Princeton Univ. Press, 1968); and John W. Crowley, *The Black Heart's Truth: The Early Career of William Dean Howells* (Chapel Hill: Univ. of North Carolina Press, 1985). A more recent work that provocatively explores the conflict between what are described as "Howells's divided sympathies" (187), his social criticism and a competing impulse toward elitism, is Elsa Nettels, *Language, Race, and Social Class in Howells's America* (Lexington: Univ. Press of Kentucky, 1988), 187.

4. This incongruity reflects an apparent fusion of disparate genres. As Kenneth Burke describes it, whereas the didactic and the jeremiad, with their demands for change and adherence to ideals, reject the world as it is, the comic mode promotes acceptance of the world (Kenneth Burke, *Attitudes toward History,* rev. ed. [Boston: Beacon, 1959], 39-91).

5. For a publication history, see Clara and Rudolf Kirk's introductory essay to William Dean Howells, *The Altrurian Romances*, vol. 20 of *A Selected Edition*, ed. Edwin H. Cady, Ronald Gottesman, and David J. Nordloh (Bloomington: Indiana Univ. Press, 1968), xi-xxxiv; also see Cady, *Realist at War*, 197-200. Howells spelled *traveller* with two *l*'s when the essays were published serially in the *Cosmopolitan.* He changed the spelling to one *l* when *A Traveler* appeared in book form, perhaps in an attempt to distinguish the American style from the British (Clara Kirk, *W.D. Howells, Traveler from Altruria* [New Brunswick, N.J.: Rutgers Univ. Press, 1962], 90). In this discussion, the form chosen by Howells for his book title will be used except when specific reference is made to the essays.

6. The most extensive critical treatment of the Altrurian Romances remains Clara Kirk's *W.D. Howells, Traveler from Altruria,* which describes in detail the contemporary political milieu. The formal structure of these writings is treated in George Uba, "Howells and the Practicable Utopia: The Allegorical Structure of the Altrurian Romances," *The Journal of Narrative Technique* 13 (1983): 118-30. The Altrurian Romances are compared with Herbert Marcuse's writings and thus treated as sophisticated ideological criticism in Sam Girgus, *The Law of the Heart: Individualism and the Modern Self in American Literature* (Austin: Univ. of Texas Press, 1979), 73-83. For a study that situates the Altrurian Romances in a literary tradition of pastoral utopias, designed less to promote political change than to suggest changes in individual consciousness, see Jean Pfaelzer, *The Utopian Novel in*

America, 1886-1896: The Politics of Form (Pittsburgh: Univ. of Pittsburgh Press, 1984), chapter 3. Most other critical discussions deal only briefly with the Altrurian Romances in the context of Howells's other writings. In this study, the Altrurian Romances will be treated whole (as presented in the Indiana edition). This follows Howells's expressed wish to have the two novels published together in one volume; the inclusion of the first five "Letters" simply complements part 1 of *Through the Eye*.

7. Howells, *The Altrurian Romances*, 30; hereafter cited in text.

8. Clara Kirk asserts that "Mr. Homos and Mr. Twelvemough are two sides of Howells himself" (Kirk, *W.D. Howells*, 4); also see Jay Martin, *Harvests of Change: American Literature, 1865-1914* (Englewood Cliffs, N.J.: Prentice-Hall, 1967), 228. The unusual names of the narrators have also sparked some critical speculation. The name *Twelvemough* refers to duodecimo volumes used for novels (Kirk, *W.D. Howells*, 4, 13). And as Kirk observes about the Altrurian, "The phrase 'Aristides the Just' comes at once to the reader's mind, and also the fact that 'homos' implies 'common man' or Man in the abstract" (Kirk, *W.D. Howells*, 83). Kirk further remarks that the third narrator, Eveleth Strange, is "Eve in search of a lost paradise, from which she had wandered into a strange world" (Kirk, *W.D. Howells*, 141). Aristides Homos will be referred to here by his surname as he is called in *A Traveler*. Eveleth Strange Homos will be called by her given name, as she is referred to in *Through the Eye*. No first name is ever given for Twelvemough.

9. Nettels, *Language, Race, and Social Class,* 184. Howells's response to this contradiction, the ethical ideals of the Altrurian Romances, can be described as a kind of Christian Socialism. Howells makes frequent reference to the Bible and the "'ideal realized by the earliest Christians, who loved one another and who had all things in common'" (146) as Altruria's conceptual basis. See Kirk, *W.D. Howells*, 15-33; also see Louis Budd, "Altruism Arrives in America," *American Quarterly* 8 (1956): 43-48.

10. Vanderbilt, *Achievement*, 108. Cf. Pfaelzer, *Utopian Novel*, 63, and the identification of Howells's vision as "a recycled Jeffersonianism."

11. George Meredith, "An Essay on Comedy," in *Comedy*, ed. Wylie Sypher (New York: Doubleday, 1964), 52.

12. Henri Bergson, "Laughter," in *Comedy*, ed. Wylie Sypher (New York: Doubleday, 1964), 188.

13. Ibid., 73, 74. Bergson's formula of comedy is based on the idea that life consists of a balance between "tension" and "elasticity" (72). If either is lacking, a social response, the comic, serves as a homeostatic device. Although Bergson, like George Meredith, focuses on the way in which comedy serves a stabilizing function—Meredith would regard the destabilizing aspect of comedy as satire—his attention to the way comedy "corrects" rigidity suggests the subversive aspects of the genre. The essay "Laughter" appeared in 1900, though Bergson had published his thoughts on the subject as early as 1884.

14. Sigmund Freud, *Jokes and Their Relationship to the Unconscious,* trans. James Strachey (New York: Norton, 1963), 97. In this work, Freud's emphasis was on unconscious motivation. Accordingly, he perceived a close relationship between jokes and "dream-work," particularly condensation and displacement (159-80). Jokes, like dreams, also contain a strong element of disguised wish fulfillment.

15. Ibid., 143.

16. Louis J. Budd documents how this literally occurred with the founding of a community called Altruria near Santa Rosa, California, in 1894 (Budd, "Altruism," 49-50). Howells sent money, but the community disbanded within a year. In

addition several organizations, such as the Altruria Co-Operative Union (Oakland, 1895), the Altrurian League of New York City (1895-97), the Altrurian Society (Boston, 1895), and the Association of Altruists (New Jersey, 1900), came into being in the years following the publication of *A Traveler.*

17. The classic account of evolutionary theory in American social thinking is Richard Hofstadter, *Social Darwinism in American Thought*, rev. ed. (Boston: Beacon, 1955). Also see Flower and Murphy, *History of Philosophy*, 2: 517-63; and Schneider, *History of American Philosophy*, 321-415.

18. The late-nineteenth-century struggle in the United States over the discipline of psychology will be treated in greater detail in the next chapter. For a description of American responses to empiricism and physiological psychology, see Fay, *American Psychology*, 129-69.

19. Stanley Edgar Hyman notes that Darwin borrowed the idea of the struggle for existence from Malthus (Stanley Edgar Hyman, *The Tangled Bank: Darwin, Marx, Frazer and Freud as Imaginative Writers* [New York: Atheneum, 1962], 4). Hofstadter makes a similar observation, noting points where Darwin's and Spencer's social ideas converge and diverge (Hofstadter, *Social Darwinism*, 38-39, 90-91). Also see Gillian Beer, *Darwin's Plots: Evolutionary Narrative in Darwin, George Eliot, and Nineteenth-Century Fiction* (London: Routledge and Kegan Paul, 1983).

20. Herbert Spencer, *Social Statics, or the Conditions Essential to Human Happiness Specified and the First of Them Developed* (1851; reprint, New York: Augustus M. Kelley, 1969), 412. Adaptation also had more general moral implications to Spencer: "All evil results from the non-adaptation of constitution to conditions. This is true of everything that lives" (Spencer, *Social Statics*, 59).

21. Herbert Spencer, *The Principles of Psychology*, 3d ed. (New York: Appleton, 1899), 1: 293-94.

22. See ibid., 1: 427-53. William James observes, however, that evolutionary psychology, notwithstanding its supposedly materialistic analysis, demands a primal "mind-stuff," which can then be shaped by evolutionary forces. In this way the higher mental processes posited by Christian (and other) thinkers exist as a possibility from the start and infuse evolutionary psychology with a supernatural component. See James, *Principles*, 148-64.

23. John Fiske, *Outlines of Cosmic Philosophy based on the Doctrine of Evolution, with Criticisms on the Positive Philosophy* (Boston: Houghton Mifflin, 1892), 2: 201; hereafter cited in text as *Outlines*. Fiske first met Howells in 1867. In 1871, while Howells was editor, Fiske proofread for the *Atlantic Monthly*; in 1872, he was asked to edit its science department. Fiske is identified as "Howells' chief potential source of Darwinism" by Harry Hayden Clark ("The Role of Science in the Thought of W. D. Howells," *Transactions of the Wisconsin Academy of Sciences, Arts and Letters* 42 [1953]: 264).

24. In the 1872 edition of *Psychology*, Spencer first included a discussion of egoistic and altruistic sentiments (Spencer, *Psychology*, 2: 578-626), which Fiske adapted to his own purposes.

25. Donald Pizer notes that two main tenets of Howells's realist criticism in *Criticism and Fiction* (1891) are that literature is a product of the society in which it is found and that change in both society and literature is slowly but inevitably progressive. Pizer further observes that when Howells was at the *Atlantic* (1866-81) he "read, reviewed, or editorially supervised many works and articles on Taine and evolution" (Donald Pizer, *Realism and Naturalism in Nineteenth-Century American Literature*, rev. ed. [Carbondale: Southern Illinois Univ. Press, 1984],

72, 75). For a detailed account of the influence of science on Howells, see Clark, "Role of Science"; and Jane Marston, "Evolution and Howellsian Realism in *The Undiscovered Country,*" *American Literary Realism* 14 (1981): 231-41.

26. William Dean Howells, "Recent Literature," *Atlantic Monthly* 33 (1874): 622.

27. William Dean Howells, "John Fiske," *Harper's Weekly* 20 (July 1901): 732.

28. William Dean Howells, "Recent Literature," *Atlantic Monthly* 30 (1872): 366.

29. Howells "steered a nimble course between scientific adaptation in the natural world, on the one hand, and the claims of moral freedom and Divine Providence on the other," according to Vanderbilt, *Achievement*, 85. The tension between the two is further suggested by the novelistic counterpoint to the morally transcendent acts in *The Rise of Silas Lapham* and *The Minister's Charge,* the earlier *A Modern Instance* (1882). This novel's relatively modern tone derives in part from its seemingly inexorable plot, in which neither effectual action nor appreciable insight may be found among the main characters, but it does resemble Howells's other writings insofar as it criticizes its characters' self-absorption. In addition, as Amy Kaplan observes, this novel, like *A Hazard of New Fortunes* and *The Rise of Silas Lapham,* raises issues about American realism with its treatment of the representation of culture in the mass media. See Amy Kaplan, *The Social Construction of American Realism* (Chicago: Univ. of Chicago Press, 1988), chapters 1 and 2.

30. In *Looking Backward,* Bellamy also uses the family metaphor to characterize the ideal country; see Thomas, *Alternative America,* 242-43). Despite this similarity and the essentially Christian nature of both utopian visions, Howells and Bellamy differ on the important issue of human nature, which Bellamy treats as a relatively static individualistic entity.

31. Bergson, "Laughter," 65. The joke, insofar as it temporarily promotes an "absence of feeling" (63), serves to defuse potentially upsetting situations by indirection and thereby helps to maintain social fictions. Howells himself notes this function of laughter when he has Homos comment of another character, "In his reply he took refuge in that humor peculiar to the Americans: a sort of ether where they may draw breath for a moment free from the stifling despair which must fill every true man among them when he thinks how far short of their ideal their reality has fallen" (207-8).

32. See Maldwyn Allen Jones, *American Immigration* (Chicago: Univ. of Chicago Press, 1960), 208.

33. Quoted in ibid., 259.

34. On working-class nativism, see Gwendolyn Mink, *Old Labor and New Immigrants in American Political Development: Union, Party and State, 1875-1920* (Ithaca: Cornell Univ. Press, 1986), 51-64. Also see Jones, *American Immigration,* 207-77 passim, on more general nativist responses to immigration.

35. Ironically, in *A Traveler* Homos criticizes labor unions because they did not involve themselves in electoral politics the way European labor organizations traditionally did. On the issue of "American exceptionalism" from European working-class political tendencies, see J. David Greenstone, *Labor in American Politics* (New York: Knopf, 1969), 3-38; also see Herbert G. Gutman, *Work, Culture and Society in Industrializing America: Essays in American Working-Class History and Social History* (New York: Knopf, 1976), 3-78; and Hubert Perrier,

"The Socialists and the Working Class in New York, 1890-96," in *American Labor and Immigration History, 1877-1920s: Recent European Research,* ed. Dirk Hoerder (Urbana: Univ. of Illinois Press, 1983).

36. Cahan had achieved renown among the Yiddish-speaking Jewish population as editor of *The Forward,* a prominent Yiddish newspaper. Cahan's *The Rise of David Levinsky* displays an intellectual debt to Howells even in its title. Howells's contradictory impulses in relation to Cahan are described as a defense of traditional American culture and a simultaneous desire to include new voices, in Jules Chametsky, *Our Decentralized Literature: Cultural Mediation in Selected Jewish and Southern Writers* (Amherst: Univ. of Massachusetts Press, 1986), 29-36. Vanderbilt offers an insightful discussion of Howells's anxiety about immigration in which he notes the fervent anti-Semitism of Howells's friends—Henry Adams, Charles Eliot Norton, and James Russell Lowell—and Howells's relative insensitivity about this issue; see Vanderbilt, *Achievement* 96-126.

37. William Dean Howells, "Doorstop Acquaintance," *Atlantic Monthly* 23 (1869): 492.

38. William Dean Howells, "By Horse-Car to Boston," *Atlantic Monthly* 25 (1870): 122.

39. William Dean Howells, "A Pedestrian Tour," *Atlantic Monthly* 24 (1869): 595, 595, 594, 596.

40. Howells was using the conventional slang meaning of *white* to denote "honourable; square-dealing" (*Oxford English Dictionary,* 3764). Howells's treatment of miscegenation in *An Imperative Duty* (1891) is noteworthy here. In this short novel, a Boston woman agonizes over the moral issue of whether to tell her niece that the young woman had a black great-grandparent. When informed, the young woman rejects her suitor, although she later marries him; the couple then goes to live in Italy. Although Howells's decision to write on this topic may seem bold, he relies on racial stereotypes and considerable melodrama. Howells also encouraged the African American poet Paul Laurence Dunbar, and he was a founding member of the NAACP in 1909 (see Cady, *Realist at War,* 161-62). Elsa Nettels offers a nuanced discussion of Howells's complex relationship to Paul Dunbar and the question of his relative sensitivities and insensitivities regarding race; see Nettels, *Language, Race, and Social Class,* 80-86.

41. On the presence of Krupp in the White City, see Kirk, *W.D. Howells,* 112. David Minter, in his discussion of "Chicago's Dream City," notes that in addition to the exclusion of foreign peoples from the city itself only a single structure next to the Children's Building was dedicated to women and that African Americans, limited to formal recognition on a single day, were totally denied any official physical presence. See David Minter, *A Cultural History of the American Novel: Henry James to William Faulkner* (New York: Cambridge Univ. Press, 1994), 23-31.

42. John Fiske, "Manifest Destiny," *Harper's New Monthly Magazine* 70 (1885): 578.

43. Ibid., 579.

44. Ibid., 578, 588.

45. The association between immigrants and urban industrial workers, noted only obliquely in Homos's displeased comments about New York, has validity because in 1880, 80 percent of New Yorkers were either immigrants or children of immigrants; see Gutman, *Work, Culture and Society,* 40.

46. Yehoshua Arieli, *Individualism and Nationalism in American Ideology* (Cambridge: Harvard Univ. Press, 1964), 28.

5 The Ironic Construction of Selfhood

1. Howells's solution was consistent with contemporary psychological thought: "Historically, the 'back to Kant' movement in the latter part of the nineteenth century owed much to the post-Darwinian effort to save the human 'will' from the deterministic implications of evolutionary naturalism" (William Woodward, "Stretching the Limits of Psychology's History," in *The Problematic Science*, ed. Woodward and Ash, 4).

2. Critics generally have treated James's writing from a thematic perspective. For discussions that situate James in a tradition of idealistic individualism, see Quentin Anderson, "Practical and Visionary Americans," *American Scholar* 45 (1976): 405-18; also see Frederick Hoffman, "William James and the Modern Literary Consciousness," *Criticism* 4 (1962): 1-13. William James's thought is evaluated from the perspective of Henry James's modernist literary experimentation, in Ross Posnock, *Henry James, William James, and the Challenge of Modernity* (New York: Oxford Univ. Press, 1991). For a study that focuses on the effects of James's ideas of consciousness on Gertrude Stein, see Lisa Ruddick, *Reading Gertrude Stein: Body, Text, Gnosis* (Ithaca, N.Y.: Cornell Univ. Press, 1990); on his influence on his brother Henry, see Richard A. Hocks, *Henry James and Pragmatistic Thought* (Chapel Hill: Univ. of North Carolina Press, 1974).

Scholars also have explored the cultural implications of James's thought. James is understood to offer a "humanistic understanding of experience" that can help the individual cope with the world in Girgus, *Law of the Heart*, 134. Frank Lentricchia similarly locates in James an impetus for action—"Philosophy should be trying to change, not interpret the world"—in *Ariel and the Police: Michel Foucault, William James, Wallace Stevens*, 105. Lentricchia treats *The Principles* primarily to discuss the metaphor of private property in James's idea of the self. Walter Benn Michaels also centers his discussion around this metaphor. Unfortunately Michaels misidentifies the psychology of the time as "introspective"; he resultantly pigeonholes James as "the most influential exponent of that psychology" and elsewhere oversimplifies James's thought (e.g., "James thus imagines the will as everywhere triumphant"); see Walter Benn Michaels, *The Gold Standard and the Logic of Naturalism: American Literature at the Turn of the Century* (Berkeley: Univ. of California Press, 1987), 241, 242.

3. James, *Principles*, 15; hereafter cited in text.

4. Rush himself strongly believed in the importance of environment. In an essay published in 1786, "The Influence of Physical Causes upon the Moral Faculty," Rush stressed the physical to support the idea that insanity was treatable. Later Common Sense psychologists, however, lacking Rush's (and James's) background in medicine, concentrated solely on mentation, without much regard for physical factors.

5. Quoted in Fay, *American Psychology*, 166.

6. Quoted in ibid., 163.

7. Howard M. Feinstein, *Becoming William James* (Ithaca, N.Y.: Cornell Univ. Press, 1984), 322. Feinstein describes James's political maneuverings at Harvard and tells how James pressured Harvard by allowing Johns Hopkins University to court him (332-40). This period in James's career is also treated in Sheldon

Stern, "William James and the New Psychology," in *Social Sciences at Harvard, 1860-1920,* ed. Paul Buck (Cambridge: Harvard Univ. Press, 1965), 175-195.

8. Unless otherwise noted, emphases are James's.

9. Jacques Barzun similarly calls *The Principles* "the narrative of a search"; see Jacques Barzun, *A Stroll with William James* (New York: Harper and Row, 1983), 34. Barzun's unfamiliarity with nineteenth-century psychology limits his awareness of how this search operates in relation to the discipline that James plainly is writing about. As an illustration of Barzun's unfamiliarity with the state of the discipline at that time we may note that he calls James's use of examples from literature "very provoking," when, in fact, the use of literary material was utterly typical of philosophical psychology texts (Barzun, *Stroll,* 2). Accordingly, Barzun concludes that the search ends less than a quarter of the way through the book, and he ignores the structure of the remaining text.

10. The chapter on the will is followed by a supplement that treats a topic closely related to questions of the will, hypnosis, a subject that perplexed advocates of the free will. A general conclusion then follows.

11. In one respect, the shorter, one-volume *Psychology,* published in 1892, even more closely resembles faculty psychology texts—it discusses sensation at the start and treats the senses in the same orderly fashion as does Upham's *Abridgement.* The shorter *Psychology,* though, more clearly charts a progression from constraint, whether of mentation or of action, to freedom. It opens with his discussion of habit and progresses to a treatment of voluntary behaviors and the will.

12. Kenneth Burke, "The Four Master Tropes," in *A Grammar of Motives* (1945; reprint, Berkeley: Univ. of California Press, 1969), 503-17.

13. In its original form, this concept suggested that the neural pathway remained intact so long as it was a functional response to a given stimulus. John Dewey's 1896 discussion of the reflex arc, to be discussed later in this chapter, broke from this dualism of stimulus and response by arguing that experience is always mediated by mental constructs and that what had been labeled response should properly be regarded as an attempt to act on the environment. See John Dewey, "The Reflex Arc Concept in Psychology," in *The Early Works, 1882-1898,* vol. 5, ed. Jo Ann Boydston (Carbondale: Southern Illinois Univ. Press, 1972), 96-109.

14. James's desire to rescue introspection from the intuitions of faculty psychologists and place it at the service of an empirical psychology has led some philosophers to align his work with that of Franz Brentano and Carl Stumpf as a precursor to phenomenology; see Aron Gurwitsch, *The Field of Consciousness* (Pittsburgh: Duquesne Univ. Press 1964); Hans Linschoten, *On the Way toward a Phenomenological Psychology: The Psychology of William James* (Pittsburgh: Duquesne Univ. Press, 1968); Bruce Wilshire, *William James and Phenomenology: A Study of* The Principles of Psychology (Bloomington: Indiana Univ. Press, 1968); and Richard Stevens, *James and Husserl: The Foundations of Meaning* (The Hague: Martinus Nijhoff, 1974). In *The Principles,* James, like these other psychologists, regards introspection as fallible but essential to psychology; see Herbert Spiegelberg, *The Phenomenological Movement: A Historical Introduction,* 3d ed. (The Hague: Martinus Nijhoff, 1982), 33-36, 62-63, 100-104.

15. William James, *The Letters of William James,* ed. Henry James (Boston: Atlantic Monthly Press, 1920), 1: 147. References to this episode are a critical commonplace; see Ralph Barton Perry, *The Thought and Character of William James* (Boston: Little, Brown, 1935), 1: 320-32; William Woodward, "William

James's Psychology of Will: Its Revolutionary Impact on American Psychology," in *Explorations in the History of Psychology in the United States,* ed. Josef Brozek (Lewisburg, Pa.: Bucknell Univ. Press, 1984), 149; John Anderson, "'The Worst Kind of Melancholy': William James in 1869," *Harvard Library Bulletin* 30 (1982): 369-86; William Barrett, "Our Contemporary, William James," *Commentary* 60.6 (1975): 59; S. P. Fullinwider, "William James's Spiritual Crisis," *Historian* 13 (1975): 39-57; and Gerald E. Myers, *William James: His Life and Thought* (New Haven: Yale Univ. Press, 1986), 45-53.

Myers defends Perry's notion of a philosophical cure by appealing to a holistic vision: "James would have argued that the important consideration is not whether a physical, psychological, or philosophical condition is a cause or a symptom, but whether the whole constellation of a severe depression, which may include elements of all these categories, can be significantly altered by improving the philosophical condition" (Myers, *William James,* 46). Howard Feinstein is more skeptical: "Perry's version provides a pleasing structure for the biography of an important philosopher. It is a tale of rebirth typical of Christian spiritual biography" (Feinstein, *Becoming,* 307-8). Feinstein also notes that the "crisis" was not unique and that there was no concomitant change in James's health. Similar doubts about the unique quality and importance of this episode are voiced in Daniel W. Bjork, *William James: The Center of His Vision* (New York: Columbia Univ. Press, 1988), 88-90.

16. Gordon Allport has noted "the fact that the famous chapter on Habit is not consistent with James's concept of a purposive self endowed with a selective consciousness" (Gordon Allport, "The Productive Paradoxes of William James," *Psychological Review* 50 [1943]: 104). Dewey notes more generally the "double strain in the *Principles of Psychology.* One strain is official acceptance of epistemological dualism. . . . But James's analysis of special topics tends, on the contrary, to reduction of the subject matter to a vanishing point" (John Dewey, "The Vanishing Subject in the Psychology of James," *Journal of Philosophy* 37 [1940]: 589). Dewey further remarks that this conflict is most prominent in James's discussion of the self.

17. Coincidentally, the drainage-channel image also calls to mind the fact that James's grandfather, William James, made his fortune in industry and land speculation along the Erie Canal.

18. On Freud's use of this metaphor, see Jean Laplanche, *Life and Death in Psychoanalysis,* trans. Jeffrey Mehlman (Baltimore: Johns Hopkins Univ. Press, 1976). Laplanche ultimately criticizes Freud for sublimating empirical findings in favor of figural consistency.

19. Charles S. Peirce, *Selected Writings: Values in a Universe of Chance,* ed. Philip P. Wiener (New York: Dover, 1958), 99.

20. The second half of the chapter contains a lengthy rejection of earlier philosophical schools and an outdated discussion of abnormal mental states.

21. Although James disagrees with Hume on a number of points (such as the division of ideas into the categories of simple and complex), their shared attention to experience is noteworthy, particularly because James persuasively refuted the philosophy of Common Sense, which itself originated in the attempt to refute Hume.

22. This idea is central to the structure of *The Principles* and to James's later work. On the relationship between Hume's and James's thought, see Flower and Murphy, *History of Philosophy,* 1: 249-51.

23. The distinction is also a source of the questionable belief that James ultimately abandoned the ideas in *The Principles* in favor of radical empiricism. Some maintain that *The Principles* provides the basis for his later thought; for example, see John Dewey, "William James as Empiricist," in *In Commemoration of William James, 1842-1942* (New York: Columbia Univ. Press, 1942), 48-57. More popular, however, especially among philosophers, is the belief that as James moved beyond *The Principles* his philosophy would culminate in pragmatism and radical empiricism; see Myers, *William James*, chapter 11 passim; also see Herbert Schneider, "Healthy Minds with Sick Souls," in *The Philosophy of William James*, ed. Walter Robert Corti (Hamburg: Felix Meiner, 1976), 357-77. The problem with this latter position emerges when the essay "Does 'Consciousness' Exist?" (1904) is examined. In this piece, later incorporated into *Essays in Radical Empiricism*, James argues that upon analysis the distinction between mind and object disappears from view. This is not substantially different from the ideas James advances in "The Stream of Thought." The primary difference between these two essays is that they are responses to different types of questions, the philosophical and the psychological. In *The Principles,* James is reluctant to distinguish between the source and objects of consciousness: "I do not wish just yet to 'commit myself' about the existence or non-existence of the ego, but I do contend that we need not invoke it" (268). But because psychology traditionally dealt with the source of consciousness, James has been inappropriately credited with too high a regard for subjectivity.

24. With respect to the semiotic implications of James's psychology, Woodward notes that James's view of language "was close to that of the hermeneutic tradition, in which expressive movements, signs, and language became the foundation for the human sciences (*Geisteswissenschaften*). His successors, including George Herbert Mead, Charles Morris, and Jean Piaget, attempted to add a social meaning to James's conception of a science of language" (William Woodward, "Introduction," in William James, *Essays in Psychology* [Cambridge: Harvard Univ. Press, 1983], xxx). By citing those who developed the explicitly social dimension of James's thought, Woodward refutes the notion that the implications of James's theory were necessarily individualistic.

6 Selfhood, Pragmatism, and Literary Studies

1. William James, *Psychology: The Briefer Course*, ed. Gordon Allport (1961; reprint, Notre Dame, Ind.: Univ. of Notre Dame Press, 1985), 43. "The Self," chapter 3 of *Psychology*, is a pared-down version of "The Consciousness of Self" in the two-volume *Principles of Psychology*. The emphasis in the earlier, longer work is on overturning an essentialist concept of the self; this is subordinated in the later version to his discussion of the self as actor/observer (the "I") as opposed to the self as object of study (the "me").

2. James, *Psychology: The Briefer Course*, 46.

3. George Herbert Mead, *Mind, Self, and Society: From the Standpoint of a Social Behaviorist*, ed. Charles W. Morris (Chicago: Univ. of Chicago Press, 1936), 138. Mead, like James, also distinguishes between the "I" and the "me" as components of the self, but Mead's distinction is more complex than that of James. To Mead, the "me" is more closely identified with social attitudes, whereas the "I" is that which reacts to these attitudes. As Mead states, "The 'I' is the response of the organism to the attitudes of others; the 'me' is the organized set of attitudes which

one himself assumes" (175). The ultimate importance of the "I" for Mead is that it is his name for the capacity for spontaneous action or initiative, although what it furnishes in the name of freedom it lacks in the self-awareness available only through the "me" phase of selfhood.

4. Ibid., 136.

5. Herbert Blumer, "Society as Symbolic Interaction," in *Symbolic Interaction: Perspective and Method* (Englewood Cliffs, N.J.: Prentice-Hall, 1969), 79.

6. John R. Hall revealingly contrasts the symbolic interactionist approach with the reliance on the idea of an objective historical matrix characteristic of the *Annales* school (among others). According to Hall, from a symbolic interactionist perspective, time is "subjectively and socially constructed, and it is meaningful action and interaction that gives time its shape" (John R. Hall, "Social Interaction, Culture, and Historical Studies," in *Symbolic Interaction and Cultural Studies*, ed. Howard S. Becker and Michael McCall [Chicago: Univ. of Chicago Press, 1990], 19). This provides a discontinuous vision of events that does not purport to be objective but which also, insofar as it designates meaning as socially constructed, does not simply assert that all accounts are equally valid. The great concern of those anxious about abandoning the ideal of objectivity is thus noted by Hall. A most impressive discussion of the ideal of objectivity and the corresponding fear of subjectivism is offered by Richard J. Bernstein in *Beyond Objectivism and Relativism: Science, Hermeneutics, and Praxis* (Philadelphia: Univ. of Pennsylvania Press, 1985).

7. James, *Psychology: The Briefer Course*, 58.

8. Charles S. Peirce, "How to Make Our Ideas Clear," in *Selected Writings*, ed. Wiener, 121.

9. Jacques Derrida, *Margins of Philosophy*, trans. Alan Bass (Chicago: Univ. of Chicago Press, 1982), 209.

10. Tompkins, *Sensational Designs*, 123, 124. Interestingly, one of the critics Tompkins criticizes, Leslie Fiedler, had, like Tompkins, appreciated *Uncle Tom's Cabin* as "an astonishingly various and complex book" (Fiedler, *Love and Death*, 264). His study of the sentimental novel was generated by his interest in the form as a cultural artifact, however, one that finally was complicit with the hegemony of middle-and upper-class values and did not comprise a self-consciously oppositional form, as Tompkins insists. Some of Fiedler's criticisms of Stowe have returned to the current debate, though, in play with Tompkins's ideas of the sentimental as ideological critique. See, for example, Budick, *Engendering Romance*, 109-13.

11. Graff, *Professing Literature*, 173. Graff discusses the limits of explication as pedagogy, noting that certain New Critics, such as Austin Warren and René Wellek were aware that in effect the New Criticism took for granted some degree of literary history and traditions. Elizabeth Freund, in discussing the problematic legacy of the New Criticism, raises a difficult question and provides an equally difficult answer: "Why should a discredited critical method continue to trouble us so persistently? Partly, no doubt (as many have said), because the academy is reluctant to relinquish its indubitable pedagogical successes" (Elizabeth Freund, *The Return of the Reader: Reader-Response Criticism* [New York: Methuen, 1987], 64). These kinds of successes are difficult to abandon because there seems to be no alternative but a substantial reorganization of classroom practices, a reorganization that only begins with canon reformation. In a time when quantitative results are more aggressively demanded by business-oriented critics of education, such a reorganization promises to inspire spirited opposition. This sort of oppositional position

on the social functions of pedagogy and its relationship to theory is exemplified by the introductory essay of Henry Giroux, *Redrawing Educational Boundaries* (Albany: State Univ. of New York Press, 1990); see also the discussion of the relationship of postmodernism to teaching in Lester Faigley, *Fragments of Rationality: Postmodernity and the Subject of Composition* (Pittsburgh: Univ. of Pittsburgh Press, 1992), chapter 4.

12. Richard J. Bernstein uses this phrase as a capsulized description of Dewey's concept of the educative process (Richard J. Bernstein, "Dewey, Democracy: The Task ahead of Us," in *Post-Analytic Philosophy*, ed. John Rajchman and Cornel West [New York: Columbia Univ. Press, 1985], 54). Bernstein also notes the prevalent, distorted perception of Dewey's educational theory, bluntly stating, "There is still a popular myth that Dewey, the so-called father of progressive education, advocated a child-centered conception of education that sentimentalizes and idealizes the child's development. This is one of the extremes he opposes" (54). Familiarity with any of Dewey's writings on education reinforces Bernstein's corrective characterization of Dewey's thought. An admirably clear description of his educational philosophy is offered in John Dewey, *Democracy and Education* (New York: Free Press, 1966).

13. Joan D. Hedrick, "'Peaceable Fruits': The Ministry of Harriet Beecher Stowe," *American Quarterly* 40 (September 1988): 307.

14. Jehlen, "The Family Militant," 385.

15. Harriet Beecher Stowe, *Uncle Tom's Cabin, or Life among the Lowly,* in *Three Novels* (New York: Library of America, 1982), 190.

16. Henry F. May, "Harriet Beecher Stowe's *Oldtown Folks:* An Introduction," in *The Divided Heart: Essays on Protestantism and the Enlightenment in America* (New York: Oxford Univ. Press, 1991), 98.

17. Harriet Beecher Stowe, *Pink and White Tyranny: A Society Novel* (New York: New American Library, 1988), 146; hereafter cited in text.

18. John Dewey, *Individualism, Old and New,* vol. 5 of *The Later Works,* ed. Jo Ann Boydston (Carbondale: Southern Illinois Univ. Press, 1978), 49.

19. Dewey, *Individualism,* 76-77.

20. John Dewey, "My Pedagogic Creed," *The Philosophy of John Dewey,* ed. John J. McDermott (Chicago: Univ. of Chicago Press, 1973), 452.

21. Bernstein, "Dewey," 49.

22. Nancy Fraser, *Unruly Practices: Power, Discourse and Gender in Contemporary Social Theory* (Minneapolis: Univ. of Minnesota Press, 1989), 108.

Index

164